SQL Query Design P
Best Practices

A practical guide to writing readable and maintainable SQL queries using its design patterns

Steve Hughes

Dennis Neer

Dr. Ram Babu Singh

Shabbir H. Mala

Leslie Andrews

Chi Zhang

BIRMINGHAM—MUMBAI

SQL Query Design Patterns and Best Practices

Publishing Product Manager: Arindam Majumdar
Senior Editor: Tiksha Abhimanyu Lad
Technical Editor: Sweety Pagaria
Copy Editor: Safis Editing
Project Coordinator: Farheen Fathima
Proofreader: Safis Editing
Indexer: Sejal Dsilva
Production Designer: Arunkumar Govinda Bhat
Marketing Coordinator: Nivedita Singh

First published: February 2023
Production reference: 2190423

Published by Packt Publishing Ltd.
Livery Place
35 Livery Street
Birmingham
B3 2PB, UK.

ISBN 978-1-83763-328-9

www.packtpub.com

Contributors

About the authors

Steve Hughes is a senior director of data and analytics at 3Cloud. In this role, he focuses on growing the teams' skills and capabilities to deliver data projects with Azure. He has worked with technology for over 20 years, with much of that time spent on creating **business intelligence** (**BI**) solutions and helping customers implement leading BI and cloud solutions. He is passionate about using data effectively and helping customers understand that data is valuable and profitable. Steve has recently been diagnosed with ALS but continues to work and share with others what he has learned. Steve is also the founder of Data on Wheels where he blogs with one of his daughters on topics such as data, analytics, and work enablement.

I want to thank my family, friends, and peers for supporting me through my health changes, and I am especially thankful to Sheila, my wife. I could not do this without her support and encouragement.

Dennis Neer is a senior architect of data and analytics at 3Cloud. In this role, he focuses on working with clients to design Azure solutions for their data and analytic needs so that they may use that data to make business decisions based on that data. This includes using tools such as SQL Server databases, Synapse, data lakes, and Power BI. He has worked with technology for over 30 years, with 25 years in designing and building database and visualization solutions. He is passionate about data and helping businesses to understand the information contained in their data and how it can be used to make important decisions regarding their business to improve the strength of their business.

I want to thank my wife, Jeanie, for all of the support and encouragement she has given me throughout my career, and while working on this book; I couldn't do this without you.

Dr. Ram Babu Singh is an accomplished data analytics and data science professional with a Ph.D. in computer science and a Microsoft Certified Professional designation. With over 2 decades of experience in data platforms, he is recognized as an expert in his field. As the lead data architect at 3Cloud, he has developed complex data analytics and data science solutions for high-profile clients such as Microsoft, Accenture, and HP. An accomplished academic with published papers in international journals, he has a patent in artificial intelligence, highlighting his innovative problem-solving approach. With over 10 years of leadership experience in data and analytics, he has earned a reputation as a thought leader and mentor in the industry.

I want to thank my wife, Dr. Nirmal Lodhi, for supporting me throughout my journey, and my son Rudra and daughter Riddhima for letting me steal their family time. I also want to thank my colleagues for their support.

Shabbir H. Mala is a director of data and analytics at 3Cloud. He has over 23 years of experience in thought leadership and consulting, developing complex data solutions, business systems, and processes using Azure Data Services and Power BI. He currently manages a data architecture team of over 40 principals and senior architects focusing on business growth, successful project delivery, and client experience. He loves and has done talks at Power BI conferences and local Power BI user groups. He has been awarded Microsoft FastTrack Solution Architect for the last 2 consecutive years, in 2021 and 2022. He was born and raised in Mumbai (India), and came to the United States in 2006 and is currently living in Chicago. He is married with three kids.

Leslie Andrews is a lead data architect of data and analytics at 3Cloud. Working in the IT sector for over 20 years in local government, electrical supply, law enforcement, and healthcare, she has broad experience to draw from to assist clients in making data more accessible for end users. Leslie's expertise includes SQL development, ETL, data warehousing, data modeling, and analytics. Leslie currently holds several Microsoft certifications related to Azure technologies for data engineering. She approaches each day as an opportunity to use data and technology to make it easier for others to do their daily work. Leslie has been doing public speaking since 2015, was an IDERA ACE in 2019, and is a supporter of and contributor to the SQL community.

Chi Zhang is a lead data architect at 3Cloud. After completing her master's degree at Carnegie Mellon University, she worked in data consulting for the past 5 years. She has helped clients from various industries to deliver customized data solutions within Azure. Focusing on ETL, data warehousing, data modeling, and BI reporting, Chi solves data problems for clients and builds data solutions that provide business users with better operational insights and a smoother experience. Recently, she has continued to grow her footprint in the Azure community: earning certifications in Azure data engineering and data science, giving her first public tech talk, co-authoring a technical book, and becoming an active contributor to the SQL community.

I want to thank my husband, Joey, for all the help and company he has been giving me throughout my life so far. You push me to be a better person, and I'd do this all over again with you.

About the reviewers

Paul Turley is a competency lead director for the 3Cloud solutions BI&A practice, and Microsoft Data Platform MVP. He consults, writes, speaks, teaches, and blogs about BI and reporting solutions. He works with companies to model data and visualize and deliver critical information to make informed business decisions, using the Microsoft Data Platform and business analytics tools. He is the director of the Oregon Data Community PASS chapter and user group, the author and lead author of *Professional SQL Server 2016 Reporting Services*, and 14 other titles from Wrox & Microsoft Press. Paul is a FastTrack Recognized Solution Architect and holds several certifications related to the Microsoft Data Platform and BI.

Christopher J Knapp is a cloud solutions director at 3Cloud. For the last 17 years, he has worked primarily in the healthcare industry in all aspects of data, including transformation, storage, data modeling, BI, advanced analytics, and machine learning. He has spoken in multiple settings across the nation on various data topics. More recently, CJ has focused on Spark-based ETL and analytical methods, as well as cloud-based data platform systems at scale for healthcare. He is a father, husband, polyglot, and constant consumer of culture outside of work. He spends the majority of his free time having adventures with his family, traveling, and mixing craft cocktails at home. Sometimes, he even manages to mix them well.

Andie Letourneau is a cloud solution consultant with over 25 years of experience specializing in MS SQL Server databases, data warehousing, and BI. She has Azure Data Fundamentals and Azure Administrator Associate Microsoft certifications. She has presented at numerous SQL user group meetings and SQL Saturday events. She lives with her husband in beautiful Cave Creek, AZ.

Table of Contents

3

Formatting Your Results for Easier Consumption 31

4

Manipulating Data Results Using Conditional SQL 45

Part 2: Solving Complex Business and Data Problems in Your Queries

5

Using Common Table Expressions 65

6

Analyze Your Data Using Window Functions   77

7

Reshaping Data with Advanced Techniques   95

8

Impact of SQL Server Security on Query Results   111

Part 3: Optimizing Your Queries to Improve Performance

9

10

Part 4: Working with Your Data on the Modern Data Platform

11

Appendix

Preface

SQL was created to support **relational database management systems (RDBMSs)**. It was not created just for SQL Server. SQL, or as it is typically pronounced *sequel*, has been the de facto standard for working with relational databases for nearly 50 years. The structure and understanding of this language have been established as a standard in both ANSI and ISO.

While the language has a standard and well-established set of syntax rules and capabilities, it has been implemented in many ways throughout the years by various RDBMS vendors. Microsoft implemented **Transact-SQL (T-SQL)** in SQL Server and has continued to use it as the primary SQL version, used in the various Azure SQL Database implementations.

While the focus of our book is primarily around retrieving data from databases efficiently, SQL is not limited to just data retrieval. SQL can be used to manipulate the database structure, manipulate data, and retrieve data. SQL can also be used to issue commands to the underlying database system depending on what the language supports.

As we move into the **modern data estates**, relational data is not the only data within the environment. We are seeing more document-style databases and other non-relational datasets used in common practice. What is interesting about this is that there is always a push to get back to SQL-supported datasets. The tabular nature of the data returned by SQL is the easiest data to consume in numerous tools available in the marketplace today and is easy for users to understand. Languages and document sets such as **JSON** are highly flexible and support a less structured version of data. However, those sets often must be converted to a tabular format to be easily consumed by various tools and understood by the users consuming that data. Think of it like JSON a machine and developer-friendly data storage format, but tabular formats used by SQL make it easy for you to understand what is in it.

As we move into some of these modern scenarios and even in some older scenarios such as MDX, we find the SELECT... FROM... WHERE format of the SQL language has been implemented to make it easier to work with data. As a developer, it is important for you to understand the best formats and most efficient methods of writing these queries to get the results you need. A lot of these efficiencies are true for whatever database system you work in. This book will focus on working with SQL Server and T-SQL in particular; however, many of the principles will apply across all relational systems.

Who this book is for

This book is for the SQL developer who is ready to take their query development skills to the next level. This includes report writers, data scientists, or similar data gatherers and allows users to expand their skills for complex querying and build more efficient and performant queries. This book also seeks to advance their knowledge of the modern data estate and introduce query techniques for pulling data from data lakes. For those just learning SQL, this book can help you accelerate your learning and prevent you from making common mistakes.

What this book covers

The book is organized into four parts, with multiple chapters in each part. The book is designed to grow your experience from beginning to end if you choose to read it in that fashion. One of the greatest values is that each chapter is self-standing and can be used as a reference if you come across a situation where you need to improve your query writing specifically with that scenario. This also allows you to engage this book at whichever point makes the most sense for your query writing capabilities and skills.

In *Chapter 1, Reducing Rows and Columns in Your Result Sets*, the focus is on reducing your rows and columns to build an efficient dataset that can be used in reporting and other use cases.

The focus shifts to aggregating your results in *Chapter 2, Efficiently Aggregating Data in Your Results*. You can return a much more refined dataset that is easier to consume by effectively aggregating results to the right granularity in the content you need to pass along.

In *Chapter 3, Formatting Your Results for Easier Consumption*, the focus shifts to formatting your results. Often when working with data coming from a database, it must support levels of granularity or specific types of data to be efficient or inclusive. However, this comes at the price of storing data in a format that is not necessarily conducive to end users. Common formatting difficulties include handling currencies and dates. In this chapter, you will learn how to effectively format your data for more efficient use outside the database.

We expand on query efficiency by using conditional SQL in *Chapter 4, Manipulating Your Data Results Using Conditional SQL*. This will allow you to refine results even further for your end user. SQL Server supports several conditional logic statements that will be explored in this chapter.

Chapter 5, Using Common Table Expressions, delves into the world of **common table expressions** (**CTEs**) as they are commonly referred to. This technique is used to reduce subqueries and support other complex scenarios. In this chapter, you will learn how to build efficient CTEs to solve complex business problems.

Chapter 6, Analyze Your Data Using Window Functions, introduces you to window functions inside SQL. These functions allow you to do inline query aggregations or other techniques, such as row numbers. Some of the problems that are solved using window functions include building and running totals in your results.

Chapter 7, Reshaping Your Data with Advanced Techniques, dives into advanced techniques for **reshaping** your data. This includes handling hierarchical data and working with the PIVOT and UNPIVOT commands.

Chapter 8, Impact of SQL Security on Query Results, helps you deal with the impact of **security** on your query results. Citizen developers are often unaware of the impact security might have on the data they are pulling into their results. This chapter looks at the various implications of security and how to understand that impact on the results that you get and deliver to your end user.

Chapter 9, Understanding Query Plans, describes how to understand query plans. In this chapter, you will be introduced to the query plan itself and how to read it to determine what you can do to improve the performance and the query that you're writing.

We then move on to understanding the impact of indexes on your query design in *Chapter 10, Understanding the Impact of Indexes on Your Query Design*. While we will not dive into authoring indexes, understanding the impact of indexes, including which indexes will improve your query performance, is the focus here. This will help you communicate your index needs to those that own the database design.

JSON data or NoSQL data has been disruptive to SQL writers around the world. In *Chapter 11, Handling JSON Data in SQL Server*, we will walk through the various functions and capabilities of SQL in SQL Server that supports JSON.

In *Chapter 12, Integrating File Data and Data Lake Content with SQL*, we will walk through techniques to integrate file and data lake content in your queries. This more complex technique is becoming very necessary in the new modern data platform.

We then have *Chapter 13, Organizing and Sharing Your Queries with Jupyter Notebooks*, covering Jupyter notebooks. Jupyter notebooks are available in **Azure Data Studio** and Synapse Workspace. These notebooks can be used to organize and share queries and their results more efficiently than **SQL Server Management Studio** (**SSMS**). In this chapter, we will walk you through notebook creation and sharing.

In the *Appendix, Preparing Your Environment*, we will walk you through setting up your environment to support the exercises in this book.

To get the most out of this book

Software/hardware covered in the book	Operating system requirements
Microsoft Azure Storage Explorer	Windows, macOS, or Linux
SQL Server 2022 or Azure SQL Database	Windows, macOS, or Linux
Azure Data Studio	Windows, macOS, or Linux

This book covers many illustrations and examples of working with SQL to improve your overall writing and performance. To make this simple for all our users, we have chosen to use the `Wide World Importers` sample databases available from Microsoft. Therefore, depending on the nature of the query that we are constructing and providing examples for, one of the two databases (operational: **WideWorldImporters**; data warehouse: **WideWorldImportersDW**) provided by Microsoft will be used. Bear in that means you will have *two* databases to run the exercises created within this book.

It is recommended that you install the following tools on your device, as these will be used with the exercises in this book:

- SSMS and Azure Data Studio installation. You'll find the installation instructions at the following location: `https://learn.microsoft.com/en-us/sql/ssms/download-sql-server-management-studio-ssms`. Be sure to install both SQL Server Management Studio and Azure Data Studio in the installation process.

- **Microsoft Azure Storage Explorer** is used to move files in and out of Azure. You'll find the installation instructions at this location: `https://azure.microsoft.com/en-us/products/storage/storage-explorer/`.

- You can use either **SQL Server 2022** or **Azure SQL Database** for your database platform. If you need to install SQL Server 2022 or set up Azure SQL Database, refer to the *Appendix* for detailed instructions.

- All examples in this book will be using the `Wide World Importers` sample databases provided by Microsoft and found here: `https://github.com/Microsoft/sql-server-samples/releases/tag/wide-world-importers-v1.0`. We will be using the full backups for SQL Server and the standard backups for Azure SQL DB.

If you are using the digital version of this book, we advise you to type the code yourself or access the code from the book's GitHub repository (a link is available in the next section). Doing so will help you avoid any potential errors related to the copying and pasting of code.

Full instructions for installation and database configuration can be found in the *Appendix*.

Download the example code files

You can download the example code files for this book from GitHub at `https://github.com/PacktPublishing/SQL-Query-Design-Best-Practices`. If there's an update to the code, it will be updated in the GitHub repository.

We also have other code bundles from our rich catalog of books and videos available at `https://github.com/PacktPublishing/`. Check them out!

Download the color images

We also provide a PDF file that has color images of the screenshots and diagrams used in this book. You can download it here: `https://packt.link/Xxotr`.

Conventions used

There are a number of text conventions used throughout this book.

`Code in text`: Indicates code words in text, database table names, folder names, filenames, file extensions, pathnames, dummy URLs, user input, and Twitter handles. Here is an example: "All window functions can utilize the PARTITION BY expression of the OVER clause, which is always optional."

A block of code is set as follows:

```
SELECT TOP (3) [Order Key]
      , [Description]
  FROM [Fact].[Order]
```

When we wish to draw your attention to a particular part of a code block, the relevant lines or items are set in bold:

```
SELECT TOP(3) FORMAT( [Date], 'D', 'en-US' ) 'US English'
      ,FORMAT( [Date], 'D', 'en-gb' ) 'British English'
      ,FORMAT( [Date], 'D', 'de-de' ) 'German'
      ,FORMAT( [Date], 'D', 'zh-cn' ) 'Chinese Simplified
(PRC)'
  FROM [Dimension].[Date]
```

Bold: Indicates a new term, an important word, or words that you see onscreen. For instance, words in menus or dialog boxes appear in **bold**. Here is an example: "Next you will expand the **Security** and **Users** folders and find your login ID."

> **Tips or important notes**
> Appear like this.

Get in touch

Feedback from our readers is always welcome.

General feedback: If you have questions about any aspect of this book, email us at customercare@packtpub.com and mention the book title in the subject of your message.

Errata: Although we have taken every care to ensure the accuracy of our content, mistakes do happen. If you have found a mistake in this book, we would be grateful if you would report this to us. Please visit www.packtpub.com/support/errata and fill in the form.

Piracy: If you come across any illegal copies of our works in any form on the internet, we would be grateful if you would provide us with the location address or website name. Please contact us at copyright@packt.com with a link to the material.

If you are interested in becoming an author: If there is a topic that you have expertise in and you are interested in either writing or contributing to a book, please visit authors.packtpub.com.

Share Your Thoughts

Once you've read *SQL Query Design Pattern Best Practices*, we'd love to hear your thoughts! Scan the QR code below to go straight to the Amazon review page for this book and share your feedback.

https://packt.link/r/1-837-63328-2

Your review is important to us and the tech community and will help us make sure we're delivering excellent quality content.

Download a free PDF copy of this book

Thanks for purchasing this book!

Do you like to read on the go but are unable to carry your print books everywhere? Is your eBook purchase not compatible with the device of your choice?

Don't worry, now with every Packt book you get a DRM-free PDF version of that book at no cost.

Read anywhere, any place, on any device. Search, copy, and paste code from your favorite technical books directly into your application.

The perks don't stop there, you can get exclusive access to discounts, newsletters, and great free content in your inbox daily

Follow these simple steps to get the benefits:

1. Scan the QR code or visit the link below

https://packt.link/free-ebook/9781837633289

2. Submit your proof of purchase
3. That's it! We'll send your free PDF and other benefits to your email directly

Part 1: Refining Your Queries to Get the Results You Need

The goal of the four chapters in this part is to help you become a more efficient query writer. One of the areas we commonly see where people struggle is building queries to get the results that they need without including additional content in their query results just because they might need it later:

- *Chapter 1, Reducing Rows and Columns in Your Result Sets*
- *Chapter 2, Efficiently Aggregating Data in Your Results*
- *Chapter 3, Formatting Your Results for Easier Consumption*
- *Chapter 4, Manipulating Your Data Results Using Conditional SQL*

1
Reducing Rows and Columns in Your Result Sets

Today the sources of data that a data analyst has access to have grown to the point that the amount of data that is available to you is unlimited. The challenge that a data analyst faces today is to determine how to generate a result set that is manageable and has the information that ensures that it will meet the needs of the analyst for their reports and analysis. If there is too much data, the result set will become unmanageable and unusable due to information overload; too little data and the data will have gaps, and the end user will lose trust in the data.

In this chapter, we will review how you determine how much data and what data you should keep in your result set and how to filter that data efficiently. We will also review how to determine which columns you should keep and how you can efficiently select the correct columns. The chapter will then wrap up with a short discussion on how these activities will impact future data aggregations.

By the end of this chapter, you will understand how to identify the data and columns that you need and the most efficient method for getting the data into a usable result set that can easily be recreated.

In this chapter, we will cover the following main topics:

- Identifying data to be removed from the dataset
- Understanding the value of creating views versus removing data
- Exploring the impact of row and column reductions on aggregations

Technical requirements

To work with the examples and illustrations in this chapter, you will need to have SQL Server Management Studio installed. We will be working with the `WideWorldImportersDW` database on SQL Server. Please refer to the *Appendix* for tool installation and database restoration guidance.

You will find the code from this chapter on GitHub: `https://github.com/PacktPublishing/SQL-Query-Design-Best-Practices/tree/main/Chapter01`

Identifying data to remove from the dataset

With the amount of data that is freely available today, databases are getting larger and larger, and that makes it a challenge for data analysts to analyze the data properly. A challenge that data analysts face is determining what data is required to be able to produce a dataset that provides the information that is relevant for analysis. In this chapter, you will learn how to reduce the amount of data and columns that are contained in a dataset without affecting the result set.

To do this, you will need to first understand what data is required through interviews with the people requesting the result set. The interview process will help you to understand what the person requesting the result set wants to accomplish and give you an idea of where to find the data and what database and table contain the information that is required. With this knowledge, you will need to perform some initial analysis of the data in the database tables to determine how much and what columns of data are needed. This is often done through simple queries that perform row counts and table descriptions. The following are examples of the type of queries that may be used.

The following is a query to get an idea of the data in a table:

```
SELECT TOP (1000) *
  FROM database.schema.table;
```

This type of query will give you an idea of what data is available in a particular table by showing you up to the first 1,000 rows in the table, and if the table has fewer than 1,000 rows, it will show you all of the rows in the table.

The following query will show you all of the columns and their data types in a particular schema:

```
SELECT Table_name as [Table] ,
       Column_name as [Column] ,
       Table_catalog as [Database],
       table_schema as [Schema]
FROM   information_schema.columns
WHERE  table_schema = 'Fact'
ORDER BY Table_name, Column_name;
```

This type of query will read the system tables in the database to return the names of all of the Column instances that each table in the schema contains. The table that we are interested in is the information_schema.columns table. With this information, you can determine what columns are available for you to use.

With this information, let's look at an example for solving the following sample request that was determined by interviewing a user. For the examples in this chapter, we will assume that the interview has resulted in the following analysis:

We want to be able to analyze the number of orders that resort in a back-order item being created by each year and month and how many customers were impacted.

How do we go about this? Let us check in the following sections.

Reducing the amount of data

We start by determining which tables seem to contain the data that is required as just described:

```
SELECT Table_name as [Table] ,
       Column_name as [Column] ,
       Table_catalog as [Database],
       Table_schema as [Schema]
FROM information_schema.columns
Where Table_schema = 'fact'
AND Table_name = 'Order'
ORDER BY Table_name, Column_name;
```

Figure 1.1 shows the results of the query:

Table	Column	Database	Schema
Order	City Key	WideWorldImportersDW	Fact
Order	Customer Key	WideWorldImportersDW	Fact
Order	Description	WideWorldImportersDW	Fact
Order	Lineage Key	WideWorldImportersDW	Fact
Order	Order Date Key	WideWorldImportersDW	Fact
Order	Order Key	WideWorldImportersDW	Fact
Order	Package	WideWorldImportersDW	Fact
Order	Picked Date Key	WideWorldImportersDW	Fact
Order	Picker Key	WideWorldImportersDW	Fact
Order	Quantity	WideWorldImportersDW	Fact
Order	Salesperson Key	WideWorldImportersDW	Fact
Order	Stock Item Key	WideWorldImportersDW	Fact
Order	Tax Amount	WideWorldImportersDW	Fact
Order	Tax Rate	WideWorldImportersDW	Fact
Order	Total Excluding Tax	WideWorldImportersDW	Fact
Order	Total Including Tax	WideWorldImportersDW	Fact
Order	Unit Price	WideWorldImportersDW	Fact
Order	WWI Backorder ID	WideWorldImportersDW	Fact
Order	WWI Order ID	WideWorldImportersDW	Fact

Figure 1.1 – Results of the query to show all columns in a table

Based on the results, the Fact.Order table is a good candidate to start with, so let's run the following query:

```
SELECT TOP (1000) *
  FROM [WideWorldImportersDW].[Fact].[Order];
```

In *Figure 1.5*, you will notice that the following results are the same as you saw in the preceding result, and you do not have to include the filters because they are already included in the view:

Order Year	Order Month	Order	Stock Item	Customer	WWI Order	WWI Backorder
2013	1	26	176	330	12	54
2013	1	407	195	61	177	222
2013	1	809	173	125	334	421
2013	1	1578	165	258	558	592
2013	1	2287	192	197	768	858
2013	2	6908	168	162	2156	2163
2013	3	11187	195	25	3483	3523
2013	3	11417	201	207	3555	3585
2013	3	11599	168	379	3610	3675
2013	3	13017	173	206	4056	4094
2013	3	13187	199	170	4114	4160
2013	3	13692	170	11	4272	4305
2013	3	14125	198	34	4403	4428
2013	3	14278	171	313	4454	4471
2013	4	14738	166	7	4606	4645
2013	4	14945	196	303	4667	4703
2013	4	15446	183	380	4829	4885
2013	4	15920	186	177	4982	5007
2013	4	16517	181	7	5171	5223
2013	4	17541	192	46	5504	5551
2013	4	19192	187	87	6030	6052
2013	4	19321	188	372	6068	6106

Figure 1.5 – Result set using a view

This can save you the time of having to create the query in the future once the initial query has been created, and you can be assured that the data is correct. Most things that you can do in a query can also be done in a view, and you can use the view as though it is a table and just select columns from the view as you would in the table.

Now let's look at how this filtering impacts any aggregations that you may plan to do with the result set.

Exploring the impact of row and column reductions on aggregations

Now you know how to reduce the number of rows and specify the columns that you need in your result set, let's talk about what the impact will be on any aggregations that you may be interested in.

First of all, based on this result set, you can view the number of backorders by any combination of columns. For example, to see the number of backorders based on year and month, you could use the following query:

```
SELECT Year([Order Date Key]) as "Order Year",
       Month([Order Date Key]) as "Order Month",
```

```
   COUNT([WWI Backorder ID]) as "Number of backorders",
   COUNT(distinct [Customer Key]) as "Impacted Customers",
   COUNT([Order Key]) as "Number of orders"
FROM [WideWorldImportersDW].[Fact].[Order]
WHERE [WWI Backorder ID] IS NOT NULL
GROUP BY Year([Order Date Key]),
         Month([Order Date Key])
ORDER BY Year([Order Date Key]),
         Month([Order Date Key]);
```

You could also run the following query using the view that you created, and you will get the same results:

```
SELECT [Order Year],
       [Order Month],
   COUNT([WWI Backorder]) as "number of backorders",
   COUNT([customer]) as "number of impacted customers",
   COUNT([Order]) as "number of orders"
FROM v_backorders
GROUP BY [Order Year],
     [Order Month];
```

Figure 1.6 shows a subset of the results from the query:

Order Year	Order Month	number of backorders	number of impacted customers	number of orders
2015	4	556	556	556
2013	2	209	209	209
2013	7	495	495	495
2014	5	575	575	575
2014	10	602	602	602
2015	6	603	603	603
2016	1	571	571	571
2013	9	466	466	466
2014	7	544	544	544
2013	11	442	442	442
2014	11	498	498	498
2013	5	510	510	510
2014	3	398	398	398
2014	4	486	486	486
2015	5	561	561	561
2016	3	512	512	512
2015	1	523	523	523
2013	1	481	481	481
2015	8	531	531	531
2013	3	378	378	378
2014	1	453	453	453

Figure 1.6 – Subset of results from the earlier queries

On closer investigation, you will notice that the values in the number of backorders and number of orders columns are the same. Why is this? The answer is in the filter; it only returns records that have an associated backorder, so you will not get the actual number of orders that have been placed, and any calculations will not be accurate. So, to get an accurate number of orders, you will need to get all the orders in the table, not just the orders associated with a backorder. You will also see that the order of the result set is different for the query that uses the view and the query that does not use the view. This is due to the query that uses the view being stored in a memory heap from the view and accessed on demand, whereas the query that does not use the view is stored on the disk in the primary key order of the table.

This is the impact of using a filter; to get around this, you can add a subquery to remove the filter. So here is how you can update your query to get that additional information:

```sql
SELECT Year([Order Date Key]) as [Order Year],
       Month([Order Date Key]) as [Order Month],
   COUNT(distinct [Customer Key]) as [Impacted Customers],
   COUNT(distinct [Stock Item Key]) as [Backorder Items],
   COUNT([WWI Backorder ID]) as [Number of backorders],
   fo.orders,
       fo.Customers
FROM [WideWorldImportersDW].[Fact].[Order] o,
     (select  Year([Order Date Key]) as [Order Year],
             Month([Order Date Key]) as [Order Month],
             COUNT (distinct [Order Key]) as [orders],
             COUNT (distinct [customer Key]) as [Customers]
       FROM [WideWorldImportersDW].[Fact].[Order]
   GROUP BY Year([Order Date Key]),
             Month([Order Date Key])) as fo
WHERE [WWI Backorder ID] IS NOT NULL
AND year(o.[Order Date Key]) = fo.[Order Year]
AND month(o.[Order Date Key]) = fo.[Order Month]
GROUP BY Year([Order Date Key]),
         Month([Order Date Key]),
    fo.orders,
    fo.Customers
ORDER BY Year([Order Date Key]),
         Month([Order Date Key]);
```

This will give you the following result set, as seen in *Figure 1.7*. Notice you now see values in the orders, Impacted Customers, Number of backorders, and Customers columns for each Order Month:

Order Year	Order Month	Impacted Customers	Backorder Items	Number of backorders	orders	Customers
2013	1	105	189	481	5281	367
2013	2	44	139	209	3726	340
2013	3	81	175	378	5389	375
2013	4	105	190	487	5314	373
2013	5	108	201	510	5699	373
2013	6	75	190	390	5338	364
2013	7	107	199	495	5896	375
2013	8	88	187	393	4819	358
2013	9	94	192	466	5099	364
2013	10	85	187	433	5171	361
2013	11	82	188	442	4957	350
2013	12	83	186	411	4966	356
2014	1	99	191	453	5682	375
2014	2	80	191	419	4830	352
2014	3	78	176	398	5118	362
2014	4	99	197	486	5513	371
2014	5	112	203	575	6027	377
2014	6	114	199	585	5888	374
2014	7	111	200	544	6310	371
2014	8	94	195	454	5130	360
2014	9	88	185	453	5117	357

Figure 1.7 – Results of using filters in a query

This can be done for any number of columns as long as the subquery is grouped by the same fields as the main query. To simplify this query, you could very easily create a view of all the orders and then use the views to get the same results with less query development.

Here is a sample of the query to create the order view that you can use in future queries:

```
CREATE VIEW [dbo].[v_orders] AS
SELECT Year([Order Date Key]) as [Order Year],
      MONTH([Order Date Key]) as [Order Month],
      COUNT(distinct [Order Key]) as [orders],
      COUNT(distinct [customer Key]) as [Customers]
FROM [WideWorldImportersDW].[Fact].[Order]
GROUP BY Year([Order Date Key]),
        Month([Order Date Key])
```

Here is a sample of the query that uses the two views (v_Backorders and v_orders) that have been created in this chapter:

```
SELECT o.[Order Year],
       o.[Order Month],
       o.Customers,
       o.orders,
   COUNT(b.[WWI Backorder]) as [total backorders],
   COUNT(distinct b.[customer]) as [impacted customers]
FROM [WideWorldImportersDW].[dbo].[v_Backorders] b,
[WideWorldImportersDW].[dbo].[v_orders] o
WHERE b.[Order Year] = o.[Order Year]
AND b.[Order Month] = o.[Order Month]
GROUP BY o.[Order Year],
         o.[Order Month],
o.Customers,
o.orders
ORDER BY o.[Order Year],
         o.[Order Month];
```

The following is the result of the query:

Order Year	Order Month	Customers	orders	total backorders	impacted customers
2013	1	367	5281	481	105
2013	2	340	3726	209	44
2013	3	375	5389	378	81
2013	4	373	5314	487	105
2013	5	373	5699	510	108
2013	6	364	5338	390	75
2013	7	375	5896	495	107
2013	8	358	4819	393	88
2013	9	364	5099	466	94
2013	10	361	5171	433	85
2013	11	350	4957	442	82
2013	12	356	4966	411	83
2014	1	375	5682	453	99
2014	2	352	4830	419	80
2014	3	362	5118	398	78
2014	4	371	5513	486	99
2014	5	377	6027	575	112
2014	6	374	5888	585	114
2014	7	371	6310	544	111
2014	8	360	5130	454	94
2014	9	357	5117	453	88

Figure 1.8 – Sample results of using multiple views in a query

So as you can see, it is easy to reduce the amount of data that you bring into your result, but sometimes, you will need to include other data that may have been filtered out. This is where views come in handy and allow you to include data that may have been filtered in previous activities. You will need to use caution when deciding between using a view over a subquery due to the performance implications. In this example, the data size is small enough that the performance implications are negligible.

As you can see from this section, there are multiple ways in which you will be able to create result sets and get the same results.

Summary

In this chapter, we discussed how to determine what data you need in your result set to meet your analysis needs.

We started with some simple queries to identify what table we needed to get the data we needed, and then we queried the table to get a sample of data that was contained in it. Next, we created a query that would create a result set that met the needs of the request and showed how it could be turned into a view that makes the query easily reusable. We then wrapped up the chapter by showing how there may be a need to get data that is not available because it was filtered out.

In the next chapter, we will expand upon this knowledge to look at how to efficiently aggregate the data so that your queries will run more efficiently.

2
Efficiently Aggregating Data

In the previous chapter, you learned how to reduce the number of rows and columns contained in your dataset so that you have the data required to do the analysis that you are interested in. The next step that you will want to do is to aggregate your data so that you have summarized information making it easier to show the information in an easy-to-consume dataset.

In this chapter, you will learn the what, when, and how of data aggregation in SQL so that the dataset can be used by most end users to do successful analytics. We will start with what data should be aggregated, followed by a discussion on when the data should be aggregated and the different methods of aggregating the data. The chapter will wrap up with a short discussion on how to develop aggregations that are efficient and have minimal impact on your SQL server resources.

In this chapter, we will cover the following main topics:

- Identifying data to be aggregated
- Determining when to aggregate data
- Methods to aggregate data
- Improving performance when aggregating data

By the end of this chapter, you will understand the different methods to aggregate data, when to aggregate the data, and how to best aggregate the data.

Technical requirements

To work with the examples and illustrations in this chapter, you will need to have SQL Server Management Studio installed. We will be working with the `WideWorldImportersDW` database on SQL Server. Please refer to the *Appendix* for tool installation and database restoration guidance.

You will find the code from this chapter here on GitHub: `https://github.com/ PacktPublishing/SQL-Query-Design-Best-Practices/tree/main/Chapter02`

Identifying data to be aggregated

To identify the data that you are going to aggregate in the initial dataset that you have created, it is important to understand the story that you are trying to tell about the data. Some items will need to be counted, some will need to be summarized, and some will need to be aggregated by summarizing and counting. For example, if you are interested in doing an analysis of the data showing how many times an item has been ordered, then this would be an example of when you would aggregate the data by performing counts. If you are looking at data to see how many sales have occurred or the profits that have been made, this would be an example of summarizing the data. In addition, you may be interested in the average profit for a time period or the earliest and latest that an order has been delivered.

With these aggregations in place, the size of the dataset will be reduced, and you will be able to perform several other calculations based on these aggregations.

The following SQL has examples of aggregations and the type of calculations that could be performed from the aggregations:

```sql
SELECT [Invoice Date Key]
     ,[Delivery Date Key]
     ,SUM([Quantity]) as "# of items sold"
     ,SUM([Profit]) as profit
     ,SUM ([Total Including Tax]) as "total bill with taxes"
  FROM [WideWorldImportersDW].[Fact].[Sale]
  GROUP BY [Invoice Date Key], [Delivery Date Key]
```

Figure 2.1 depicts the results from the preceding SQL:

Invoice Date Key	Delivery Date Key	# of items sold	profit	total bill with taxes
2013-02-08	2013-02-09	7434	79058.6	178077.76
2013-02-25	2013-02-26	4925	41569.15	93578.39
2013-03-02	2013-03-03	3736	43854.85	88493.94
2013-03-14	2013-03-15	14002	119923.05	250612.44
2013-03-20	2013-03-21	9334	86824.65	185902.85
2013-03-26	2013-03-27	5714	47061.4	114092.32
2013-05-11	2013-05-12	4596	28995.75	71460.65
2013-05-21	2013-05-22	7531	96755.95	217180.22
2013-05-27	2013-05-28	10093	97419.9	214008.99
2013-05-28	2013-05-29	12974	110398.7	242219.34
2013-06-14	2013-06-15	9012	95209.8	217710.55
2013-06-26	2013-06-27	6914	76876.65	186906.23
2013-07-18	2013-07-19	6936	62780.8	153203.6
2013-08-21	2013-08-22	11592	75627.8	185726.16
2013-08-26	2013-08-27	9811	79456.7	183368.28
2013-08-27	2013-08-28	6490	59667.85	141011.2
2013-09-26	2013-09-27	6661	72937	161039.4
2013-10-18	2013-10-19	4715	39938.65	89821.57
2013-11-04	2013-11-05	8177	62764.95	146858.6
2013-11-14	2013-11-15	6670	60927	136476.5

Figure 2.1 – Sample of aggregations

Figure 2.2 is an example of a type of calculation that can be done with the result set:

Date	Average profits by date	Average bill amount by date
2013-02-08	10.63	23.95
2013-02-05	8.44	19

Figure 2.2 – Sample of calculations performed on aggregations

You may have noticed a new clause in the SQL query to create the aggregation; this is the GROUP BY line. The purpose of this line is to identify what you want to aggregate your data by; in this case, we are aggregating by invoice date and delivery date. Any column that is included in your query that is not being aggregated will need to be included in the GROUP BY clause of the query. We will go into more detail regarding the SQL to create these aggregations in the *Methods to aggregate data* section later in this chapter. In the meantime, let's look into when the data should be aggregated.

Determining when data should be aggregated

Now that we know what data we want to aggregate, when should this aggregation be performed? The aggregation should occur once you have identified the level of granularity you require. So, what does the level of granularity mean? It refers to the level of detail that an aggregation is completed to; for example, you want to know your profits at a daily level or monthly level. Other examples include aggregating to the day, month, year, store location, product, and so on.

Going back to *Figure 2.1*, we have the aggregations based on the invoice date, but we really want to know the totals based on the year, so you would then want to perform the aggregation based on the created dataset. Refer to the following query for how to do this:

```
SELECT YEAR([Invoice Date Key]) as Year
      ,SUM([Quantity]) as "# of items sold"
      ,SUM([Profit]) as profit
      ,SUM([Total Including Tax]) as "total bill with taxes"
   FROM [WideWorldImportersDW].[Fact].[Sale]
   GROUP BY year([Invoice Date Key])
```

The following is an example of the aggregation based on the invoiced year along with the resulting dataset:

Year	# of items sold	profit	total bill with taxes
2013	2401657	22768352.25	52563272.64
2016	1241304	11174765.55	25971029.11
2014	2567401	24828462.45	57418916.89
2015	2740266	26957600.65	62090220.81

Figure 2.3 – Sample of aggregations by invoice year

So, the answer to the question of when an aggregation should be performed is once you know what you want to aggregate. At that point, you will need to remove the fields that are not related to the aggregation so that you have the aggregation at the granularity required. Once the unnecessary columns have been removed, you add the GROUP BY clause in the query, as shown in *Figure 2.3*. Since Delivery Date Key was not part of the requirement for the granularity, it has been removed from the SQL. The reason for this is that every column that is not being aggregated will need to be included in the GROUP BY clause. This would impact the aggregation and give you results that are not desired. For an example of this, refer to the following query:

```
SELECT YEAR([Invoice Date Key]) as Year
      ,([Delivery Date Key]) as [Deliver Date]
    ,SUM([Quantity]) as [# of items sold]
    ,SUM([Profit]) as profit
    ,SUM([Total Including Tax]) as [Total bill will taxes]
FROM [WideWorldImportersDW].[Fact].[Sale]
GROUP BY YEAR([Invoice Date Key])
        ,[Delivery Date Key]
```

Figure 2.4 shows what the result set would look like should Delivery Date Key be included:

Year	Deliver Date	# of items sold	profit	Total bill will taxes
2013	2013-01-04	8256	70075.75	155966.93
2013	2013-02-09	7434	79058.6	178077.76
2013	2013-02-26	4925	41569.15	93578.39
2013	2013-04-17	11898	118855.4	269476.07
2013	2013-04-18	11710	92089.45	210607.35
2013	2013-04-24	9884	96883.3	222505.81
2013	2013-05-05	6253	58012.65	124110.89
2013	2013-06-06	9526	112814.35	250679.35
2013	2013-07-12	12607	149956.9	358280.5
2013	2013-07-27	6487	72803.85	175664.82
2013	2013-09-18	6900	68950.05	160869.91
2013	2013-10-03	6912	69076.05	150202.66
2013	2013-10-22	9164	79122.95	193849.8
2013	2013-03-15	14002	119923.05	250612.44
2013	2013-07-21	5998	42889.25	103548.25
2013	2013-03-30	5115	45994.8	115153.42
2013	2013-05-22	7531	96755.95	217180.22
2013	2013-10-29	9297	82435.65	195568.9
2013	2013-11-08	5139	50314	113162.37
2013	2013-11-23	4283	42874	95749.82
2013	2013-12-29	1509	14555.7	34713.84

Figure 2.4 – Sample of aggregations by invoice year and delivery date

Notice the differences in the result set from *Figure 2.3* and *Figure 2.4*; there are many more rows in the result set due to `Delivery Date Key` being included in the aggregation. This is an example of how aggregation can change based on the level of granularity.

You may recall that the delivery date did not have anything to do with the originally desired aggregation for the invoice year, so it was removed from the SQL shown in *Figure 2.3*.

Now that you know when to perform aggregations, let's look at the various types of aggregations that can be done.

Methods to aggregate data

Now that you know what data you want to aggregate and when you should or should not aggregate the data, let's take a look at the different methods that can be used to aggregate the data. There are multiple options to aggregate the data in SQL, and *Figure 2.5* shows a subset of some of the most common types of aggregation that can be used in SQL:

```
AVG()
COUNT()
MAX()
MIN()
SUM ()
```

Figure 2.5 – Aggregation functions

For a more extensive list you can refer to this link: `https://learn.microsoft.com/en-us/sql/t-sql/functions/aggregate-functions-transact-sql?view=sql-server-ver16`.

In the following sections, we will see an example of each of these aggregations.

The AVG() function

This function is used to produce an average of all of the values in the column that are being aggregated. It should be used on columns containing numeric values and will return a numeric value based on the data that is in the column. NULL values in a column will be ignored. The following SQL is a sample using the AVG () function, and *Figure 2.6* shows the associated result set:

```
SELECT YEAR([Invoice Date Key]) as Year,
       MONTH([Invoice Date Key]) as Mnth,
       AVG([Quantity]) as [Average # of Items Sold]
From [WideWorldImportersDW].[Fact].[Sale]
GROUP BY YEAR([Invoice Date Key]),
         MONTH([Invoice Date Key])
ORDER BY YEAR([Invoice Date Key]),
         MONTH([Invoice Date Key])
```

Here is the output:

Year	Month	Average # of Items Sold
2013	1	36
2013	2	38
2013	3	38
2013	4	40
2013	5	41
2013	6	40
2013	7	39
2013	8	40
2013	9	37
2013	10	38
2013	11	39
2013	12	39
2014	1	38
2014	2	38
2014	3	38

Figure 2.6 – Sample result set of the AVG() function

The SUM() function

This function is used to produce the total of the values in the column that are being aggregated. This function should be used on columns containing numeric values and will return a numeric value based on the data in the column. The following SQL is a sample using the SUM() function:

```
SELECT YEAR([Invoice Date Key]) as Year,
       MONTH([Invoice Date Key]) as Mnth,
       SUM([Quantity]) as [Total # of Items Sold]
FROM [WideWorldImportersDW].[Fact].[Sale]
GROUP BY YEAR([Invoice Date Key]),
         MONTH([Invoice Date Key])
ORDER BY YEAR([Invoice Date Key]),
         MONTH([Invoice Date Key])
```

The following is the associated result set:

Year	Month	Total # of Items Sold
2013	1	193271
2013	2	142120
2013	3	207486
2013	4	212995
2013	5	230725
2013	6	213468
2013	7	232599
2013	8	192199
2013	9	190567
2013	10	198476
2013	11	194290
2013	12	193461
2014	1	216337
2014	2	182103
2014	3	196451

Figure 2.7 – Sample result set of the SUM() function

The COUNT() function

This function is used to produce a count of the number of occurrences for the column that is being aggregated. Rows that include NULL values will be included in the total count, so this function will return the total number of rows in the table, whether the column has a value or not. This function can be used on any column data type and returns a number. The following SQL is a sample using the COUNT() function, and *Figure 2.8* shows the associated result set:

```
SELECT YEAR([Invoice Date Key]) as Year,
       MONTH([Invoice Date Key]) as Mnth,
       COUNT([Stock Item Key]) as [# of Items Sold]
FROM [WideWorldImportersDW].[Fact].[Sale]
GROUP BY YEAR([Invoice Date Key]),
         MONTH([Invoice Date Key])
ORDER BY YEAR([Invoice Date Key]),
         MONTH([Invoice Date Key])
```

The following is the result of the COUNT() function:

Year	Month	# of Items Sold
2013	1	5246
2013	2	3707
2013	3	5330
2013	4	5254
2013	5	5617
2013	6	5287
2013	7	5834
2013	8	4767
2013	9	5021
2013	10	5097
2013	11	4899
2013	12	4909
2014	1	5610
2014	2	4768
2014	3	5070

Figure 2.8 – Sample result set of the COUNT() function

The MAX() function

This function is used to return the largest value in the column that is being aggregated. Any row containing a NULL value will be ignored. Any column type can be used with this function. The following SQL is a sample using the MAX() function, and *Figure 2.9* shows the associated result set:

```
SELECT [Invoice Date Key],
       MAX([Quantity]) as [# of Items Sold]
FROM [WideWorldImportersDW].[Fact].[Sale]
GROUP BY [Invoice Date Key]
ORDER BY [Invoice Date Key]
```

The following is the result of the MAX() function:

Invoice Date Key	# of Items Sold
2013-01-01	96
2013-01-02	288
2013-01-03	260
2013-01-04	250
2013-01-05	216
2013-01-07	288
2013-01-08	360
2013-01-09	260
2013-01-10	252
2013-01-11	324
2013-01-12	225
2013-01-14	260
2013-01-15	288
2013-01-16	260
2013-01-17	216

Figure 2.9 – Sample result set of the MAX() function

The MIN() Function

This function is the opposite of the MAX() function and is used to return the smallest value in the column that is being aggregated. Any row containing a NULL value will be ignored. Any column type can be used with this function. The following SQL is a sample using the MIN() function:

```
SELECT YEAR([Invoice Date Key]) as Year,
       MIN([Delivery Date Key]) as [Earliest Delivery Date]
```

```
    FROM [WideWorldImportersDW].[Fact].[Sale]
    GROUP BY Year([Invoice Date Key])
    ORDER BY Year([Invoice Date Key])
```

The following is the output of the MIN() function:

Year	Earliest Delivery Date
2013	2013-01-02
2014	2014-01-02
2015	2015-01-02
2016	2016-01-02

Figure 2.10 – Sample result set of the MIN() function

With these functions, you can aggregate your dataset to meet the needs of the analysis you need to perform.

Now that you are aware of the functions that are used for aggregation, let's discuss how to do this efficiently so as to not impact the performance of the SQL query.

Improving performance when aggregating data

Developing SQL queries to aggregate data is a relatively simple process if you understand the granularity that you want to achieve. But there are times that you will need to rework your SQL to enable it to perform more efficiently; this mostly happens when there are many columns that are part of many aggregations. For example, if the result set contains aggregations that are part of another aggregation, you would want to develop the SQL query containing a subquery that creates the initial aggregations and then performs the final aggregation. An alternative would be to create multiple queries to aggregate the data appropriately for each aggregation and then use a MERGE function to create a single dataset to be able to perform your analysis. Here is a sample SQL query that uses subqueries to create an aggregation from two different subjects:

```
SELECT YEAR([Invoice Date Key]) as [Invoice Year]
      ,MONTH([Invoice Date Key]) as [Invoice Month]
    ,COUNT([Customer Key]) as [# of Customers with Orders]
    ,d.[# of Customers] as [# of Customers Received Orders]
FROM [WideWorldImportersDW].[Fact].[Sale],
    (SELECT YEAR([Delivery Date Key]) as [Delivery Year]
        ,MONTH([Delivery Date Key]) as [Deliver Month]
     ,COUNT([Customer Key]) as [# of Customers]
 FROM [WideWorldImportersDW].[Fact].[Sale]
 GROUP BY YEAR([Delivery Date Key])
```

```
            ,MONTH([Delivery Date Key])) d
WHERE YEAR([Invoice Date Key]) = d.[Delivery Year]
AND MONTH([Invoice Date Key]) = d.[Deliver Month]
GROUP BY YEAR([Invoice Date Key])
        ,MONTH([Invoice Date Key])
   ,[# of Customers]
ORDER BY YEAR([Invoice Date Key])
        ,MONTH([Invoice Date Key]);
```

Figure 2.11 shows a sample of the result set from the preceding query. In this case, the aggregation of invoices to deliveries by year and month:

Invoice Year	Invoice Month	# of Customers with Orders	# of Customers Received Orders
2013	7	5834	5637
2013	8	4767	4877
2013	9	5021	4934
2013	10	5097	5092
2013	11	4899	5022
2013	12	4909	4675
2014	1	5610	5595
2014	2	4768	4911
2014	3	5070	5006
2014	4	5443	5427
2014	5	5930	6053
2014	6	5798	5772
2014	7	6227	6229
2014	8	5059	5202
2014	9	5059	4914

Figure 2.11 – Aggregation function and results using a subquery

Here is a sample SQL query that uses a JOIN function to bring the data together in a single result set:

```
SELECT YEAR([Invoice Date Key]) as [Invoice Year]
        ,MONTH([Invoice Date Key]) as [Invoice Month]
    ,COUNT([Customer Key]) as [# of Customers with Orders]
    ,d.[# of Customers] as [# of Customers Received Orders]
FROM [WideWorldImportersDW].[Fact].[Sale]
JOIN (SELECT YEAR([Delivery Date Key]) as [Delivery Year]
        ,MONTH([Delivery Date Key]) as [Deliver Month]
     ,COUNT([Customer Key]) as [# of Customers]
```

```
FROM [WideWorldImportersDW].[Fact].[Sale]
 GROUP BY YEAR([Delivery Date Key])
        ,MONTH([Delivery Date Key])) d
ON YEAR([Invoice Date Key]) = d.[Delivery Year]
AND MONTH([Invoice Date Key]) = d.[Deliver Month]
GROUP BY YEAR([Invoice Date Key])
        ,MONTH([Invoice Date Key])
  ,[# of Customers]
ORDER BY YEAR([Invoice Date Key])
        ,MONTH([Invoice Date Key]);
```

Figure 2.12 shows the result set from running the preceding SQL query:

Invoice Year	Invoice Month	# of Customers with Orders	# of Customers Received Orders
2013	1	5246	5013
2013	2	3707	3805
2013	3	5330	5465
2013	4	5254	4992
2013	5	5617	5648
2013	6	5287	5518
2013	7	5834	5637
2013	8	4767	4877
2013	9	5021	4934
2013	10	5097	5092
2013	11	4899	5022
2013	12	4909	4675
2014	1	5610	5595
2014	2	4768	4911
2014	3	5070	5006
2014	4	5443	5427
2014	5	5930	6053
2014	6	5798	5772
2014	7	6227	6229
2014	8	5059	5202
2014	9	5059	4914

Figure 2.12 – Aggregation function and results using a JOIN function

Notice that both methods return the same result set; the first is more of an older style, while the second is the more modern approach that is often used today. The older style is included here in case an analyst comes across some older queries in their work.

The choice of which option to use is based on the complexity of the two SQL queries and whether the SL queries will have the same information. These options can be used with any of the aggregation functions discussed previously. With these methods, you can break down your SQL queries into smaller and simpler ones to make the entire SQL easier to maintain and troubleshoot.

Summary

In this chapter, we discussed when and how you aggregate which data that will be collected in your dataset.

We started by discussing what data you should be aggregating to make your data easier to analyze once the dataset is created. We followed that up with a brief discussion of when you should aggregate the data. Once we learned what data to aggregate and when it should be aggregated, we discussed the various functions that can be used to aggregate the data. We then wrapped up the chapter by discussing how a SQL query could be broken down into multiple SQL queries to make them easier to troubleshoot and maintain. Then we showed how the queries could be combined using a subquery or a JOIN function to combine the results of multiple queries into a single result set.

You now have the necessary skills to collect data and aggregate it into a result set that will be easy to analyze. In the next chapter, we will continue your SQL journey by learning how to format the data that you are collecting for the result set.

3

Formatting Your Results for Easier Consumption

In the world of business intelligence, business analysts often get very specific requirements from the end users on what they want to see in the reports. As data analysts/business intelligence engineers, we want to make sure we have the skills to fulfill that need, for example, by getting into details such as the language the report uses, the decimal precision for the total spending of a customer, to the specific date format for a quarterly payout. These are all things we should gather requirements for from our end users and have the skill to deliver. Creating easily readable results is almost as important as the data itself!

In this chapter, we'll learn to format a few different fields by going through some examples that display the breadth and flexibility available to us. Starting with dates, as they would be seen in different countries around the world and in the many different day, month, quarter, and year combos possible. Next, we will look at various number formats and the functions we can use to adjust them. Finally, in this chapter, we will also discuss the importance of giving our result columns meaningful aliases to help end users. It won't be an exhaustive review of all the options but enough to make sure we have a good foundation to continue in this book.

In this chapter, we will cover the following main topics:

- Using the FORMAT() function
- Formatting dates and numbers with CAST(), CONVERT(), and ROUND(), among others
- Comparing FORMAT(), CONVERT(), and CAST()
- Aliasing columns with meaningful names

Technical requirements

To work with the examples and illustrations in this chapter, you will need Azure Data Studio or SQL Server Management Studio installed. We will be working with the `WideWorldImportersDW` database on SQL Server or Azure SQL Database. Please refer to the *Appendix* for tool installation and database restoration guidance.

You will find the code from this chapter here on GitHub: `https://github.com/PacktPublishing/SQL-Query-Design-Best-Practices/tree/main/Chapter03`

Using the FORMAT() function

`FORMAT()` is an extremely versatile function for changing how certain strings, dates, and numeric values look. We will consider a few popular things we can do with `FORMAT()` in this section.

For the examples in this section, we will mainly leverage the dimension date table and the fact sales table from the `WideWorldImportersDW` database discussed in previous chapters to showcase date and number formatting possibilities. Let's check out some of the possibilities in the following sections.

Format() with culture

Let's start with a simple example of culture formatting.

The `FORMAT()` function comes with preset culture-specific formats we can pass in as a parameter. This is a great way for us to start with our initial draft of the report to show to the business users and get more specific requirements on each element.

Now let us try the following code in conjunction with the World Wide Importer database:

```
SELECT TOP(3) FORMAT( [Date], 'd', 'en-US' ) 'US English'
       ,FORMAT( [Date], 'd', 'en-gb' ) 'British English'
       ,FORMAT( [Date], 'd', 'de-de' ) 'German'
       ,FORMAT( [Date], 'd', 'zh-cn' ) 'Chinese Simplified
(PRC)'
  FROM [Dimension].[Date]
```

As we can see, the function takes in the following three arguments:

- The value we are trying to format. In this case, the Date field from [Dimension].[Date] table.

- A format string that could be a standard format string such as d, D, or g. In this case, we chose d, which means short date format. A comprehensive list of strings accepted can be found here `https://learn.microsoft.com/en-us/dotnet/standard/base-types/standard-date-and-time-format-strings`.

- An optional culture argument that's used to specify the culture of the format we are trying to present here. If this value is not set, then the language of the session is used as the default. A commonly supported list of cultures can be found at `https://learn.microsoft.com/en-us/bingmaps/rest-services/common-parameters-and-types/supported-culture-codes`.

Here is an example for this:

	US English	British English	German	Chinese Simplified (PRC)
1	1/1/2013	01/01/2013	01.01.2013	2013/1/1
2	1/2/2013	02/01/2013	02.01.2013	2013/1/2
3	1/3/2013	03/01/2013	03.01.2013	2013/1/3

Figure 3.1 – Results of the query

Looking at the returned result, we can see there could be a sharp difference between cultures. It is a great idea to start with any of these based on business users' location to show them the values and gather more specific requirements on more detailed format needs.

Try the following code with the same database:

```
SELECT TOP(3) FORMAT( [Date], 'D', 'en-US' ) 'US English'
       ,FORMAT( [Date], 'D', 'en-gb' ) 'British English'
       ,FORMAT( [Date], 'D', 'de-de' ) 'German'
       ,FORMAT( [Date], 'D', 'zh-cn' ) 'Chinese Simplified
(PRC)'
  FROM [Dimension].[Date]
```

We only changed one argument in this example; the d format string in this example was switched to D. In this case, we chose D, which means the results returned for the date value are in long date format. It provides a longer and more descriptive date and returns in the local language of the cultural value. Have a look at the following results:

	US English	British English	German	Chinese Simplified (PRC)
1	Tuesday, January 1, 2013	01 January 2013	Dienstag, 1. Januar 2013	2013年1月1日
2	Wednesday, January 2, 2013	02 January 2013	Mittwoch, 2. Januar 2013	2013年1月2日
3	Thursday, January 3, 2013	03 January 2013	Donnerstag, 3. Januar 2013	2013年1月3日

Figure 3.2 – Results of the query

As we can see, formatting numbers is easy using the built-in functions. Let's also walk through an example of numbers with the simple `FORMAT()` function:

```
SELECT TOP(3) FORMAT([Quantity],'D','fr-FR' ) 'Quantity'
       ,FORMAT([Unit Price],'C','fr-FR' ) 'Unit Price'
```

```
    ,FORMAT([Tax Rate]/100, 'P', 'fr-FR') 'Tax Rate'
  FROM [Fact].[Sale]
```

Now, in the following example, we are using a few more standard format strings to change the way a numeric value looks. As we can see, D is used for formatting a number to an integer. C stands for currency, and SQL automatically adjusts the associated currency sign for display based on the culture code passed in. P is for percentage; the results add a % sign to the end of the number passed in:

	Quantity	Unit Price	Tax Rate
1	10	230,00 €	15,00 %
2	9	13,00 €	15,00 %
3	9	32,00 €	15,00 %

Figure 3.3 – Results of the query

These are just a few examples to showcase what the FORMAT() functions can do with the standard passed-in values. There are many more combinations you can experiment with and adjust based on end-user feedback. It's highly recommended you try more of them out with the help of the previously mentioned links from Microsoft Learn (*Figure 3.1*). It is important to note that another change takes place in the background when we use FORMAT(). All of the data types, regardless of what they were originally, become the NVARCHAR datatype. Keep this in mind for downstream queries, as you may need to perform a transformation to have it work correctly!

Now that we have a good understanding of the basics of FORMAT(), let us take a look at some of the more advanced uses.

Format() with custom formatting strings

Sometimes business users want a completely different format of dates or numbers because of company conventions or other internal reasons; a simple format might not be sufficient in this case. What should we do then?

The FORMAT() function might still be able to help in this situation since it also supports custom formatting. By passing in a custom string pattern, it adjusts the string's sequence and separators based on the pattern. In the following sections, we'll go through a few examples for time-related data types and a few more for numeric data types.

Format() with time data types

For example, if we run the following code in the World Wide Importer database:

```
SELECT TOP(3) FORMAT( [Date], 'MM-dd-yyyy') AS 'Date'
FROM [Dimension].[Date]
```

We get the result back as shown in *Figure 3.4*:

	Date
1	01-01-2013
2	01-02-2013
3	01-03-2013

Figure 3.4 – Results of the query

Without having to pass in the culture code, the function knows exactly what to do with the format based on the pattern string passed in. MM stands for month value, dd for day, and yyyy for the number of years. It is important to note that case matters for these variables; switching MM to mm would result in the query trying to format the month as minutes, which we know doesn't make sense. We can certainly switch the pattern string up to get different results as needed.

Try the following code on your own to get a better understanding:

```
SELECT FORMAT( [Date], 'yyyy/MM/dd') AS 'Date'
FROM [Dimension].[Date]
```

The results are as follows:

	Date
1	2013/01/01
2	2013/01/02
3	2013/01/03

Figure 3.5 – Results of the query

Let's look at another example:

```
SELECT TOP(3) FORMAT( [Date], 'yyyy') AS 'Year'
FROM [Dimension].[Date]
```

The result returned is shown as follows:

	Year
1	2013
2	2013
3	2013

Figure 3.6 – Results of the query

As shown, since we passed in a pattern that represents four digits for the year, we got back just the year part of the dates. Another good example could be the following:

```
SELECT TOP(3) FORMAT( [Date], 'MM/dd/yyyy HH:mm tt') AS 'Date'
FROM [Dimension].[Date]
```

In this case, we are adding hour, minutes, and AM/PM indicators to the mix. The result we get back looks like the following:

	Date
1	01/01/2013 00:00 AM
2	01/02/2013 00:00 AM
3	01/03/2013 00:00 AM

Figure 3.7 – Results of the query

Because dates in the dimension date table do not have an explicit time element attached in the string, we receive the default **00:00 AM** value for hour and minute here.

Format() with numeric types

Format() also supports custom patterns for numeric values. Refer to the following code:

```
SELECT TOP 3 FORMAT([Tax Rate]/100,'00.00%') 'Tax Rate'
FROM [Fact].[Sale]
```

With 0 as the placeholder in the custom string, the result returned is as follows:

	Tax Rate
1	15.00%
2	15.00%
3	15.00%

Figure 3.8 – Results of the query

As we can see, the function converts a decimal value into a percentage format, as we included the % sign at the end of the custom string. We can also use # as the placeholder to accomplish the same task.

For percentage conversion, we can also use the following pattern: starting the custom string with % or # followed by the number format we expect to receive, FORMAT converts the decimal number into a percentage format as well:

```
SELECT FORMAT(0.15,'#0.0%') [Tax]
```

The result returned is as follows:

	Tax
1	15.0%

Figure 3.9 – Results of the query

There are certainly more things we can do with dates and numeric formats with the FORMAT() function.

> **Note**
>
> Reference for more patterns can be found at https://learn.microsoft.com/en-us/dotnet/standard/base-types/custom-numeric-format-strings.

While the FORMAT() function provides us with great flexibility with conversions in languages and preset formats, we need to bear in mind that the return type of this function is nvarchar() or null. So it is of great importance for us to learn about the functions mentioned in the next section as well to facilitate changing the nvarchar() back to a DATETIME type or an integer type transformation.

Formatting dates and numbers with functions

Besides using the FORMAT() function to reformat dates and numbers, we can also use CONVERT() to achieve the same goals. In the meantime, numbers can be manipulated by using functions such as ROUND(), CEILING(), and FLOOR(). We'll take a closer look at these functions in the following sections.

Formatting dates and numbers with CONVERT() and CAST()

The CONVERT() function takes in three arguments. The first argument is the data field data type, which is used to define the target data type the query returns. The second is the data field we want to change the format of. The third argument is a style code. It is an integer expression that specifies how the CONVERT() function will translate the *expression*. For a NULL style value, NULL is returned. The data type determines the range. CAST() will also be used briefly in the examples because sometimes our data does not include time elements and we want to attach hour and minute information to the result, and CAST() will help a lot in these types of situations.

Formatting dates with CONVERT() and CAST()

Let's take a look at the following example:

```
SELECT TOP(3) CONVERT(VARCHAR, [Date],  112) AS 'Date'
FROM [Dimension].[Date]
```

Here's what we get back from the database:

	Date
1	20130101
2	20130102
3	20130103

Figure 3.10 – Results of the query

As we can see, the - instances between year, month, and date from the original date format were taken out automatically with this style code, as 112 is the ISO code for dates. Let's look at another one of these examples:

```
SELECT TOP 3 CONVERT(VARCHAR, [Date],  12) AS 'Date'
FROM [Dimension].[Date]
```

When we take out 1 from 112, we retrieve the following data:

	Date
1	130101
2	130102
3	130103

Figure 3.11 – Results of the query

As shown in the result, we no longer have a four-digit year number. Instead, a two-digit representation was returned. This consistently happens when we use 2 instead of 102 and 3 instead of 103 as style codes.

Another example worth looking at is the following:

```
SELECT TOP 3 CONVERT(VARCHAR, CAST([Date] AS Datetime),  113)
AS 'Date'
FROM [Dimension].[Date]
```

Instead of using 112 as the style code, we are going to try out 113, and we are casting the date field to a data type of Datetime, meaning we are attaching hour and minute values to the field now:

	Date
1	01 Jan 2013 00:00:00:000
2	02 Jan 2013 00:00:00:000
3	03 Jan 2013 00:00:00:000

Figure 3.12 – Results of the query

As shown, 113 gives us a shorthand descriptive *MM dd yyyy* format with a defaulted standard *HH:mi:ss:mmm* (24-hour) format.

There are a few more style codes for dates available to use, and they can be found here for reference https://learn.microsoft.com/en-us/sql/t-sql/functions/cast-and-convert-transact-sql?view=sql-server-ver16#date-and-time-styles.

Format numbers with CONVERT() and CAST()

Let's start with an example of CONVERT():

```
SELECT CONVERT(DECIMAL(10,2), 102.55268) AS Number
```

In this case, we are trying to limit the length of the decimal number, also known as accuracy or precision. The result looks like this:

Figure 3.13 – Results of the query

As instructed, the function effectively chops off all the digits after the second number to the right of the decimal point. We can change the 2 in DECIMAL(10,2) to adjust the number of digits we preserve from the number. Another comparison we should look at is in the following query. In this example, we will compare the numeric and int arguments' impact on the results.

Run the following query and see whether you notice the difference:

```
SELECT CONVERT(numeric, 102.55268) AS NumericNumber,
CONVERT(int, 102.55268) AS IntegerNumber
```

The result looks like the following:

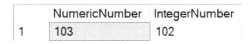

Figure 3.14 – Results of the query

We can easily tell that the conversion of a decimal number to numeric type does a round up (if the digit to the right of the decimal point is larger than 4), and the conversion to an integer simply takes away the numbers to the right of the decimal point.

We could also convert a number to a string, shown as follows, with currency signs in front for easier readability:

```
SELECT '$'+ CONVERT(nvarchar(10), 102.55268) AS Number
```

The result we receive looks like this:

Figure 3.15 – Results of the query

Since we are converting a decimal number to nvarchar, we need to pay attention to the length of nvarchar we assign to the output data type. If we don't allocate enough length to the string, the arithmetic overflow error will appear.

Now let's talk about the CAST() function. It is not too different from CONVERT() when it comes to number conversions. The function takes two arguments. The first is the field or number we want to convert, then we use the AS keyword and specify the second argument, which is the final output data type we are looking for.

Run the following code in any SQL database:

```
SELECT CAST(102.55268 as numeric(10,2)) AS [number]
```

As expected, the result returns us a decimal number with only two digits to the right of the decimal point:

	number
1	102.55

Figure 3.16 – Results of the query

As long as we stick to the syntax of CAST(), the behavior of how it outputs integer and numeric numbers is the same as CONVERT().

Formatting numbers with ROUND() and CEILING()

Besides CONVERT() and CAST(), we can leverage a few more functions when it comes to numbers.

The ROUND() function rounds the decimal number we are looking for to the digit we specify when we call the function.

Here is an example of ROUND():

```
SELECT ROUND(102.55268, 1) AS Number
```

The result is as follows:

	Number
1	102.60000

Figure 3.17 – Results of the query

It doesn't take out the zeros after the decimal point, but it stops the number from going on too long. If we wish to remove the zeros, we can wrap the ROUND() function inside a CONVERT() function as follows:

```
SELECT CONVERT(numeric(10,1),ROUND(102.55268,1)) AS Number
```

This would return the following result:

	Number
1	102.6

Figure 3.18 – Results of the query

When checking with FLOOR(), the result is as follows:

```
SELECT FLOOR(102.55268) AS Number
```

The lower integer, which the decimal input number is the closest to, is returned:

	Number
1	102

Figure 3.19 – Results of the query

And as we probably have guessed, CEILING() does the opposite of FLOOR():

```
SELECT CEILING(-102.55268) AS Number
```

The result returned is as follows:

	Number
1	-102

Figure 3.20 – Results of the query

In conclusion, formatting numbers with TSQL can be very easy using the built-in functions. Next, we explain the functions in depth by drawing comparisons.

Comparing FORMAT(), CONVERT(), and CAST()

Now that we've learned about the frequently used functions for formatting purposes, it might be helpful if we break down the pros and cons of using them.

First off, FORMAT() provides us with the most flexibility and the more intuitive methods to use. However, it only returns nvarchar or null type values, which require more transformation using CONVERT() or CAST() for us to change the field's data type. Also, it can be relatively more expensive to use from a performance perspective and can be very hard on our CPUs. Realistically, though, it is still nice to be able to perform the translations with just the function itself. It is important we recall using this function when that need emerges.

Moving on to CONVERT() and CAST(), these two functions are very similar in many ways. The CONVERT() function can be a bit more flexible as it accepts an optional style parameter that is used for formatting. Because of this extra flexibility, CONVERT() is more popular when datetime() formatting is required. Given CAST() is designed to be more user-friendly as there's not too many things we can do with it, and there's no performance loss using CAST() compared with CONVERT(), we advise you to apply it to all basic conversions.

Now, let us see how aliasing columns with names help the query results.

Alias columns with meaningful names

To ensure our SQL query results are easily presentable and readable, it almost goes without saying that we should always try our best to name the fields with meaningful content to the business. While figuring out what to name the column can be science plus art, there's not much to the actual aliasing process itself. Most of the queries in this chapter ended up with the AS keyword with an alias following. This is all that is needed to ensure the results from a column have a different name.

A simple example is as follows:

Original query:

```
SELECT TOP (3) [Order Key]
     ,[Description]
  FROM [Fact].[Order]
```

Original results:

	Order Key	Description
1	1	Ride on toy sedan car (Black) 1/12 scale
2	2	Developer joke mug - old C developers never die (...
3	3	USB food flash drive - chocolate bar

Figure 3.21 – Results of the query

Aliased query:

```
SELECT TOP (3) [Order Key]
     ,[Description] AS [Product Description]
  FROM [Fact].[Order]
```

Aliased results:

	Order Key	Product Description
1	1	Ride on toy sedan car (Black) 1/12 scale
2	2	Developer joke mug - old C developers never die (...
3	3	USB food flash drive - chocolate bar

Figure 3.22 – Results of the query

Aliasing columns is easy to do but can be tricky to master. To capture the result of a query and decide on a meaningful name for it is something that takes practice; however, as you progress through the book you'll have many opportunities to try!

Summary

In this chapter, we walked through various examples of how we can format dates and numbers using a few different functions, such as FORMAT(), CONVERT(), and CAST(). They should help us to deliver what the business requires from a reporting perspective on data formats. With all these functions, we should be able to handle all of the requirements stakeholders send our way. Just remember to always start from available default formats for the initial walkthrough of the report, and then go into the specifics with the end users to get more detailed requirements and adjust as needed. This not only simplifies the initial build of the report but also allows us to continue with any other queries we may be running without having to worry about data types (remember the FORMAT function turns all inputted data into varchar). It will also save both the developer and business user valuable time.

In the next chapter, we will look at manipulating the results using conditional SQL, further building our toolkit to present the data in a readable format to the consumer.

4

Manipulating Data Results Using Conditional SQL

In previous chapters, we learned how to use the WHERE clause and a series of functions to filter down and format the data results. Now, what if we must give certain field values a new definition to make them more understandable? For example, the state names in the database were stored in abbreviations, however, the reports the data serve are meant to serve international stakeholders. So then, how can we present *IL* as *Illinois* and *CA* as *California* without having to add a column into the database taking up permanent storage space? Or perhaps, for better grouping purposes, we want to be able to provide the report users with a country-level sales revenue number instead of just state-level details. This is when we head into the conditional query world, by defining the grouping rules at query runtime.

In this chapter, we will learn about when and how to use the CASE, COALESCE, and ISNULL statements, noting the advantages and disadvantages they may have over each other in certain use cases.

The main topics we will look at in this chapter are as follows:

- Using the CASE statement
- Using the COALESCE() function
- Using the ISNULL() function

Technical requirements

To work with the examples and illustrations in this chapter, you will need to have Azure Data Studio or **SQL Server Management Studio (SSMS)** installed. We will be working with the WideWorldImportersDW database on SQL Server or Azure SQL Database. Please refer to the *Appendix* for tool installation and database restoration guidance.

You will find the code from this chapter on GitHub: https://github.com/PacktPublishing/SQL-Query-Design-Best-Practices/tree/main/Chapter04

Using the CASE statement

A CASE statement is a widely used expression that takes in a list of conditions, evaluates the database column(s) referred to in the expression and, based on the evaluation of the field value, returns transformed values according to the rules defined.

It is a powerful and versatile tool that can be used to evaluate multiple conditions and return different results based on those conditions. It can be especially useful in scenarios where we need to handle different data types or values in a flexible and efficient way. It can be used in a few places in a SQL statement.

In this section, we'll go through a few examples to showcase how to use it in SELECT, ORDER BY, UPDATE, and HAVING.

Using a simple CASE expression in a SELECT statement

The first way to use this expression is a simple version where the expression only looks at one field and only searches for the value from that field:

```
SELECT TOP(3) [Stock Holding Key], [Bin Location],
[BinLocationDetailed] =
CASE [Bin Location]
  WHEN 'L-1' THEN 'LowerLevel1'
  WHEN 'L-2' THEN 'LowerLevel2'
  WHEN 'L-3' THEN 'LowerLevel3'
  ELSE 'N/A'
END,
  [Target Stock Level]
FROM [Fact].[Stock Holding]
```

The results are as follows:

	Stock Holding Key	Bin Location	BinLocationDetailed	Target Stock Level
1	1	L-1	LowerLevel1	100
2	2	L-1	LowerLevel1	100
3	3	L-2	LowerLevel2	120

Figure 4.1 – Results of the query

In this example, we use the [Bin Location] field from the [Fact].[Stock Holding] table to demonstrate how a simple CASE statement can be called. We first define the name of the new field we are trying to create (in this case, BinLocationDetailed) followed by the = sign. The first part of a CASE statement identifies which field from the dataset we want to add additional context to. Then, WHEN/THEN combinations – just like they sound, the logic of the rules are ingested here into the statement.

For any row of record containing the value after WHEN, the expression will return the value after the respective THEN. When we finish listing all but one grouping, we use the ELSE keyword to define the rest of the return value outside of the specific values that we are looking for from the existing field. Refer to the previous example to help understand the syntax! The statement finishes with the END keyword.

Using a searched CASE expression in a SELECT statement

Using this CASE expression, we are ingesting logic into the query to help with the grouping of a specific field we chose to use the range with.

Here, we are using a range of values instead of a specific one to drive that grouping:

```
SELECT TOP(3) [Order Key], [WWI Order ID], [Total Excluding
Tax],
  CASE WHEN [Total Excluding Tax] >= 1500 THEN 'Extra Large'
      WHEN [Total Excluding Tax] >= 500 AND [Total Excluding
Tax] < 1500 THEN 'Large'
      WHEN [Total Excluding Tax] >= 100 AND [Total Excluding
Tax] < 500 THEN 'Medium'
      ELSE  'Small' END AS [Sales Size]
FROM [Fact].[Order]
```

In this case, we are trying to group orders with a total amount higher than 1500 as Extra Large, orders with a total amount between 500 and 1500 as Large, orders that have a total amount of 100 to 500 as Medium, and all orders that have a total amount of less than 100 as Small. As we can see in the following top three results, the groupings of the sales order sizes are accurately presented as defined:

	Order Key	WWI Order ID	Total Excluding Tax	Sales Size
1	1	1	2300.00	Extra Large
2	2	2	117.00	Medium
3	3	2	288.00	Medium

Figure 4.2 – Results of the query

Using CASE in an ORDER BY statement

Just like how we can leverage a CASE expression in SELECT statements for extra logic ingestion, it is also doable in ORDER BY statements. It can be used to specify the order in which the query results should be returned. This enables us to control the sorting of the query results based on multiple criteria or conditions. For example, consider the following:

```
SELECT TOP (1000) [Employee Key]
  ,[WWI Employee ID]
```

```
    , [Employee]
    , [Is Salesperson]
FROM [Dimension].[Employee]
WHERE [Valid To] >= getdate()
AND [Employee Key] <> 0
ORDER BY CASE WHEN [Is Salesperson] = 0 THEN [Employee Key]
END ASC,
    CASE WHEN [Is Salesperson] = 1 THEN [WWI Employee ID] END
DESC
```

In this example, we are ordering the employees from the [Dimension].[Employee] table by grouping them into two groups: salespeople and non-salespeople. Then, we order the two groups by descending employee key sequence. If the employee's salesperson flag is 1, then order the non-salesperson's employee key in ascending order. We can observe the results in the return here:

	Employee Key	WWI Employee ID	Employee	Is Salesperson
1	212	20	Jack Potter	1
2	208	16	Archer Lamble	1
3	207	15	Taj Shand	1
4	206	14	Lily Code	1
5	205	13	Hudson Hollinworth	1
6	200	8	Anthony Grosse	1
7	199	7	Amy Trefl	1
8	198	6	Sophia Hinton	1
9	195	3	Hudson Onslow	1
10	194	2	Kayla Woodcock	1
11	196	4	Isabella Rupp	0
12	197	5	Eva Muirden	0
13	201	9	Alica Fatnowna	0
14	202	10	Stella Rosenhain	0
15	203	11	Ethan Onslow	0
16	204	12	Henry Forlonge	0
17	209	17	Piper Koch	0
18	210	18	Katie Darwin	0
19	211	19	Jai Shand	0

Figure 4.3 – Results of the query

As we expected, all the employees with an [Is Salesperson] flag as 1 were returned in descending order by their employee keys. Employees with an [Is Salesperson] flag equal to 0 were returned in ascending order by WWI Employee ID.

The following is another example that showcases the more direct approach of assigning values to certain fields and ordering by that assigned value:

```
SELECT [Employee Key]
      , [Employee]
    , [Preferred Name]
FROM [Dimension].[Employee]
WHERE [Valid To] >= getdate()
  AND [Employee Key] <> 0
ORDER BY CASE WHEN [Preferred Name] LIKE 'H%' OR [Preferred
Name] LIKE 'K%' THEN 1
      WHEN [Preferred Name] LIKE 'A%' THEN 2
      WHEN [Preferred Name] LIKE 'D%' OR [Preferred Name] LIKE
'P%' THEN 3
      ELSE 4
END ASC, [Employee] ASC
```

The result is as follows:

	Employee Key	Employee	Preferred Name
1	204	Henry Forlonge	Henry
2	205	Hudson Hollinworth	Hudson
3	195	Hudson Onslow	Hudson
4	210	Katie Darwin	Katie
5	194	Kayla Woodcock	Kayla
6	201	Alica Fatnowna	Alica
7	199	Amy Trefl	Amy
8	200	Anthony Grosse	Anthony
9	208	Archer Lamble	Archer
10	209	Piper Koch	Piper
11	203	Ethan Onslow	Ethan
12	197	Eva Muirden	Eva
13	196	Isabella Rupp	Isabella
14	212	Jack Potter	Jack
15	211	Jai Shand	Jai
16	206	Lily Code	Lily
17	198	Sophia Hinton	Sophia
18	202	Stella Rosenhain	Stella
19	207	Taj Shand	Taj

Figure 4.4 – Results of the query

In this example, the CASE statement is used in the ORDER BY clause to specify the order in which the [Preferred Name] field should be sorted. The CASE() statement assigns a numerical value to certain letters of the alphabet with which [Preferred Name] starts. With H and K assigned the same lowest value of 1, A with 2, and D and P with 3, we make sure that the query results are sorted first by [Preferred Name], with H and K being returned on the top of the list, A follows, then D and P, and then all the rest listed in alphabetical order.

Overall, using the CASE statement in the ORDER BY clause can be a useful way of controlling query result sorting and getting the results returned in desired orders. This can be especially helpful when sorting criteria are complex and difficult to express using the typical ORDER BY syntax.

Using CASE in an UPDATE statement

The CASE expression can be used in an UPDATE statement to specify the new values to be assigned to a field based on desired conditions. This allows us to add extra logic to our update query and handle different data types or values in a flexible and efficient way.

For example, currently, the top 10 records returned from the query are as follows:

```
SELECT TOP(10)
    [City]
      ,[State Province]
      ,[Sales Territory]
  FROM [Dimension].[City]
  WHERE City <> 'Unknown'
```

This returns the following result:

	City	State Province	Sales Territory
1	Carrollton	New York	Mideast
2	Carrollton	Virginia	Southeast
3	Carrollton	Illinois	Great Lakes
4	Carrollton	Missouri	Plains
5	Carrollton	Ohio	Great Lakes
6	Carrollton	Kentucky	Southeast
7	Carrollton	Georgia	Southeast
8	Carrollton	Alabama	Southeast
9	Carrollton	Mississippi	Southeast
10	Carrollton	Texas	Southwest

Figure 4.5 – Results of the query

Now, let's write and execute an UPDATE statement like the following:

```
UPDATE [Dimension].[City]
SET [Sales Territory] =
 (CASE
 WHEN [State Province] = 'New York' THEN 'Eastcoast'
 WHEN [State Province] = 'Illinois' THEN 'Midwest'
 WHEN [State Province] = 'Missouri' THEN 'Midwest'
   END
  )
 WHERE [State Province] IN ('New York', 'Illinois',
'Missouri')
```

The result returned by SELECT changes to the following:

	City	State Province	Sales Territory
1	Carrollton	New York	Eastcoast
2	Carrollton	Virginia	Southeast
3	Carrollton	Illinois	Midwest
4	Carrollton	Missouri	Midwest
5	Carrollton	Ohio	Great Lakes
6	Carrollton	Kentucky	Southeast
7	Carrollton	Georgia	Southeast
8	Carrollton	Alabama	Southeast
9	Carrollton	Mississippi	Southeast
10	Carrollton	Texas	Southwest

Figure 4.6 – Results of the query

As we can see, the CASE statement takes the [State Province] field value as input and defines new [Sales Territory] values for the respective fields. Notice that when the UPDATE statement was run, the returned message showed 13328 rows affected. This reflects the fact that all rows with [State Province] as New York, Illinois, or Missouri were updated. And if we compare closely, the row with New York in [State Province] has [Sales Territory] as Eastcoast now. The same thing happened to Illinois and Missouri.

Now that we know how the CASE statement can be used in UPDATE() queries, let's run the following query to reset the table to its original state for future demonstrations in the book:

```
UPDATE [Dimension].[City]
  SET [Sales Territory] =
```

```
  (CASE
   WHEN [State Province] = 'New York' THEN 'Mideast'
   WHEN [State Province] = 'Illinois' THEN 'Great Lakes'
   WHEN [State Province] = 'Missouri' THEN 'Plains'
  END
   )
  WHERE [State Province] IN ('New York', 'Illinois',
'Missouri')
```

Using CASE in a HAVING statement

The CASE statement can be used in a HAVING clause to ingest specific conditional logic for filtering the results of a query based on aggregated values.

Here is an example of it:

```
SELECT TOP(20) [Customer Key],
    SUM([Total Excluding Tax]) AS [Customer Total Spending]
FROM [Fact].[Transaction]
WHERE [Customer Key] <> 0
GROUP BY [Customer Key]
HAVING
CASE
   WHEN SUM([Total Excluding Tax]) >= 150000 THEN 'High'
   WHEN SUM([Total Excluding Tax]) >= 10000 AND SUM([Total
Excluding Tax]) < 150000 THEN 'Medium'
   ELSE 'Low'
END = 'High'
ORDER BY [Customer Total Spending] ASC
```

The following are the results:

	Customer Key	Customer Total Spending
1	378	154555.45
2	374	169931.60
3	111	181002.15
4	197	183277.70
5	227	183321.40
6	340	185707.00
7	66	188680.45
8	292	190017.30
9	305	195208.05
10	258	197314.45
11	225	198555.45
12	369	199441.80
13	358	201364.45
14	251	203346.30
15	126	203960.40
16	91	204303.60
17	348	204815.50
18	303	205312.55
19	24	206388.85
20	175	207512.50

Figure 4.7 – Results of the query

When a CASE expression is used in a HAVING clause as we can see, it enables us to determine the groups of customers we are trying to categorize the data into. We can pick the specific group we want to see in the filter and get the final result the business users are looking for. It largely makes things easier for us from a data manipulation perspective, as the logic is no longer stored in a field specifically, but instead, in something we create dynamically. In this case, with ORDER BY at the end of the query demanding an ascending sort for the final results, all of our results are over the lower limit of 150,000 as a high spending group, meaning the CASE statement in the HAVING clause helped us sort out the grouping.

Of course, the same logic of using a CASE expression in a HAVING clause can be done with a SUM and GROUP BY statement nested within a SELECT statement as well.

Let's try the following code:

```
SELECT TOP(20) [Customer Key],
    [Customer Total Spending],
    [Spending Group]
FROM (
```

```
SELECT [Customer Key],
   SUM([Total Excluding Tax]) AS [Customer Total Spending],
   CASE
     WHEN SUM([Total Excluding Tax]) >= 150000 THEN 'High'
     WHEN SUM([Total Excluding Tax]) >= 10000 AND SUM([Total
Excluding Tax]) < 150000 THEN 'Medium'
     ELSE 'Low'
   END AS [Spending Group]
 FROM [Fact].[Transaction]
 WHERE [Customer Key] <> 0
 GROUP BY [Customer Key]
) AS CustomerGroup
WHERE [Spending Group] = 'High'
ORDER BY [Customer Total Spending] ASC
```

The results are as follows:

	Customer Key	Customer Total Spending	Spending Group
1	378	154555.45	High
2	374	169931.60	High
3	111	181002.15	High
4	197	183277.70	High
5	227	183321.40	High
6	340	185707.00	High
7	66	188680.45	High
8	292	190017.30	High
9	305	195208.05	High
10	258	197314.45	High
11	225	198555.45	High
12	369	199441.80	High
13	358	201364.45	High
14	251	203346.30	High
15	126	203960.40	High
16	91	204303.60	High
17	348	204815.50	High
18	303	205312.55	High
19	24	206388.85	High
20	175	207512.50	High

Figure 4.8 – Results of the query

As we can deduce from the results, the two ways of using CASE statements generate the exact same result. The HAVING clause has the advantage of being easier to read. For more information on HAVING clauses, take a look at https://learn.microsoft.com/en-us/sql/t-sql/queries/select-having-transact-sql?view=sql-server-ver16.

In general, CASE statements help us ingest the logic into the grouping of data without us having to store the logic as a physical field in the database. This greatly increases the flexibility we have with our report creation.

In the next section, we will take a look at how using COALESCE() statements can help when working with Null values.

Using the COALESCE() expression

The COALESCE() expression allows us to specify a list of values and return the first non-null value in the list. To produce meaningful data, we start by analyzing the dataset, exploring the data values, and transforming values as required. It is very important that we understand how to handle NULL values in datasets, as they can potentially affect the results of our queries, our calculations, and ultimately, the reports we are presenting to the end users. COALESCE() was primarily designed to help us with NULL value handling. We'll walk through a few examples in this section and talk about the differences between COALESCE() and CASE.

How to use COALESCE()

Let's go through a few simple examples to get an understanding of how it works:

```
SELECT COALESCE(NULL, NULL, 8,12,13) AS [Output]
```

The result is as follows:

Figure 4.9 – Result of the query

Just as we expected, the output value of the query is 8 since it is the first non-null value from the list we sent in. The expression ignores the first two NULL values, and 12 and 13 instances occur after 8.

We can try this out with a different data type as well:

```
SELECT COALESCE(NULL, NULL, NULL, 'A','B', NULL, NULL) AS
[Output]
```

The result returned is as follows:

Figure 4.10 – Result of the query

Again, A is the first non-null value in the list, so it gets returned. The expression ignored the three NULL instances in front of A and the B value, as well as the extra two NULL instances.

However, even though the COALESCE() statement can take multiple expressions, it gets a little more complicated when trying to use it on several different data types simultaneously.

Let's run the following code in SSMS:

```
SELECT COALESCE(NULL, NULL, 2, 3, 'A', NULL, NULL) AS [Output]
```

The output of the query looks as follows:

	Output
1	2

Figure 4.11 – Result of the query

From the previous result, it seems as though we can pass in different data types to the expression. So let's try this one as well:

```
SELECT COALESCE(NULL, NULL, 'A', 2, 3, NULL, NULL) AS [Output]
```

The result returned is as follows:

```
Msg 245, Level 16, State 1, Line 1
Conversion failed when converting the varchar value 'A' to data type int.
```

Figure 4.12 – Result of the query

This time, unfortunately, the result we get is an error message. It's important we take a minute to remember this example. Depending on the order of the data types passed in, we may get an error from the expression. As we can tell from the two examples, the expression evaluates each data type and returns the data type with the highest precedence; if we pass in a varchar value before an integer, the result will error out because it doesn't know how to convert the varchar value to an integer to compare them. It is best to avoid mixing data types when we use COALESCE(). However, if we have to, we should always pass in the integer fields to the expression before any varchar fields. To learn more about data type precedence, check out this page from Microsoft: https://learn.microsoft.com/en-us/sql/t-sql/data-types/data-type-precedence-transact-sql?redirectedfrom=MSDN&view=sql-server-ver16.

Using the `WideWorldImporters` database, let's walk through a popular use case of COALESCE() for concatenating strings.

Run the following code:

```
SELECT [Transaction Key] AS [TransactionKey],
  [WWI Invoice ID] AS [WWIInvoiceID],
  [WWI Customer Transaction ID] AS [WWICustomerTransactionID],
  '00000' + CAST([Transaction Key] AS VARCHAR(3)) +
COALESCE(CAST([WWI Invoice ID] AS VARCHAR(3)),'00') + CAST([WWI
Customer Transaction ID] AS VARCHAR(3)) AS  [WWI ID],
  '00000' + CAST([Transaction Key] AS VARCHAR(3)) + CAST([WWI
Invoice ID] AS VARCHAR(3)) + CAST([WWI Customer Transaction ID]
AS VARCHAR(3)) AS [WWI ID with NULL]
FROM [Fact].[Transaction]
WHERE [Transaction Key] IN (40,41,42,43)
```

In this example, we can tell we are trying to define a new column, concatenating the transaction key, `WWI Invoice ID`, and `WWI Customer Transaction ID` together to generate a new field called `WWI ID`. However, some of the `WWI Invoice ID` values are NULL. Using COALESCE(), we avoided NULL values showing up in the new `WWI ID` field.

The result returned is as follows:

	TransactionKey	WWIInvoiceID	WWICustomerTransactionID	WWI ID	WWI ID with NULL
1	40	40	127	000004040127	000004040127
2	41	41	130	000004141130	000004141130
3	42	NULL	231	000004200231	NULL
4	43	NULL	232	000004300232	NULL

Figure 4.13 – Results of the query

As shown, using COALESCE(X, '00'), we can replace the X field's NULL value with 00 and avoid the ID field having NULL concatenated into the string. This is one of the most leveraged use cases of COALESCE() in real life. It is important to note that concatenating a NULL value into a string results in returning NULL. In the next section, we will look at the similarities and differences between COALESCE() and CASE.

Comparing COALESCE() and CASE()

Now that we learned about both the COALESCE() and CASE expressions, you might be wondering, *What is the difference between the two? Are they really that different?*

The answer is they are not really that different. The COALESCE() expression is just a shortcut for the CASE expression, specifically for NULL values.

Look at the following CASE statement (do not run, this is a syntactical demonstration):

```
CASE WHEN X1 IS NOT NULL THEN Y1
     WHEN X2 is NOT NULL THEN Y2
...
     ELSE Yn
END
```

With this CASE statement, the input values are evaluated N times because an expression that contains subqueries is evaluated twice. It's not enough for the SQL engine to determine what values are really to be returned if it doesn't go through all scenarios. Different results can be returned between the first evaluation and the second one.

More details on this can be found here if you are interested to know more about it: https://learn.microsoft.com/en-us/sql/t-sql/language-elements/coalesce-transact-sql?view=sql-server-ver16.

Generally speaking, the COALESCE() expression gives us great flexibility in dealing with NULL values and is very frequently leveraged. It is important we try to utilize it when we see fit. COALESCE() is able to help us find the NULL values: however, in the next section, we will look at a statement capable of determining what NULL is.

Using ISNULL() function

The ISNULL() function is used to return the defined input value in case the passed-in expression has NULL as its value. It only accepts two parameters and only evaluates the passed-in expression. We will walk through a few simple examples of it and do a comparison between ISNULL() and COALESCE() in this section.

How to use ISNULL()

Let's jump into the examples!

Run the following code in SSMS:

```
SELECT ISNULL('Hello', 'World') AS [Output]
```

The result returned is as follows:

Figure 4.14 – Result of the query

As we can see, when we pass in two `VARCHAR` values, the function evaluates the first one (in this case, `Hello`) and determines it is not a `NULL` value, so it returns the `Hello` value itself as result.

Now, run the following chunk of code:

```
SELECT ISNULL(NULL, 'World') AS [Output]
```

The result we get this time is as follows:

Figure 4.15 – Result of the query

This time, we received `World` as a result of the query because the first value passed in is `NULL`. Ultimately, the function is evaluating the first value and deciding which value to send out. If the first value is `NULL`, then the second value will be used as the result, and vice versa.

Let's try to run a third one just to make sure we are understanding this correctly:

```
SELECT ISNULL('Hello', NULL) AS [Output]
```

As we expected, the result returned is as follows :

Output
1   Hello

Figure 4.16 – Result of the query

This proves our theory of how the function behaves. It is as simple as we described earlier. All it does is determine whether the first value is `NULL`, in which case, it will return the second defined value as a result.

If we do this in the `WideWorldImportersDW` database, an example could be as follows:

```
SELECT [Transaction Key],
  [WWI Invoice ID],
  ISNULL([WWI Invoice ID],'0') AS [WWIInvoiceID]
FROM [Fact].[Transaction]
WHERE [Transaction Key] IN (40,41,42,43)
```

The result came back as follows:

	Transaction Key	WWI Invoice ID	WWIInvoiceID
1	40	40	40
2	41	41	41
3	42	NULL	0
4	43	NULL	0

Figure 4.17 – Results of the query

The NULL values from the WWI Invoice ID field are all replaced by the 0 value as defined in the second parameter in the query.

NULL can be a tricky value to handle from time to time. If you are not familiar with the concept, check out these two pages before building out your use cases with ISNULL():

https://learn.microsoft.com/en-us/sql/t-sql/language-elements/null-and-unknown-transact-sql?view=sql-server-ver16

https://www.red-gate.com/hub/product-learning/sql-prompt/the-null-mistake-and-other-sql-null-heresies

Comparing ISNULL() and COALESCE()

We have learned about how to use ISNULL() and saw how it can be put to work. Let's do a comparison between the two expressions that help us with NULL value handling and do a quick summary:

- ISNULL() takes two parameters (and only two), whereas COALESCE() can take more than two.

- ISNULL() is a function where the value in it only gets evaluated once, and in the previous section, we discussed how COALESCE() might get evaluated multiple times because of the existence of subqueries. Although based on multiple sources of performance checks, ISNULL() and COALESCE() perform quite similarly when used to solve the same problem.

- ISNULL() takes a NULL value and converts it into an integer; it also only evaluates the first parameter passed in. While using COALESCE(), however, the data type has to be provided, and it returns the data type of the value with the highest precedence. That's also why, in some cases, we see data type conversion difficulties resulting in errors.

For more details on this topic, please visit https://learn.microsoft.com/en-us/sql/t-sql/language-elements/coalesce-transact-sql?view=sql-server-ver16.

With this, we have seen how we can apply the ISNULL() function to be used with conditional applications.

Summary

In this chapter, we walked through a few examples of conditional statements. Some of them allow us to add more complicated logic to the dataset we are trying to deliver, while some of them help us with handling NULL values.

To summarize, conditional statements provide us with great convenience when it comes to defining logic on what is to be executed on what condition. With them, data professionals like us can finally begin to ingest logic into any data queries on the fly. By allowing added complexity, they enable more sophisticated techniques to be leveraged on changing and viewing the information within a database. Being able to fluently use the common conditional statements will certainly give us a leg up in our daily operations on query writing and report building.

In the next chapter, we will take a look at common table expressions that will help us better utilize the knowledge we gained here.

Part 2:
Solving Complex Business and Data Problems in Your Queries

In this part, we begin to expand into more advanced query solutions. The four chapters in this section focus on complex query construction to solve specific business needs. Often these techniques are either improperly implemented or not even used to solve complex business problems, which results in inefficient queries:

- *Chapter 5, Using Common Table Expressions*
- *Chapter 6, Analyze Your Data Using Window Functions*
- *Chapter 7, Reshaping Your Data with Advanced Techniques*
- *Chapter 8, Impact of SQL Security on Query Results*

5

Using Common Table Expressions

Common Table Expressions (CTEs) are a powerful way to compartmentalize and organize your complex queries into bite-sized chunks that you can then manipulate the final output required by your process. CTEs can also be used to create recursive/hierarchal relationships to report on common parent/child scenarios, such as manager/employee.

In this chapter, we will learn how to use CTEs as one of the techniques to solve complex business and data problems. We'll cover the best practices for creating and organizing CTEs, creating recursive queries for use in hierarchies, and reviewing other situations where CTEs can be used.

We are going to cover the following main topics in this chapter:

- Creating CTEs
- Using CTEs in recursive relationships
- Recursive alternatives for Synapse

By the end of this chapter, you will understand why CTEs are important for query creators, how to create and use them, and how to utilize them to create meaningful outputs for your business problems.

Technical requirements

To work with the examples and illustrations in this chapter, you will need to have Azure Data Studio and or SQL Server Management Studio installed. We will be working with the `WideWorldImporters` database and/or the `WideWorldImportersDW` database on SQL Server or Azure SQL Database. Please refer to the *Appendix* section for tool installation and database restoration guidance.

You will find the code from this chapter on GitHub: `https://github.com/PacktPublishing/SQL-Query-Design-Best-Practices/tree/main/Chapter05`

Creating CTEs

Creating a CTE is not a complex process. It is a simple query that defines the name of the CTE and then uses it:

```
;   --previous line must have a ; terminator
WITH
ISODates as (
SELECT distinct [Date]
      ,[ISO Week Number] as [ISOWeekNumber]
  FROM [Dimension].[Date])


SELECT Date, [ISOWeekNumber]
FROM ISODates
```

The query gets the distinct list of Date instances and ISO Week Number from Date Dimension in the WorldWideImportersDW database sample. The start of the query is the with keyword, which has a semi-colon terminating the line before it. Next is the name you will use to refer to the CTE in any future queries, in this case, ISODates. The query renames ISO Week Number to ISOWeekNumber. The final step is to write a query that selects from or uses the CTE table that was created. Refer to the following figure:

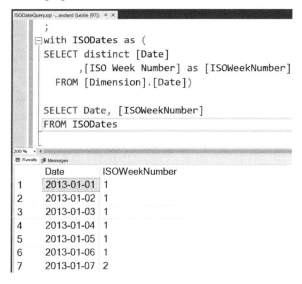

Figure 5.1 – A complete CTE query and the result set from the
WorldWideImportersDW sample database

You can now create a CTE and display the results.

A great technique for creating complex queries that utilize CTEs is set theory. By thinking about the results of the queries as sets and how to combine them, we will limit the records that need to be analyzed, increase the efficiency of the query engine, and make our queries easier for others to understand.

Set theory for queries

Before we move into a little more complicated query, let's talk a little bit about set theory and how it can be applied to creating queries. When you think of a set of something, you usually think about the shared characteristics or attributes of the items in the set where the order of the items is not relevant. When we are working with queries, we can create CTEs that represent the set that we are trying to identify. We can then use JOIN statements for the CTE to get the attributes about the items in that set that we are interested in including in our final output.

Think back to your school days when you learned about Venn diagrams:

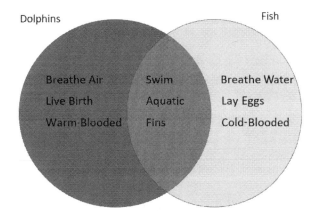

Figure 5.2 – A Venn diagram showing attributes of dolphins and fish

In this example, we have a group of facts about dolphins and a group of facts about fish. Some facts apply to both groups. That is the concept you are trying to implement in your queries. Try to think about how you can group your data into sets that you can then apply a left-hand, inner, or right-hand join to add or eliminate records from your final data result set.

By thinking about the parts of the query as different sets and combining them based on the attributes they share, you can create a result set that is very specific to your use case.

Creating a more complex CTE

Let's apply what we have learned about CTEs and set theory to a real-world example. The `Sales` table in the `WorldWideImportersDW` database sample has a single record that has a value in either [Total Dry Items] or [Total Chiller Items]. We have been assigned a report that will show, for every day in a specific period, the number of total items, combining both [Total Dry Items] and [Total Chiller Items] on each day. The *sets* of data that are required to combine into a single data set are as follows:

- All the dates in the period requested

- All the sales in the period where there were [Total Dry Items] and the date they were sold

- All the sales in the period where there were [Total Chiller Items] and the date they were sold

In the following query, we have three CTEs: `ISODates`, `DryTotalQuery`, and `ChillerTotalQuery`. Each query has a `date` field that is used in `LEFT OUTER JOIN` for the full list of dates selected from `ISODates`; the other CTEs have the total number of dry items by date and the total number of chiller items by date:

```
--start of CTE queries
WITH
ISODates as (
SELECT DISTINCT [Date],[ISO Week Number] as [ISOWeekNumber]
   FROM [Dimension].[Date])
--separate multiple CTEs with comma
,DryTotalQuery as (
SELECT [Invoice Date Key] as DryInvoiceDateKey
       ,Sum([Total Dry Items]) as DailyTotalDry
   FROM [Fact].[Sale]
   WHERE [Total Dry Items] <> 0
   GROUP BY [Invoice Date Key])
   --separate multiple CTEs with comma
,ChillerTotalQuery as (
SELECT [Invoice Date Key] as ChillerInvoiceDateKey
       ,Sum([Total Chiller Items]) as DailyTotalChiller
   FROM [Fact].[Sale]
   WHERE [Total Chiller Items] <> 0
   GROUP BY [Invoice Date Key])
   --end of CTEs
```

```
--Query selecting from CTEs:
SELECT
 [Date]
, [ISOWeekNumber]
, ISNULL(DailyTotalDry,0) as DailyTotalDry
, ISNULL(DailyTotalChiller,0) as DailyTotalChiller
, ISNULL(DailyTotalDry,0) + ISNULL(DailyTotalChiller,0) as
TotalDailyItems
 FROM ISODates d
 LEFT OUTER JOIN DryTotalQuery dtq on d.[Date] = dtq.
DryInvoiceDateKey
 LEFT OUTER JOIN ChillerTotalQuery ctq on d.[Date] = ctq.
ChillerInvoiceDateKey
 WHERE YEAR(d.Date) = 2016
 ORDER BY [Date]
```

In the final query using CTEs, an ISNULL function is used to replace the NULL values with zero. There is also a formula that calculates the total number of items sold on each date.

Here is a sample result set, but we can see that there are a total of 366 records returned, 1 for every day in 2016 (a leap year!) and for those dates where there were no sales for either item, we still get the date with zeros in all 3 fields.

	Date	ISOWeekNumber	DailyTotalDry	DailyTotalChiller	TotalDailyItems
1	2016-01-01	53	5891	0	5891
2	2016-01-02	53	7260	96	7356
3	2016-01-03	53	0	0	0
4	2016-01-04	1	13140	1032	14172
5	2016-01-05	1	9942	1392	11334
6	2016-01-06	1	14130	1752	15882
7	2016-01-07	1	14388	1968	16356
8	2016-01-08	1	10934	912	11846
9	2016-01-09	1	5384	1188	6572
10	2016-01-10	1	0	0	0
11	2016-01-11	2	5733	528	6261
12	2016-01-12	2	12271	1464	13735
13	2016-01-13	2	10565	516	11081

Query executed successfully.   WideWorldImportersDW-S... 00:00:02   366 rows

Figure 5.3 – A partial result set showing the Date, ISOWeekNumber, and
Daily totals for each category for every date in the year

You can now create multiple CTEs, create data that doesn't exist in your source, and combine that data into a single dataset that has the values you need.

It is worth noting that once you have created the final query that uses the defined CTE tables, you cannot reference those CTE tables again. In *Figure 5.4*, you will see that the last line is trying to use SELECT on the CTE that was used in the prior query. This will result in an Invalid Object Name error message, as shown in the following screenshot:

```
ISODateSalesQuery...ortersDW-Standard   + X
        GROUP BY [Invoice Date Key])

    --end of CTEs

    --Query selecting from CTEs:
    SELECT
      [Date]
    , [ISOWeekNumber]
    , ISNULL(DailyTotalDry,0) as DailyTotalDry
    , ISNULL(DailyTotalChiller,0) as DailyTotalChiller
    , ISNULL(DailyTotalDry,0)  +  ISNULL(DailyTotalChiller,0) as TotalDailyItems
    FROM ISODates d
    LEFT OUTER JOIN DryTotalQuery dtq on d.[Date] = dtq.DryInvoiceDateKey
    LEFT OUTER JOIN ChillerTotalQuery ctq on d.[Date] = ctq.ChillerInvoiceDateKey
    WHERE YEAR(d.Date) = 2016
    ORDER BY [Date]
--try to reuse CTE: will fail
    SELECT * FROM ISODates
```

```
Results    Messages

  (366 rows affected)
  Msg 208, Level 16, State 1, Line 36
  Invalid object name 'ISODates'.

  Completion time: 2022-11-27T12:20:56.0445313-07:00
```

Figure 5.4 – Error message when trying to use a defined CTE that has already been used in a final query

This is because a CTE can only be used once, and then it is no longer available.

Now that we understand the basics of CTEs, we will look at how to use them to represent hierarchical information.

Creating a recursive CTE

A recursive CTE is one where the query references itself. Think of a list of employees and the person who manages them, a parent/child relationship, a bill of materials, or other organizational/hierarchical situations. These are the types of relationships you can express using a recursive CTE.

In this section, we will examine how to take that relationship and show all the levels of a hierarchy using a CTE. We will first need to create some data to use, and then we will create a query that shows all the levels of an organizational hierarchy.

Creating the hierarchical data

The WorldWideImporters database doesn't have any tables with a parent/child relationship, so we are going to create a simple Employee table and populate it with some data to use:

```
-- Create an Employee table.
CREATE TABLE dbo.Employee
(
EmpID SMALLINT NOT NULL,
FirstNm NVARCHAR(30) NOT NULL,
LastNm NVARCHAR(40) NOT NULL,
JobTitle NVARCHAR(50) NOT NULL,
ManagerID SMALLINT NULL,
CONSTRAINT PK_EmpID PRIMARY KEY CLUSTERED (EmpID ASC),
CONSTRAINT FK_Emp_ManagerID_EmpID FOREIGN KEY (ManagerID)
REFERENCES dbo.Employee (EmpID)
);
-- Populate the table with values.
INSERT INTO dbo.Employee VALUES
(1, N'Jennifer', N'Sanchez', N'Chief Executive Officer', NULL)
,(273, N'Brianna', N'Walker', N'Vice President of Sales', 1)
,(274, N'Stephanie', N'Miller', N'West US Sales Manager', 273)
,(275, N'Blythe', N'Martinez', N'Sales Representative', 274)
,(276, N'Linda', N'Mitchell', N'Sales Representative', 274)
,(285, N'Syed', N'Abbas', N'East US Sales Manager', 273)
,(286, N'Lynn', N'Tsoflias', N'Sales Representative', 285)
,(16, N'Melissa', N'Bradley', N'Human Resources Manager', 1)
,(23, N'Mary', N'Gibson', N'HR Specialist', 16);
```

Now that we have a table with a hierarchical relationship, we will look at how to create a recursive CTE.

ating the recursive CTE

in the CTE, two members are required to create the recursiveness: the anchor member and the rsive member. Here is a query that uses the recursive technique to retrieve the manager's ID, title, and level of the hierarchy:

```
--start the CTE
WITH DirectReports AS
( --the anchor member is the top level where there is no
ManagerID
SELECT ManagerID, EmpID, JobTitle,
CAST('' as nvarchar(50)) as ManagerTitle,
0 AS EmployeeLevel --create a Level field
FROM dbo.Employee
WHERE ManagerID IS NULL
UNION ALL
SELECT e.ManagerID, e.EmpID, e.JobTitle,
CAST(d.JobTitle as nvarchar(50)) as ManagerTitle,
EmployeeLevel + 1 --increase the level by 1 for each level
of recursiveness
FROM dbo.Employee AS e
  INNER JOIN DirectReports AS d --referencing the CTE
  name here is the RECURSIVE technique
  ON e.ManagerID = d.EmpID
)
SELECT ManagerID, EmpID, JobTitle, ManagerTitle, EmployeeLevel
FROM DirectReports
ORDER BY ManagerID;
```

In this query, we created a CTE named DirectReports that defines the anchor member where ManagerID IS NULL from the Employee table. The recursive member joins the Employee table to the DirectReports CTE, and for each level, it adds one to the EmployeeLevel-derived column.

We can see in these results that there are three levels of hierarchy, the employee's title, and their manager's title:

```
RecursiveQuery.sql...Importers-Standard  ⊕ ✕
  ⊟WITH DirectReports AS
    (    --the anchor member is the top level where there is no ManagerID
        SELECT ManagerID, EmpID, JobTitle, cast('' as nvarchar(50)) as ManagerTitle,
        0 AS EmployeeLevel --create a level field
        FROM dbo.Employee
        WHERE ManagerID IS NULL
        UNION ALL
        SELECT e.ManagerID, e.EmpID, e.JobTitle, cast(d.JobTitle as nvarchar(50)) as ManagerTitle,
        EmployeeLevel + 1 --increase the level by 1 for each level of recursiveness
        FROM dbo.Employee AS e
            INNER JOIN DirectReports AS d --referencing the CTE name here is the RECURSIVE technique
            ON e.ManagerID = d.EmpID
    )
    SELECT ManagerID, EmpID, JobTitle, ManagerTitle, EmployeeLevel
    FROM DirectReports
110 %  ▾
⊞ Results  ⓖ Messages
```

	ManagerID	EmpID	JobTitle	ManagerTitle	EmployeeLevel
1	NULL	1	Chief Executive Officer		0
2	1	16	Human Resources Manager	Chief Executive Officer	1
3	1	273	Vice President of Sales	Chief Executive Officer	1
4	16	23	HR Specialist	Human Resources Manager	2
5	273	274	West US Sales Manager	Vice President of Sales	2
6	273	285	East US Sales Manager	Vice President of Sales	2
7	274	275	Sales Representative	West US Sales Manager	3
8	274	276	Sales Representative	West US Sales Manager	3
9	285	286	Sales Representative	East US Sales Manager	3

⊘ Query executed successfully.

Figure 5.5 – The results of the recursive query showing ManagerID, EmpID, the employee JobTitle, ManagerTitle, and the hierarchy level of the employee

The results of the query will automatically add more levels when additional levels are added to the source!

A recursive CTE can be used to show other relationships, such as a bill of materials, parent/child, and taxidermy. As great as the recursive CTE is, unfortunately, not all versions of SQL Server support using it. Next, we will look at achieving the same results using JOIN conditions.

Recursive alternative

In most versions of SQL Server, you can reference the anchor member within the CTE; however, this functionality is not available in Azure Synapse Analytics at the time of publishing. To create a recursive relationship in this environment, you need to know the depth of the hierarchy and use INNER JOIN instances and UNION to create the results:

```
-- Query to find out employee and manager hierarchy
WITH DirectReports as (
SELECT EmpID, JobTitle, ManagerID, NULL as ManagerTitle, 0 as
Level
```

```
FROM dbo.Employee e
WHERE ManagerID IS NULL
UNION ALL
SELECT e.EmpID, e.JobTitle, e.ManagerID, m.JobTitle, Level+1 as
Level
FROM dbo.Employee e
INNER JOIN (SELECT EmpID,JobTitle,ManagerID, 0 as Level
FROM dbo.Employee e
WHERE ManagerID IS NULL) m ON e.ManagerID = m.EmpID
WHERE e.ManagerID IS NOT NULL
UNION ALL
select e.EmpID,e.JobTitle,e.ManagerID, m2.JobTitle, Level+1 as
Level
FROM dbo.Employee e
INNER JOIN (
SELECT e.EmpID,e.JobTitle,e.ManagerID, Level+1 as Level
FROM dbo.Employee e
INNER JOIN (SELECT EmpID, JobTitle,ManagerID, 0 as Level
FROM dbo.Employee e
WHERE ManagerID IS NULL) m1 ON e.ManagerID = m1.EmpID
WHERE e.ManagerID IS NOT NULL) m2 ON e.ManagerID = m2.EmpID
WHERE e.ManagerID IS NOT NULL
UNION ALL
SELECT e.EmpID,e.JobTitle,e.ManagerID, m3.JobTitle, Level+1 as
Level
FROM dbo.Employee e
INNER JOIN (select e.EmpID,e.JobTitle,e.ManagerID, Level+1 as
Level
FROM dbo.Employee e
INNER JOIN (
SELECT e.EmpID,e.JobTitle,e.ManagerID, Level+1 as Level
FROM dbo.Employee e
INNER JOIN (SELECT EmpID, JobTitle,ManagerID, 0 as Level
FROM dbo.Employee e
WHERE ManagerID IS NULL) m1 ON e.ManagerID = m1.EmpID
WHERE e.ManagerID IS NOT NULL) m2 ON e.ManagerID = m2.EmpID
WHERE e.ManagerID IS NOT NULL) m3 ON e.ManagerID = m3.EmpID
```

```
WHERE e.ManagerID IS NOT NULL)

SELECT * FROM DirectReports
```

This query produces the same results as the recursive CTE, but it requires you to know in advance how many levels are in the hierarchy. This is how you would reproduce the concept of the recursive CTE without the convenience of being able to refer to the anchor CTE. It is a much longer solution and less readable. However, it is the only way at this time to get these results for a Synapse Dedicated SQL Server.

Summary

This chapter covered how to create CTEs, how to perform some advanced techniques to associate data in creative ways, and how to create recursive CTEs, which allow us to represent hierarchical data in a meaningful way.

We will continue to build on CTE techniques in the next chapter using window functions to perform additional calculations.

6

Analyze Your Data Using Window Functions

Window functions have been part of SQL Server since the 2005 release, and while they don't let you do anything that you can't do with traditional queries, it makes those complicated queries much easier to write and read and usually executes them faster than traditional queries.

There are three different categories of window functions: ranking, value, and aggregate.

In this chapter, we will look at the different functions within each category and see what type of business problems each can be used to solve. We will examine example queries to understand what each function does and how to construct the function within the query. We will also learn the different keywords required to call the function and develop some complex outputs.

The main topics we will cover in this chapter are as follows:

- Understanding window functions
- Using window functions
- Example scenarios and business problems

Technical requirements

To work with the examples and illustrations in this chapter, you will need Azure Data Studio and/or SQL Server Management Studio installed. We will be working with the `WideWorldImporters` and/or the `WideWorldImportersDW` database on SQL Server or Azure SQL Database. Please refer to the *Appendix* for tool installation and database restoration guidance.

You will find the code from this chapter here on GitHub: `https://github.com/PacktPublishing/SQL-Query-Design-Best-Practices/tree/main/Chapter06`

Understanding window functions

A window function operates over a set of rows called a window and returns a column that is included with the other selected columns. The window becomes a partition on the table and allows the rows to retain their details while providing an aggregate. That is what makes the window function different from aggregates, even though, in some cases, it is evaluating an aggregate.

Here is a partial list of the window functions:

- Ranking:

  - `ROW_NUMBER`

  - `RANK`

  - `DENSE_RANK`

  - `NTILE`

  - `PERCENT_RANK`

  - `CUME_DISTLEAD`

  - `FIRST_VALUE`

  - `LAST_VALUE`

  - `COUNT`

  - `PERCENTILE_CONT`

  - `PERCENTILE_DIST`

- Value:

  - `LAG`

- Aggregate:

  - `AVG`

  - `SUM`

  - `MAX/MIN`

Next, we will look at the structure of the window functions and the required clauses to create them.

Using a window function in a query

To use a window function in a query, you just include it as a column in the query definition. Every window function requires an `OVER` clause and optionally can include a `PARTITION BY` clause and an `ORDER BY` clause, which is required by some functions but not all.

We will start by looking at ROW_NUMBER(). There are many situations when analyzing data where having a row number is useful.

In the following example, we will assign a row number to every InvoiceID from the WorldWideImporters-Standard database's Sales.Invoices table. ROW_NUMBER() is one of the window functions that requires an OVER clause with ORDER BY declared. By including an ORDER BY clause in the query that matches the order of the OVER clause, we can see that the results are ordered by InvoiceID, and the RowNumber field created in the query is in the correct order:

```
SELECT ROW_NUMBER() OVER (ORDER BY InvoiceID) as RowNumber
       ,[InvoiceID]
       ,[CustomerID]
  FROM [Sales].[Invoices]
  WHERE Year(InvoiceDate) = 2016
  ORDER BY InvoiceID
```

Here is a partial result set showing the row number in the order of InvoiceID:

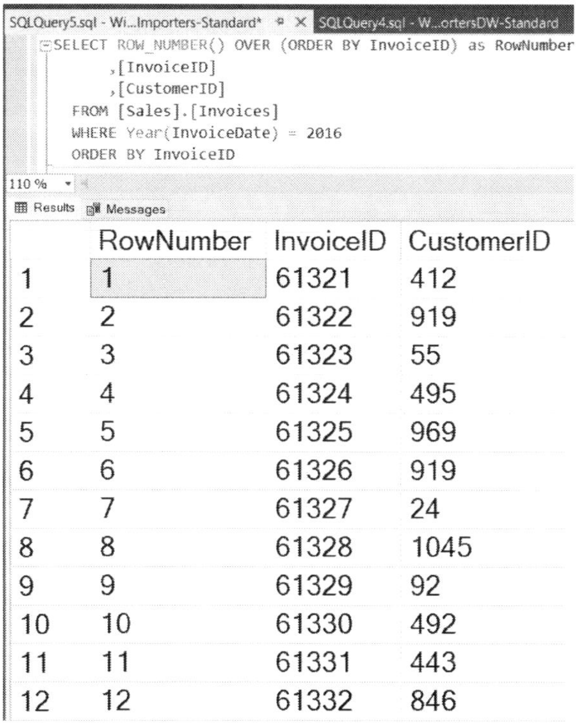

Figure 6.1 – A query example showing the RowNumber() window function based on InvoiceID and the result set from the WorldWideImporters standard sample database

By changing the ORDER BY declaration in the OVER clause, we can rearrange the calculated row number. This is shown here:

```
SELECT ROW_NUMBER() OVER (ORDER BY CustomerID) as RowNumber
      ,[InvoiceID]
      ,[CustomerID]
  FROM [Sales].[Invoices]
  WHERE Year(InvoiceDate) = 2016
  ORDER BY CustomerID
```

You can see in *Figure 6.2* that there is no guarantee of order for InvoiceID when we ORDER BY CustomerID. On row **12** in the results, we can see that InvoiceID is not correctly ordered, **68196** is *after* **69455**:

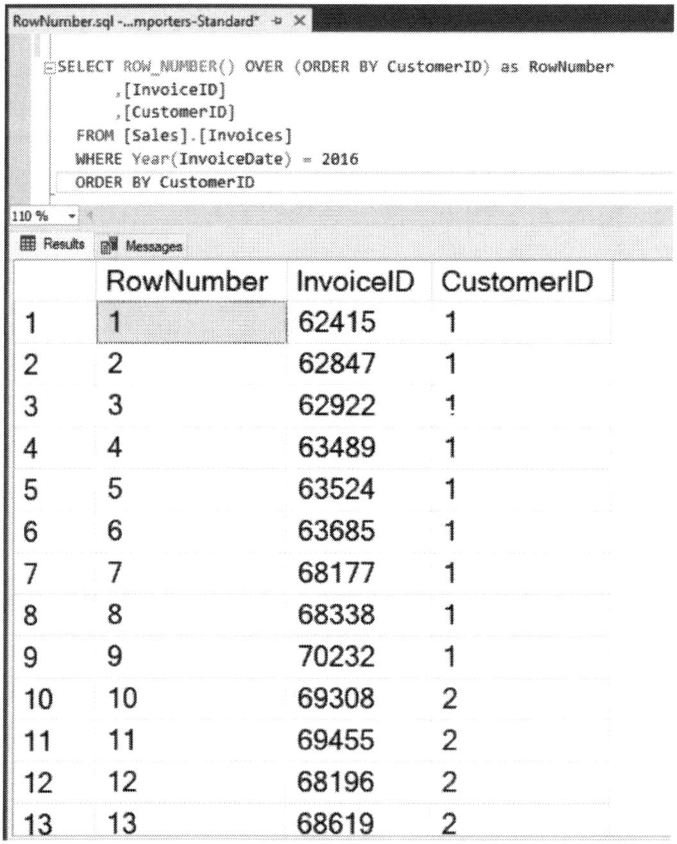

Figure 6.2 – A query example showing the RowNumber() window function based on CustomerID and the result set from the WorldWideImporters standard sample database

To guarantee the order of `CustomerID` and `InvoiceID`, both must be included in the `OVER` declaration, shown as follows:

```
SELECT ROW_NUMBER() OVER (ORDER BY CustomerID, InvoiceID) as
RowNumber
    ,[InvoiceID]
    ,[CustomerID]
FROM [Sales].[Invoices]
WHERE Year(InvoiceDate) = 2016
ORDER BY CustomerID,InvoiceID
```

In the following figure, we can see that the `RowNumber` field is now sequenced by `CustomerID` and then `InvoiceID`:

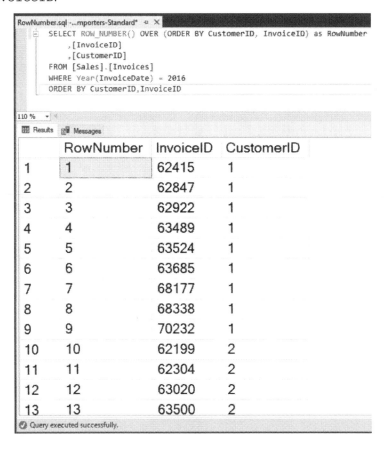

Figure 6.3 – A query example showing the RowNumber() window function based on CustomerID
and InvoiceID and the result set from the WorldWideImporters standard sample database

Now that we understand the basics of the ROW_NUMBER() function, next we will look at adding a partition to the results to get a row number within a group.

Adding a partition to the results

When we talk about partitioning regarding result sets, it means splitting a larger result set into smaller parts. In our example, in the *Using a window function in a query* section, we added the RowNumber field to the entire dataset. However, in many cases, we want to assign the row number within a group, such as a CustomerID value, that restarts with each new group.

To accomplish resetting the row number, we can add a partition to the dataset, as follows:

```
SELECT ROW_NUMBER()
OVER (PARTITION BY CustomerID
ORDER BY CustomerID, InvoiceID ) as RowNumber
    , [InvoiceID]
    , [CustomerID]
FROM [Sales].[Invoices]
WHERE Year(InvoiceDate) = 2016
ORDER BY CustomerID, InvoiceID
```

We can see in the following result that the RowNumber field restarts at **1** when CustomerID changes at record number **10**:

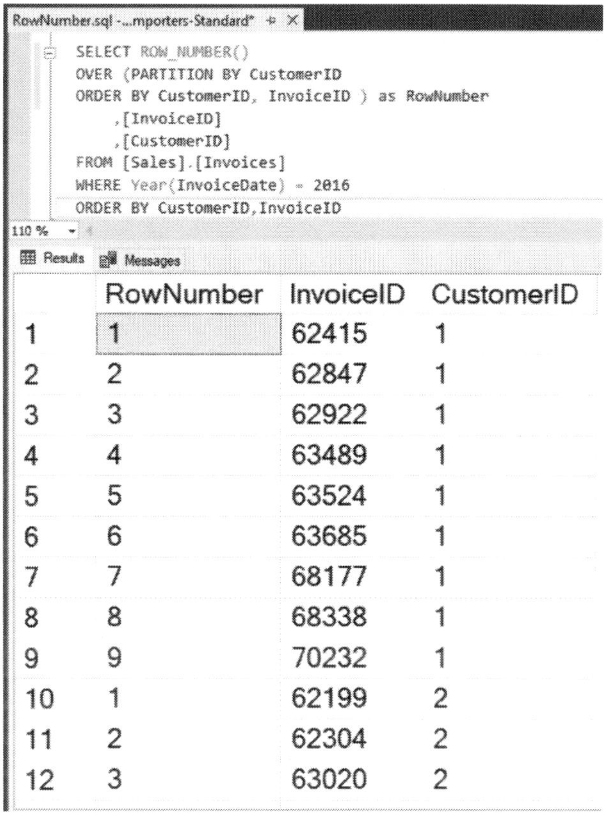

Figure 6.4 – A query example showing the RowNumber() window function with a partition based on CustomerID and the result set from the WorldWideImporters standard sample database

All window functions can utilize the PARTITION BY expression of the OVER clause, which is always optional.

Window functions with frames

Frames were introduced in SQL Server 2012 as a way to specify a window that is different from the partition type to allow for additional calculations and special requirements. They only apply to a small subset of window functions, the aggregates, and the FIRST_VALUE and LAST_VALUE offset functions.

The key terms that you need to be familiar with to work with frames are as follows:

- ROWS: One of the operators (physical) that you can use to define the frame position by looking at the position of the row

- RANGE: The other operator (logical) which looks at the value of an expression over the rows

- UNBOUNDED PRECEDING: This means that the frame starts at the first row in the set

UNDED FOLLOWING: This means that the frame ends at the final row in the set

ECEDING: This is the physical number of rows before the current row (only applies
VS)

LOWING: This is the physical number of rows after the current row (only applies to ROWS)

- CURRENT ROW: The current row

The following is the syntax for the frame definition, consisting of either ROWS or RANGE, followed by BETWEEN and then the start and end point of the frame:

```
ROWS BETWEEN <start point> AND <end point>
RANGE BETWEEN <start point> AND <end point>
```

For the window functions that support a frame, the default frame is as follows:

```
RANGE BETWEEN UNBOUNDED PRECEDING AND CURRENT ROW
```

This default frame is why adding an ORDER BY expression to an OVER clause for SUM produces a running total.

Using the ROWS expression allows you to specify the number of rows to include in the frame. You can include rows before the current row, after the current row, or before and after the current row. When it comes to performance, ROWS is usually a better choice. When ROWS is declared in the expression, the work table is created in memory, and when RANGE is used, the work table is created in tempdb. It is good to memorize that if you do not declare a frame, the default of RANGE is used and you may see degraded performance.

Now that we have reviewed the structure of the windows functions and the syntax for each of the parts of the expression, we will look at the types of scenarios that the Windows functions can help solve.

Scenarios and business problems

In this example, we are going to extract the details of customer invoices and combine them with the MIN, MAX, and COUNT instances of each customer's aggregated data. Refer to the following code:

```
SELECT CustomerID,
  InvoiceID,
  InvoiceDate,
  FORMAT(MIN(InvoiceDate) OVER (PARTITION BY CustomerID),
  'yyyy-MM-dd') as FirstOrderDate,
  FORMAT(MAX(InvoiceDate) OVER (PARTITION BY CustomerID),
  'yyyy-MM-dd') as LastOrderDate,
```

```
COUNT(*) OVER (PARTITION BY CustomerID) AS SalesCount
FROM [Sales].[Invoices]
WHERE Year(InvoiceDate) = 2016
```

Partial results, shown in *Figure 6.5*, of this query show that for each customer, there is the first invoice date, the last invoice date, and the count of invoices for the year for each customer with some details for each invoice.

	CustomerID	InvoiceID	InvoiceDate	FirstOrderDate	LastOrderDate	SalesCount
1	1	62415	2016-01-18	2016-01-18	2016-05-27	9
2	1	62847	2016-01-25	2016-01-18	2016-05-27	9
3	1	62922	2016-01-26	2016-01-18	2016-05-27	9
4	1	63489	2016-02-05	2016-01-18	2016-05-27	9
5	1	63524	2016-02-06	2016-01-18	2016-05-27	9
6	1	63685	2016-02-11	2016-01-18	2016-05-27	9
7	1	68177	2016-04-26	2016-01-18	2016-05-27	9
8	1	68338	2016-04-28	2016-01-18	2016-05-27	9
9	1	70232	2016-05-27	2016-01-18	2016-05-27	9
10	2	69308	2016-05-12	2016-01-14	2016-05-14	13
11	2	69455	2016-05-14	2016-01-14	2016-05-14	13
12	2	68196	2016-04-26	2016-01-14	2016-05-14	13
13	2	68619	2016-05-03	2016-01-14	2016-05-14	13
14	2	69158	2016-05-10	2016-01-14	2016-05-14	13
15	2	66154	2016-03-23	2016-01-14	2016-05-14	13
16	2	66600	2016-03-30	2016-01-14	2016-05-14	13

Figure 6.5 – Sample results set combining aggregate information without losing the details

This type of calculation creates a combination of details and aggregates that can then be used for reporting or other calculations.

Days between orders

A common business scenario is to determine the number of days between two events. Using the LAG window function, a value from a prior record in the dataset based on the partition and order of the window can be determined and used in the current row. In this example, the invoice date of the prior record is used in a calculation to find the duration between the orders:

```
SELECT CustomerID,
InvoiceID,
```

```
InvoiceDate,
LAG(InvoiceDate, 1) OVER (PARTITION BY CustomerID ORDER BY
CustomerID, InvoiceDate) as PriorInvoiceOrderDate,
DateDiff(d, LAG(InvoiceDate, 1) OVER (PARTITION BY
CustomerID ORDER BY CustomerID, InvoiceDate), InvoiceDate) as
DaysSinceLastOrder
FROM [Sales].[Invoices]
WHERE Year(InvoiceDate) = 2016
ORDER BY CustomerID, InvoiceDate
```

Partial results from this query show that for each customer's invoices, `DaysSinceLastOrder` is calculated for each record and resets for each change in `CustomerID`:

	CustomerID	InvoiceID	InvoiceDate	PriorInvoiceOrderDate	DaysSinceLastOrder
1	1	62415	2016-01-18	NULL	NULL
2	1	62847	2016-01-25	2016-01-18	7
3	1	62922	2016-01-26	2016-01-25	1
4	1	63489	2016-02-05	2016-01-26	10
5	1	63524	2016-02-06	2016-02-05	1
6	1	63685	2016-02-11	2016-02-06	5
7	1	68177	2016-04-26	2016-02-11	75
8	1	68338	2016-04-28	2016-04-26	2
9	1	70232	2016-05-27	2016-04-28	29
10	2	62199	2016-01-14	NULL	NULL
11	2	62304	2016-01-15	2016-01-14	1
12	2	63020	2016-01-28	2016-01-15	13
13	2	63500	2016-02-06	2016-01-28	9
14	2	64000	2016-02-17	2016-02-06	11
15	2	65606	2016-03-15	2016-02-17	27
16	2	66154	2016-03-23	2016-03-15	8

Figure 6.6 – Partial set of results for a query showing the number
of days between orders partitioned by CustomerID

Again, we can use these results to perform additional calculations or logical comparisons to increase the usefulness of these results.

Finding a pattern

Another scenario that extends the LAG window function functionality is to peek at multiple records within the window and determine a pattern. What if we wanted to find where there were more than 5 days between orders over the last 3 orders from a customer? In this sample query, the **Common Table Expression** (CTE) technique is used in conjunction with additional LAG functions to determine a pattern in the number of days between orders:

```
--use a CTE to calculate the number of days between orders
WITH daysBetweenOrders as (SELECT CustomerID,
  InvoiceID,
  InvoiceDate,
  LAG(InvoiceDate, 1) OVER (PARTITION BY CustomerID ORDER BY
  InvoiceDate) as PriorInvoiceOrderDate,
  DateDiff(d, LAG(InvoiceDate, 1) OVER (PARTITION BY CustomerID
  ORDER BY InvoiceDate), InvoiceDate) as DaysSinceLastOrder
  FROM [Sales].[Invoices]
  WHERE Year(InvoiceDate) = 2016 )

  SELECT CustomerID,
  InvoiceID,
  InvoiceDate,
  DaysSinceLastOrder,
  case
  when dayssincelastorder is NULL then 'FirstOrder'
  when dayssincelastorder >= 5 or lag(DaysSinceLastOrder, 1)
Over (PARTITION BY CustomerID ORDER BY  InvoiceDate) IS NULL
then
      case when lag(DaysSinceLastOrder, 1) Over (PARTITION BY
CustomerID ORDER BY InvoiceDate) IS NULL then 'SecondOrder'
  else
    case when lag(DaysSinceLastOrder, 1) Over (PARTITION BY
CustomerID ORDER BY InvoiceDate) > 5 then
  case when lag(DaysSinceLastOrder, 2) Over (PARTITION BY
CustomerID ORDER BY InvoiceDate) > 5 then
'Yes'
  else
    'No'
  end
    else
```

```
    'No'
      end
        end
    else
      'No'
    end
    as ThreeConsequtiveOrdersWithMoreThan5DaysBetweenOrders
  From daysBetweenOrders
  ORDER BY CustomerID, InvoiceDate
```

Partial results, shown in *Figure 6.7*, of this query show that for the first order of each `CustomerID` in `ThreeConsecutiveOrdersWithMoreThan5DaysBetweenOrders`, the `case` statement identifies the record as `FirstOrder` based on a `NULL` value in the previous record if the number of `DaysSinceLastOrder` is greater than 5 or the previous record's `DaysSinceLastOrder` is `NULL` (indicating it was the first order). If the prior record is `NULL`, then the query determines that this is `SecondOrder`. Then the next `case` statement looks at the previous record to determine whether it was more than 5 days between orders. The last `case` statement looks back 2 records to determine whether `DaysSinceLastOrder` is also more than 5; if so, then the query determines that *yes,* for 3 consecutive orders, there were more than 5-days between them:

	CustomerID	InvoiceID	InvoiceDate	DaysSinceLastOrder	ThreeConsequtiveOrdersWithMoreThan5DaysBetweenOrders
1	1	62415	2016-01-18	NULL	FirstOrder
2	1	62847	2016-01-25	7	SecondOrder
3	1	62922	2016-01-26	1	No
4	1	63489	2016-02-05	10	No
5	1	63524	2016-02-06	1	No
6	1	63685	2016-02-11	5	No
7	1	68177	2016-04-26	75	No
8	1	68338	2016-04-28	2	No
9	1	70232	2016-05-27	29	No
10	2	62199	2016-01-14	NULL	FirstOrder
11	2	62304	2016-01-15	1	SecondOrder
12	2	63020	2016-01-28	13	No
13	2	63500	2016-02-06	9	No
14	2	64000	2016-02-17	11	Yes
15	2	65606	2016-03-15	27	Yes
16	2	66154	2016-03-23	8	Yes
17	2	66600	2016-03-30	7	Yes
18	2	68196	2016-04-26	27	Yes
19	2	68619	2016-05-03	7	Yes
20	2	69158	2016-05-10	7	Yes
21	2	69308	2016-05-12	2	No
22	2	69455	2016-05-14	2	No
23	3	61871	2016-01-08	NULL	FirstOrder
24	3	64365	2016-02-23	46	SecondOrder

Figure 6.7 – Partial set of results for a query showing top five gross invoice totals by CustomerID

The results also show that the tabulation of consecutive months correctly calculate when `DaysSinceLastOrder` is not greater than 5 days, as can be seen in *Figure 6.7* between lines **304** and **308** when the result returns **Yes** and then 3 records of **No** until there are again 3 consecutive orders with more than 5 days between them.

The `LEAD` function works the same way as `LAG`, but it looks forward in the dataset to the record specified in the function parameter.

Finding first N records of every group

Another common scenario is to find the first *N* of a group, the top five largest orders by customer, for instance. This can be accomplished by combining the CTE (see *Chapter 5*, for more information) with window functions.

This query summarizes the gross sales amount by `InvoiceID` from the `InvoiceLines` table. Then, by joining to the `Invoices` table to get `CustomerID`, the gross sales total can be ranked, and the final query selects the top five:

```
--use CTE to get Invoice Gross Sale Amount
  WITH InvoiceTotals as (
  SELECT InvoiceID
  , SUM(ExtendedPrice - TaxAmount) as InvoiceTotalGrossSale
  FROM [Sales].[InvoiceLines]
  GROUP BY InvoiceID)
  --join InvoiceTotals CTE to Invoice information and rank by
Gross Sales
  ,RankedTotalsByCustomer as (SELECT CustomerID,
  I.InvoiceID,
  IT.InvoiceTotalGrossSale,
  ROW_NUMBER()
  OVER (PARTITION BY CustomerID
  ORDER BY CustomerID, InvoiceTotalGrossSale desc ) as
RowNumber
  FROM [Sales].[Invoices] I
  INNER JOIN InvoiceTotals IT on I.InvoiceID = IT.InvoiceID
  )
  --Get Top 5 records for each customer
  SELECT * FROM RankedTotalsByCustomer
  WHERE RowNumber <= 5
  ORDER BY CustomerID, RowNumber
```

Partial results of this query show the highest five records by gross invoice amount for each `CustomerID`:

	CustomerID	InvoiceID	InvoiceTotalGrossSale	RowNumber
1	1	38594	20136.50	1
2	1	36197	14388.75	2
3	1	56983	12399.60	3
4	1	46095	11507.00	4
5	1	5095	10765.20	5
6	2	55116	9990.60	1
7	2	32087	9751.25	2
8	2	37371	8176.00	3
9	2	50707	7715.00	4
10	2	55967	7263.00	5
11	3	17893	13435.00	1
12	3	31737	11633.00	2
13	3	70394	11340.00	3
14	3	1228	10301.00	4
15	3	65048	10200.00	5
16	4	38802	27306.00	1
17	4	7675	17894.60	2
18	4	29106	11932.00	3
19	4	64278	11283.00	4
20	4	48379	10182.00	5
21	5	15393	13381.00	1
22	5	68582	12429.00	2
23	5	5459	12210.75	3
24	5	60610	11655.00	4

Figure 6.8 – Partial set of results for a query showing top five gross invoice totals by CustomerID

Combining the CTE technique with windows functions allows very advanced calculations with very easy-to-read and maintained queries.

Running totals

Another common request for reporting and analysis is running totals. This is possible to accomplish with window functions, but we have to include the frame syntax. In this example, we will calculate a running 3-month sum and a 3-month average of the number of invoices created each month:

```
SELECT YEAR(InvoiceDate) as InvoiceYear, Month(InvoiceDate) as
InvoiceMonth,
COUNT(*) as InvoiceCount,
SUM(COUNT(*)) OVER (ORDER BY YEAR(InvoiceDate),
Month(InvoiceDate)
```

```
ROWS BETWEEN 2 PRECEDING and CURRENT ROW) as ThreeMonthCount,
AVG(COUNT(*)) OVER (ORDER BY YEAR(InvoiceDate),
Month(InvoiceDate)
ROWS BETWEEN 2 PRECEDING and CURRENT ROW) as ThreeMonthAverage
FROM Sales.Invoices
WHERE YEAR(InvoiceDate) = 2016
GROUP BY YEAR(InvoiceDate), Month(InvoiceDate)
ORDER BY InvoiceYear, InvoiceMonth
```

This query combines a true aggregate with a GROUP BY clause and the window function with a frame to calculate the current month's count of invoices with the window aggregates showing the 3-month rolling calculations. In the results shown in *Figure 6.9*, we can see all three calculated results:

	InvoiceYear	InvoiceMonth	InvoiceCount	ThreeMonthCount	ThreeMonthAverage
1	2016	1	1844	1844	1844
2	2016	2	1655	3499	1749
3	2016	3	1887	5386	1795
4	2016	4	1856	5398	1799
5	2016	5	1948	5691	1897

Figure 6.9 – Partial set of results for a query showing by year and month, the count, 3-month count, and 3-month average from the invoices table

First and last record in the partition

The FIRST_VALUE and LAST_VALUE functions allow you to get any column from the first or last record within the partition. This is not the same as the MIN or MAX values. However, using the correct frame is key to calculating LAST_VALUE. In the query, the LastInvoiceDate_WRONG field will demonstrate why the frame is important to correctly determine the last record within the entire frame, not just the current window:

```
SELECT CustomerID, InvoiceID, InvoiceDate,
FIRST_VALUE(InvoiceDate) OVER (PARTITION BY CustomerID ORDER BY
InvoiceID) As FirstOrderDate,
LAST_VALUE(InvoiceDate) OVER (PARTITION BY CustomerID ORDER BY
InvoiceID) as LastOrderDateWRONG,
LAST_VALUE(InvoiceDate) OVER (PARTITION BY CustomerID ORDER BY
InvoiceID ROWS BETWEEN CURRENT ROW AND UNBOUNDED FOLLOWING) As
LastOrderDate
FROM Sales.Invoices
WHERE Year(InvoiceDate) = 2016
ORDER BY CustomerID, InvoiceID
```

In the results shown in *Figure 6.9*, we can see that `LastOrderDate_WRONG` shows the last invoice date within the current window, whereas `LastOrderDate` correctly shows `LastOrderDate` within the current partition to the last record:

	CustomerID	InvoiceID	InvoiceDate	FirstOrderDate	LastOrderDateWRONG	LastOrderDate
1	1	62415	2016-01-18	2016-01-18	2016-01-18	2016-05-27
2	1	62847	2016-01-25	2016-01-18	2016-01-25	2016-05-27
3	1	62922	2016-01-26	2016-01-18	2016-01-26	2016-05-27
4	1	63489	2016-02-05	2016-01-18	2016-02-05	2016-05-27
5	1	63524	2016-02-06	2016-01-18	2016-02-06	2016-05-27
6	1	63685	2016-02-11	2016-01-18	2016-02-11	2016-05-27
7	1	68177	2016-04-26	2016-01-18	2016-04-26	2016-05-27
8	1	68338	2016-04-28	2016-01-18	2016-04-28	2016-05-27
9	1	70232	2016-05-27	2016-01-18	2016-05-27	2016-05-27
10	2	62199	2016-01-14	2016-01-14	2016-01-14	2016-05-14
11	2	62304	2016-01-15	2016-01-14	2016-01-15	2016-05-14
12	2	63020	2016-01-28	2016-01-14	2016-01-28	2016-05-14
13	2	63500	2016-02-06	2016-01-14	2016-02-06	2016-05-14
14	2	64000	2016-02-17	2016-01-14	2016-02-17	2016-05-14
15	2	65606	2016-03-15	2016-01-14	2016-03-15	2016-05-14
16	2	66154	2016-03-23	2016-01-14	2016-03-23	2016-05-14
17	2	66600	2016-03-30	2016-01-14	2016-03-30	2016-05-14

Figure 6.10 – Partial set of results for a query showing the first and last invoice date

Year-over-year growth

Another very common requirement is to calculate change over a period. In this example, we will determine the total amount of invoiced orders per month and the growth from the prior period. In this example, we will be comparing growth to the same month in the prior year, or 12 rows back, using the LAG function and the CTE:

```
WITH baseSales as (
SELECT Year(Orderdate) as OrderYear, Month(Orderdate) as
OrderMonth, SUM( ol.Quantity  * ol.UnitPrice) as OrderTotal
FROM sales.orders o
INNER JOIN sales.orderlines ol on o.orderid = ol.orderid
GROUP BY Year(OrderDate), Month(OrderDate)),


PrevSales as (SELECT OrderYear, OrderMonth, OrderTotal,
LAG(OrderTotal, 12) OVER (ORDER BY OrderYear, OrderMonth) As
PreviousYearsOrder
```

```
FROM baseSales)


SELECT OrderYear, OrderMonth, OrderTotal as TotalOrders,
PreviousYearsOrder,
FORMAT((OrderTotal - PreviousYearsOrder)/PreviousYearsOrder,
'P') as YOY_Change
FROM PrevSales
WHERE PreviousYearsOrder is not null
ORDER BY OrderYear, OrderMonth
```

The results in *Figure 6.11* show that the WHERE clause has filtered out years where there is no prior year in the outer query. The query uses a CTE to calculate the total order amount for each period in the baseSales expression, which is then used as the source for PrevSales where the LAG function looks back 12 records (or 1 year back) to perform the calculation to determine the year-over-year change:

	OrderYear	OrderMonth	TotalOrders	PreviousYearsOrder	YOY_Change
1	2014	1	4202578.80	3824842.85	9.88%
2	2014	2	3572744.40	2821282.20	26.64%
3	2014	3	3955257.55	3966078.10	-0.27%
4	2014	4	4212856.25	4155710.05	1.38%
5	2014	5	4753224.10	4562830.35	4.17%
6	2014	6	4427573.80	4150098.60	6.69%
7	2014	7	4919791.85	4502741.85	9.26%
8	2014	8	4197257.40	3601220.60	16.55%
9	2014	9	3973877.85	3916003.25	1.48%
10	2014	10	4606478.45	3879872.45	18.73%
11	2014	11	4157270.55	3819809.10	8.83%
12	2014	12	4513092.40	3728103.40	21.06%
13	2015	1	4556065.25	4202578.80	8.41%
14	2015	2	4307819.25	3572744.40	20.57%
15	2015	3	4644642.35	3955257.55	17.43%
16	2015	4	5222594.85	4212856.25	23.97%
17	2015	5	4636628.45	4753224.10	-2.45%

Figure 6.11 – Partial set of results for a query showing the total order amount by year and month, the previous year's orders for that month, and the year-over-year change

These examples have demonstrated how window functions allow you to create queries to solve some standard business problems. You can use these techniques to expand these examples to perform more complex time ranges and trending.

Summary

This chapter reviewed the types of window functions you can use, how to structure and use them, and provided some examples of business use cases. We have seen how to look at records in other locations within the partition, learned about some pitfalls to be aware of when using some functions, and combined using a CTE with using the windows functions to create complex calculations that are easy to read and maintain.

In the next chapter, you will continue to expand on your ability to reshape data with more advanced techniques.

7
Reshaping Data with Advanced Techniques

When working with data, we sometimes find that we need to reshape it in order for it to be useful for storing in a table or to use that data for reporting purposes, and to do that, we transpose data by either moving columns to rows (or vice versa) and/or storing data in a hierarchical structure.

In this chapter, you will learn three advanced ways of reshaping data—`PIVOT`, `UNPIVOT`, and hierarchies, to manipulate data into meaningful output.

We will cover each topic in three main sections:

- Working with the `PIVOT` operator
- Working with the `UNPIVOT` operator
- Understanding hierarchical data

Technical requirements

To work with the examples and illustrations in this chapter, you will need to have Azure Data Studio and/ or SQL Server Management Studio installed. We will be working with the `WideWorldImporters` and/or the `WideWorldImportersDW` database on SQL Server or Azure SQL Database. Please refer to the *Appendix* for tool installation and database restoration guidance.

To work with the examples and illustrations in this chapter, you will need to have Azure Data Studio installed as well as the `WideWorldImportersDW` database on SQL Server or Azure SQL Database.

You will find the complete SQL scripts from this chapter on GitHub here: `https://github.com/ PacktPublishing/SQL-Query-Design-Best-Practices/tree/main/Chapter07`

Working with the PIVOT operator

A PIVOT operator, simply put, transforms a table output column into rows. It rotates a table-valued expression (a table-valued expression returns output as a result set/table) by turning unique values from a selected column into multiple columns and aggregates the remaining column values in the final table output.

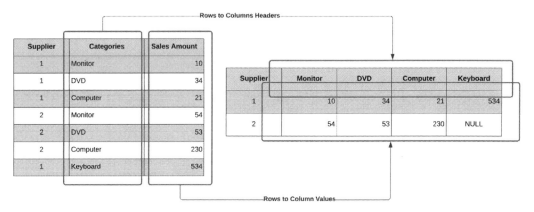

Figure 7.1 – Basic understanding of the PIVOT operator

The PIVOT operator is very similar to a CASE statement, but much simpler and more easily readable for the user.

Here is the syntax for it:

```
SELECT
<Unique Column Name(s)>
FROM
<SELECT query to produce data from table(s)>
PIVOT
(
<column to be aggregated, e.g., COUNT, AVG, etc.>
FOR
<Unique Column values that will become column headers>
);
```

> **Important**
>
> For aggregate functions in the PIVOT operator, any null values in the value column are not considered during computation.

Let's walk through an example to get a better understanding of the PIVOT operator.

The following is a very simple SELECT query that looks at our PurchaseOrders table and outputs all supplier IDs with a count of unique purchase orders:

```
---------------------------------------------------------------
--- Get Total Purchase Orders by Supplier
---------------------------------------------------------------
USE [WideWorldImporters]
GO

SELECT
[SupplierID]
, COUNT([PurchaseOrderID]) AS CTPurchaseOrder
FROM
[Purchasing].[PurchaseOrders]
GROUP BY
[SupplierID];
```

Here is the output of the query:

	SupplierID	CTPurchaseOrder
1	1	5
2	2	1
3	4	1055
4	5	13
5	7	985
6	10	10
7	12	5

Figure 7.2 – Output with supplier ID and count of purchase orders

Now, to transform this result—SupplierID rows into unique column headers—perform the PIVOT operation steps using the previously mentioned syntax. The PIVOT query would look something like the following:

```
---------------------------------------------------------------
--Using PIVOT operator, produce pivot table with Suppliers
---------------------------------------------------------------
USE [WideWorldImporters]
GO
```

```
SELECT
'Total Purchase Orders' AS TotalPurchaseOrders
, [1] AS SalesPer1, [2] AS SalesPer2, [4] AS SalesPer3
, [5] AS SalesPer4, [7] AS SalesPer5, [10] AS SalesPer6
, [12] AS SalesPer7
FROM
(
SELECT
[SupplierID]
, [PurchaseOrderID]
FROM
[Purchasing].[PurchaseOrders]
) AS SrcTbl
PIVOT
(
COUNT([PurchaseOrderID])
FOR [SupplierID] IN ([1], [2], [4], [5], [7], [10], [12])
) AS PvtTbl;
```

Here the unique SupplierID values are aliased to SalesPer1, SalesPer2..., and so on. The three main sections are highlighted to map them back to the syntax provided and for understanding:

	TotalPurchaseOrders	SalesPer1	SalesPer2	SalesPer3	SalesPer4	SalesPer5	SalesPer6	SalesPer7
1	Total Purchase Orders	5	1	1055	13	985	10	5

Figure 7.3 – Tabular output pivoting data from rows to columns

Compare this output with the first output and you will see all unique SupplierID values are now transformed into rows.

Now, let's add the next level of complexity by pulling in the supplier names from the Suppliers table.

Here, the base SELECT query—the Total Purchase Orders table will do an INNER JOIN with the Suppliers table to pull supplier names and will display actual supplier names instead of the alias we used in our last example:

```
----------------------------------------------------------------
-- Complex PIVOT operator, map Supplier name to Supplier Master
----------------------------------------------------------------
USE [WideWorldImporters]
```

```
GO

SELECT
'Total Purchase Orders' AS TotalPurchaseOrders
, [A Datum Corporation]
, [Contoso, Ltd.]
, [Fabrikam, Inc.]
, [Graphic Design Institute]
, [Litware, Inc.]
, [Northwind Electric Cars]
, [The Phone Company]

FROM
(
SELECT DISTINCT
SP.SupplierName
, PO.[PurchaseOrderID]
FROM
[Purchasing].[PurchaseOrders] PO INNER JOIN [Purchasing].
[Suppliers] SP
ON PO.SupplierID = SP.SupplierID
) AS SrcTbl
PIVOT
(
COUNT([PurchaseOrderID])
FOR SupplierName IN (
[A Datum Corporation]
, [Contoso, Ltd.]
, [Fabrikam, Inc.]
, [Graphic Design Institute]
, [Litware, Inc.]
, [Northwind Electric Cars]
, [The Phone Company]
)
) AS PvtTbl;
```

The output of this query will look like this:

	TotalPurchaseOrders	A Datum Corporation	Contoso, Ltd.	Fabrikam, Inc.	Graphic Design Institute	Litware, Inc.	Northwind Electric Cars	The Phone Company
1	Total Purchase Orders	5	1	1055	13	985	10	5

Figure 7.4 – Tabular output pivoted data with supplier names as columns

Notice the supplier names are pulled from the `Supplier's` table instead of the alias provided in the query itself.

Now, let's look at how we can dynamically specify column names as part of our query and make our statements more scalable to changes in source data.

Using PIVOT dynamically

One of the challenges with the `PIVOT` operator is the query can become very lengthy with explicit column names listed in the query itself and it can be difficult to read. This is where we have a need to build the column names dynamically, which also helps simplify the query.

In this example, what we will do is pull all column names from the `Suppliers` table, store them as a string in a temporary variable, and pass them into the `PIVOT` operation:

```
-----------------------------------------------------------------
-- Dynamic column names in a PIVOT operation
-----------------------------------------------------------------
USE [WideWorldImporters]
GO


DECLARE @pvtColumns NVARCHAR(MAX) = '';
SELECT
@pvtColumns = @pvtColumns + ', ' + QUOTENAME(Cols.SupplierName)
FROM
(
SELECT DISTINCT SP.SupplierName
FROM [Purchasing].[PurchaseOrders] PO
INNER JOIN [Purchasing].[Suppliers] SP ON PO.SupplierID =
SP.SupplierID
) Cols


SET @pvtColumns = SUBSTRING(@pvtColumns, 3, LEN(@pvtColumns));


PRINT @pvtColumns;
```

The output of this query will look like this:

```
Messages
[A Datum Corporation], [Contoso, Ltd.], [Fabrikam, Inc.], [Graphic Design Institute], [Litware, Inc.], [Northwind Electric Cars], [The Phone Company]
Completion time: 2023-02-20T13:35:04.4733395-06
```

Figure 7.5 – Pulled column names from the Suppliers table

Here, the temporary variable `pvtColumns` pulls unique supplier names from the `Suppliers` table (joined by `PurchaseOrders`) and appends a `,` character that will be used in the dynamic `PIVOT` statement to list all column names.

To extend our dynamic pivoting option, we can use the preceding column list directly in our dynamic `PIVOT` operation and execute the query using a built-in stored procedure, `sp-executesql`.

Let's walk through the following script query in three sections:

1. First, declare two variables that will be used in the SQL script to store column names and the SQL scripts:

    ```
    -----------------------------------------------------
        Dynamic column names in a PIVOT operation
    -----------------------------------------------------
    USE [WideWorldImporters]
    GO


    DECLARE
    @pvtColumns NVARCHAR(MAX) = '',
    @sql  NVARCHAR(MAX) = '';
    ```

2. Pull all `DISTINCT` supplier names and store them in the `pvtColumns` variable separated by using the `,` (comma) character:

    ```
    SELECT
    @pvtColumns = @pvtColumns + ', ' + QUOTENAME(Cols.
    SupplierName)
    FROM
    (
    SELECT DISTINCT SP.SupplierName
    FROM [Purchasing].[PurchaseOrders] PO
    INNER JOIN [Purchasing].[Suppliers] SP ON PO.SupplierID =
    SP.SupplierID
    ) Cols;
    ```

```
-- remove first comma from the list
SET @pvtColumns = SUBSTRING (@pvtColumns, 3, LEN(@
pvtColumns));
```

3. Now run the dynamic PIVOT query using column names stored in the pvtColumns variable:

```
-- dynamic PIVOT query
SET @sql =
'
SELECT
''Total Purchase Orders'' AS TotalPurchaseOrders,
' + @pvtColumns + '

FROM
(
SELECT DISTINCT
SP.SupplierName
, PO.[PurchaseOrderID]
FROM
[Purchasing].[PurchaseOrders] PO INNER JOIN [Purchasing].
[Suppliers] SP
ON PO.SupplierID = SP.SupplierID
) AS SrcTbl
PIVOT
(
COUNT([PurchaseOrderID])
FOR SupplierName IN (
' + @pvtColumns + '
)
) AS PvtTbl;
';

-- execute the dynamic sql statement
EXECUTE sp_executesql @sql;
```

The output of this query will look like the following:

TotalPurchaseOrders	A Datum Corporation	Contoso, Ltd.	Fabrikam, Inc.	Graphic Design Institute	Litware, Inc.	Northwind Electric Cars	The Phone Company
1 Total Purchase Orders	5	1	1055	13	985	10	5

Figure 7.6 – Dynamic PIVOT query output with supplier names as column names

This is the same as the one we ran without using the dynamic column names option previously and displays supplier names as columns with purchase orders aggregated to each supplier.

Working with the UNPIVOT operator

The UNPIVOT operator performs the complete opposite operation of the PIVOT operator. It rotates columns into rows. For example, in the previous section, the supplier's name [A Datum Corporation] would be rotated to record the row value and all purchase order values would be added to a new column, [PurchaseOrder].

In the following example, we have provided a SQL script to create a new table, pvtSupplierPurchaseOrder, with one record storing values, similar to the output from the dynamic PIVOT example discussed in the previous section:

```
-------------------------------------------------------------
-- Create sample table for UNPIVOT operator testing
-------------------------------------------------------------
DROP TABLE IF EXISTS [dbo].[pvtSupplierPurchaseOrder];
GO
-- Create the table and insert values as portrayed in the
previous example.CREATE TABLE pvtSupplierPurchaseOrder (
TotalPurchaseOrders VARCHAR(25)
, [A Datum Corporation] INT
, [Contoso, Ltd.] INT
, [Fabrikam, Inc.] INT
, [Graphic Design Institute] INT
, [Litware, Inc.] INT
, [Northwind Electric Cars] INT
, [The Phone Company] INT
);
GO


INSERT INTO pvtSupplierPurchaseOrder VALUES ('Total Purchase
Orders', 5, 1, 1055, 13, 985, 10, 5);
GO
```

Once you execute the preceding scripts, a new table will be created on the database, shown as follows:

	TotalPurchaseOrders	A Datum Corporation	Contoso, Ltd.	Fabrikam, Inc.	Graphic Design Institute	Litware, Inc.	Northwind Electric Cars	The Phone Company
1	Total Purchase Orders	5	1	1055	13	985	10	5

Figure 7.7 – SELECT output of the pvtSupplierPurchaseOrder table

Now, for UNPIVOT, look at the following script that is executed on the preceding table and, with it, the columns will convert into rows:

```
--------------------------------------------------------------------
-- Using UNPIVOT, produce Suppliers rows from column values
-------------------------------------------------------------
SELECT TotalPurchaseOrders, Suppliers, PurchaseOrder
FROM
     (SELECT TotalPurchaseOrders
, [A Datum Corporation]
, [Contoso, Ltd.]
, [Fabrikam, Inc.]
, [Graphic Design Institute]
, [Litware, Inc.]
, [Northwind Electric Cars]
, [The Phone Company]
    FROM pvtSupplierPurchaseOrder) p
UNPIVOT
    (PurchaseOrder FOR Suppliers IN
        ([A Datum Corporation]
, [Contoso, Ltd.]
, [Fabrikam, Inc.]
, [Graphic Design Institute]
, [Litware, Inc.]
, [Northwind Electric Cars]
, [The Phone Company])
)AS unpvt;
GO
```

The output of this query will look like this:

	TotalPurchaseOrders	Suppliers	PurchaseOrder
1	Total Purchase Orders	A Datum Corporation	5
2	Total Purchase Orders	Contoso, Ltd.	1
3	Total Purchase Orders	Fabrikam, Inc.	1055
4	Total Purchase Orders	Graphic Design Institute	13
5	Total Purchase Orders	Litware, Inc.	985
6	Total Purchase Orders	Northwind Electric Cars	10
7	Total Purchase Orders	The Phone Company	5

Figure 7.8 – Tabular output of UNPIVOT operation – columns to rows

Here, the supplier column names are converted into rows with purchase order counts for each supplier. This is the opposite to the PIVOT query output we looked at earlier in the chapter while learning about the PIVOT operator.

> **Important**
>
> If you compare both PIVOT and UNPIVOT inputs and outputs, UNPIVOT is not the exact opposite of PIVOT. PIVOT does aggregate and merge similar supplier IDs into one record but when you run UNPIVOT, it won't get back to the original table since the aggregation information is not captured.
>
> Also, any NULL value columns will be filtered in the final UNPIVOT output (for example, if we had any NULL PurchaseOrder instances in the preceding query, they won't show up in the output UNPIVOT table.

The preceding couple of sections explained the PIVOT and UNPIVOT operators with a few example queries and how to use them. We will now look at a different data shaping technique – hierarchical data and its usage.

Understanding hierarchical data

Hierarchical data, as per the name, defines data items that are related to each other by a hierarchical relationship. When we think of hierarchical data, we get a visual of a tree in our mind and a root node and one or multiple leaves; in a relational database, it's often referred to as a parent-child relation. Every child will have one parent and one parent can have one or multiple children.

Here are a few common examples of hierarchical data items in databases:

- Employee/manager relationship
- Organizational hierarchy

- Folder/files system

- Graph of links between web pages

- Tasks assigned under a project

MS SQL has a built-in data type, `hierarchyid`, and it is specially designed to store and query hierarchical data and optimized for most common cases representing tree structure hierarchical data.

There are two ways to represent nodes in this data type—string and bit representation.

The / character is used to represent a node in string representation whereas a hexadecimal value is used for bit representation.

Let's create a new `EmployeeOrganization` table and see how to use these data types:

```
---------------------------------------------------------------
-- Create a new table for Hierarchy data example
---------------------------------------------------------------
CREATE TABLE Sales.EmployeeOrganization
(
    EmpNode hierarchyid PRIMARY KEY CLUSTERED,
    EmpLevel AS EmpNode.GetLevel(),
    EmpID int UNIQUE NOT NULL,
    EmpName nvarchar(25) NOT NULL,
    EmpTitle nvarchar(25) NOT NULL
) ;
GO
```

For this example, we will insert a new root-level record where `John` is the `Manager` and has two reporting members—`Jim` and `Kim`, both with the title `Assistant Manager`. Jim has two reporting members—`Jack` and `Frank`, with the title `Team Member`:

```
---------------------------------------------------------------
-- Add John has Manager in the organization
---------------------------------------------------------------
INSERT Sales.EmployeeOrganization (EmpNode, EmpID, EmpName,
EmpTitle)
VALUES (hierarchyid::GetRoot(), 0, 'John', 'Manager');
GO


SELECT EmpNode, EmpNode.ToString() AS Text_EmpNode, EmpLevel,
EmpID, EmpName, EmpTitle
```

```
FROM Sales.EmployeeOrganization;
GO
```

The output of this query will look like this:

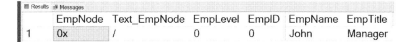

Figure 7.9 – Tabular output of EmployeeOrganization data

Here, you will see we have pulled **EmpNode** with a string and bit representation (in text output). **John** is added as a **Manager** at root **0** level.

Now, let's add Jim and Kim as Assistant Manager to John. Refer to the following query:

```
-----------------------------------------------------------------
-- Adding subordinate nodes under root node - John
-----------------------------------------------------------------
--DECLARE @vEmpNode hierarchyid, @mx hierarchyid;

SELECT @vEmpNode = EmpNode FROM Sales.EmployeeOrganization
WHERE EmpID = '0';


-- Add Jim
SELECT @mx = max(EmpNode) FROM Sales.EmployeeOrganization WHERE
EmpNode.GetAncestor(1) = @vEmpNode;


INSERT Sales.EmployeeOrganization (EmpNode, EmpID, EmpName,
EmpTitle)
    VALUES(@vEmpNode.GetDescendant(@mx, NULL), '17', 'Jim',
'Assistant Manager');


-- Add Kim
SELECT @mx = max(EmpNode) FROM Sales.EmployeeOrganization WHERE
EmpNode.GetAncestor(1) = @vEmpNode;


INSERT Sales.EmployeeOrganization (EmpNode, EmpID, EmpName,
EmpTitle)
    VALUES(@vEmpNode.GetDescendant(@mx, NULL), '24', 'Kim',
'Assistant Manager');
```

```
--   Select statement to view output
SELECT EmpNode, EmpNode.ToString() AS Text_EmpNode, EmpLevel,
EmpID, EmpName, EmpTitle
FROM Sales.EmployeeOrganization;
GO
```

The output of this query is shown as follows:

	EmpNode	Text_EmpNode	EmpLevel	EmpID	EmpName	EmpTitle
1	0x	/	0	0	John	Manager
2	0x58	/1/	1	17	Jim	Assistant Manager
3	0x68	/2/	1	24	Kim	Assistant Manager

Figure 7.10 – Tabular output after adding subordinates to a manager

Here, you will see we have **Jim** and **Kim** both added as **Assistant Manager**, reporting to **John**. The **EmpNode** field is shown as a Hex value and in string representation.

We used GetAncestor() and GetDescendant() functions to get Manager and their node details to maintain a tree structure in the organization.

You can repeat the preceding queries to add more subordinate nodes under Jim using SQL scripts. The change to this script will be just updating the employee ID to get the parent node and add two subordinates. Refer to the following queries:

```
-----------------------------------------------------------------
-- Adding subordinate nodes under root node - Jim
-----------------------------------------------------------
--DECLARE @vEmpNode hierarchyid, @mx hierarchyid;

SELECT @vEmpNode = EmpNode FROM Sales.EmployeeOrganization
WHERE EmpID = '17';

-- Add Jack
SELECT @mx = max(EmpNode) FROM Sales.EmployeeOrganization WHERE
EmpNode.GetAncestor(1) = @vEmpNode;

INSERT Sales.EmployeeOrganization (EmpNode, EmpID, EmpName,
EmpTitle)
    VALUES(@vEmpNode.GetDescendant(@mx, NULL), '32', 'Jack',
'Team Member');
```

```
-- Add Frank
SELECT @mx = max(EmpNode) FROM Sales.EmployeeOrganization WHERE
EmpNode.GetAncestor(1) = @vEmpNode;


INSERT Sales.EmployeeOrganization (EmpNode, EmpID, EmpName,
EmpTitle)
    VALUES(@vEmpNode.GetDescendant(@mx, NULL), '25', 'Frank',
'Team Member');


GO
```

To get the final output with three levels of organization structure, repeat the SELECT statement to view the output.

	EmpNode	Text_EmpNode	EmpLevel	EmpID	EmpName	EmpTitle
1	0x	/	0	0	John	Manager
2	0x58	/1/	1	17	Jim	Assistant Manager
3	0x5AC0	/1/1/	2	32	Jack	Team Member
4	0x5B40	/1/2/	2	25	Frank	Team Member
5	0x68	/2/	1	24	Kim	Assistant Manager

Figure 7.11 – Final output of the EmployeeOrganization table

We can create a stored procedure and pass the employee ID and other dynamic information and use it for adding any new members and to build the organization structure.

This concludes the details on storing hierarchical data using the hierarchyid data type. We went through an overview and walked through a few examples on how to add employees in an organization and query the hierarchical structure and discussed two very commonly used functions, GetAncestor() and GetDescendent(), to pull organization data from the hierarchyid data structure.

Summary

In this chapter, we learned how to use the PIVOT and UNPIVOT operators and how we can use them in our advanced query techniques by transforming rows into columns or vice versa. We looked at a few examples and also learned how to dynamically construct column names that are used in pivoting operations. Both of these operators are very powerful and are a very good and clean replacement for the lengthy CASE statement we studied in *Chapter 4*.

The PIVOT option is used a lot for reporting purposes and analyzing data in different formats and UNPIVOT is more for denormalizing datasets and storing them in SQL tables.

Next, we looked at the new way of storing hierarchical data, using the `hierarchyid` data type. We walked through a very typical use case of storing organization hierarchy data with examples.

In the next chapter, we will move our focus onto the security aspects of SQL queries and the things we need to take care of while querying data from a database, along with how to make sure we are using security best practices.

8

Impact of SQL Server Security on Query Results

In the previous chapters, you have learned different methods to query your data sources and create datasets that can be used to do further analytics on that data. Now you have been given a new assignment and have been asked to give your SQL query to a co-worker. One day, the co-worker comes to you and says that the SQL query that you gave them does not work. You test it out and it gives you the correct results. Why does this happen?

This chapter will start by explaining what SQL Server security is and how it can impact the result set of a query from one user to another. We will then discuss how you can verify what your security settings are for a database and will wrap up the chapter by discussing the steps that may need to be taken to modify SQL Server security for a user so that they can run an SQL query and get the correct results. This chapter will not provide the training to enable you to manage the security of a database; it will only give you an overview of SQL Server security.

In this chapter, we will be covering the following main topics:

- Why is data missing from my result set?
- Understanding SQL Server security
- Validating security settings

Technical requirements

To work with the examples and illustrations in this chapter, you will need to have SQL Server Management Studio installed. We will be working with the `WideWorldImportersDW` database on SQL Server. Please refer to the *Appendix* for tool installation and database restoration guidance.

You will find the code from this chapter on GitHub here: `https://github.com/PacktPublishing/SQL-Query-Design-Best-Practices/tree/main/Chapter08`

Why is data missing from my result set?

Your co-worker has given you a SQL query and explained what it is doing and what the expected results of the query are. They then go on an extended vacation and it is time for you to run the query. You follow the steps precisely as your co-worker explained and when you look at the results, you notice that you have not gotten the results that you were expecting. You examine the SQL query and confirm that there are no issues with the query and you are not getting any error messages when the query runs.

So what could be causing the problem? This could be a case where two co-workers do not have the same level of security. If co-workers have different security settings, then you will not get the same results when running the same query. For example, the following code shows the sample SQL query that was initially created and the results that were returned:

```
SELECT
    c.[City],
    c.[Region],
    SUM(s.[Quantity]) as Quanity,
    SUM(s.[Profit]) as Profit
FROM [Fact].[Sale] s
INNER JOIN [Dimension].[City] c
ON s.[City Key] = c.[City Key]
GROUP BY c.[City],
        c.[Region]
```

The following figure shows the results that the original analyst had returned:

City	Region	Quanity	Profit
Abbottsburg	Americas	17359	173946.95
Absecon	Americas	12415	129358.35
Accomac	Americas	16472	157768.4
Aceitunas	Americas	12693	119283
Airport Drive	Americas	16445	162500
Akhiok	Americas	30999	259554.3
Alcester	Americas	12802	127040.25
Alden Bridge	Americas	14645	152137.85
Alstead	Americas	12073	106146.95
Amado	Americas	14722	136717.8
Amanda Park	Americas	12221	117443.85
Andrix	Americas	14664	130710
Annamoriah	Americas	15326	139498.5
Antares	Americas	15363	147561.8
Antonito	Americas	12873	113055.75
Arbor Vitae	Americas	14334	135056.25

Figure 8.1 – Sample query results

Figure 8.2 shows the results that the co-worker, Jeanie, received when she ran the same query.

City	Region	Quanity	Profit
Absecon	Americas	12415	129358.35
Accomac	Americas	16472	157768.4
Airport Drive	Americas	16445	162500
Akhiok	Americas	30999	259554.3
Alcester	Americas	12802	127040.25
Alden Bridge	Americas	14645	152137.85
Amado	Americas	14722	136717.8
Amanda Park	Americas	12221	117443.85
Andrix	Americas	14664	130710
Annamoriah	Americas	15326	139498.5
Antares	Americas	15363	147561.8
Antonito	Americas	12873	113055.75
Arbor Vitae	Americas	14334	135056.25

Figure 8.2 – Sample query results when Jeanie ran the query

Notice that the results that Jeanie received did not include **Abbottsburg, Aceitunas**, or **Alstead**. This is the result of the SQL Server security that is being applied to Jeanie. In this case, she is not permitted to see information related to those cities. So what is SQL Server security? Let's look at that in the next section.

Understanding SQL Server security

SQL Server security determines what information is returned to a user who submits a query. It can be applied at the server, database, schema, table, row, or column level. Each authorized user of a database can only view data that they are authorized to see. Often, when two different people run the same query and they get different results, it is because they do not have the same access to the same tables or data.

Security is typically managed by the **database administrator** (**DBA**). If you are not getting the results that you were expecting, you may need to contact the DBA to have the access granted to you.

Security for tables and columns is applied through `Grant` or `Deny` statements run by the DBA and look like this: `GRANT SELECT ON SCHEMA.TABLE` or `DENY SELECT ON SCHEMA.TABLE`.

For column access, it is the same command with the list of columns to allow or deny access to. Here is what they look like:

```
GRANT SELECT ON SCHEMA.TABLE(COLUMN 1, COLUMN 2,....)
DENY SELECT ON SCHEMA.TABLE(COLUMN 1, COLUMN 2,....)
```

Row-level security can be done by one of the two types of security predicates: **Filter** and **Block** predicates. For details regarding this process and how to set it up, refer to `https://learn. microsoft.com/en-us/sql/relational-databases/security/row-level-security?view=sql-server-ver16`.

Now that you understand some of the ways that security can affect the query output, let's take a look at how you can validate your SQL Server security to be able to explain to a DBA what you need to have changed in your security.

Validating security settings

If you are interested in following the steps in this section in your personal environment, you will need to create a database-level login. You can refer `https://learn.microsoft.com/en-us/sql/relational-databases/security/row-level-security?view=sql-server-ver16` for the steps to create the login. The login that is created when you do an initial install of SQL Server will only create the server-level login.

Security settings will normally be controlled by the DBA and are out of scope of this book. You can reference the previous link for more details regarding SQL Server security. Before you approach your DBA, you can attempt to see whether there is any security applied to your ID by taking the following steps:

1. Start by logging in to **SQL Server Management Studio** (**SSMS**) and expand the database that you are working with. This is shown in the following screenshot:

Figure 8.3 – Log in to SSMS and expand the database

2. Next, you will expand the Security and Users folders and find your login ID:

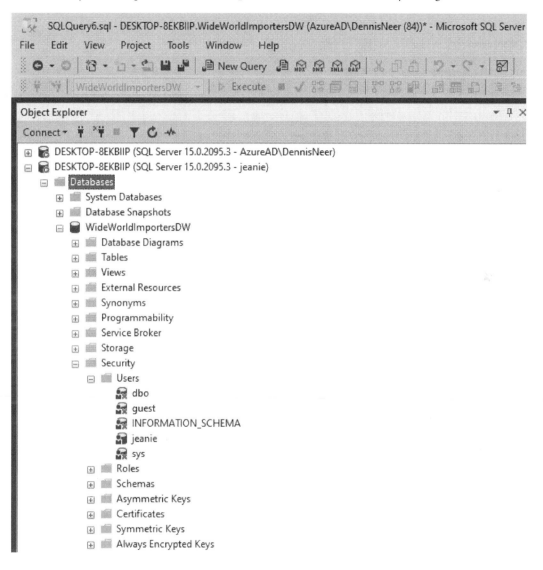

Figure 8.4 – Expand the Security and Users folders to find your login ID

3. Finally, you will right-click on your login ID and select **Properties**:

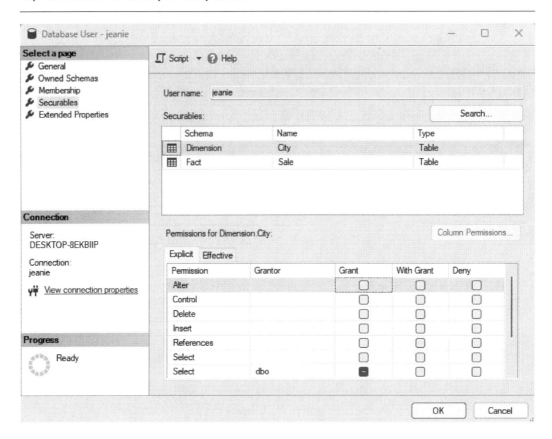

Figure 8.5 – Properties for your login ID

In *Figure 8.5*, you can see that Jeanie only has access to the **City** and **Sale** tables, which tells you that she has access to the correct tables, so that is not the issue. This indicates that row-level security applied has been and she will have to talk to the DBA to have that security changed to return all the data that she is expecting. Now, she has the information she needs to have a conversation with the DBA.

Now that you have completed this section, you can review what tables you have access to and will be ready to explain to the DBA what additional tables you may need access to. If you find that you have access to all of the tables that you need, then you can explain to the DBA what data is missing and they will be able to do additional investigation regarding your access.

Summary

In this chapter, we discussed the purpose of SQL Server security, what it is, how it can impact your result sets, and how you can verify whether you have the access you need to create your result sets.

We started by discussing how two people can run the same query and get different results and we showed an example of this happening. We then followed that up with a discussion on what SQL Server security is and the primary types of security that impact running queries. We then concluded the chapter by discussing the steps that you, as a user, can take to review your security settings before talking to the DBA to have changes made to security to get the correct results. The skills that you have developed include how to verify your SQL Server security settings, the impact of the settings on your queries, and what steps you would take to change your security settings.

With this knowledge, you are now ready to move on to the next chapter in your SQL journey. The next chapter will take you through how to review and understand query plans and what they can do to help you improve the performance of your queries.

Part 3: Optimizing Your Queries to Improve Performance

Whereas the previous two parts focused on query writing skills, this is the first chapter that focuses on performance. There are two chapters in this part to help you understand how queries are performing and how to improve that performance through query writing, query hints, and indexes:

- *Chapter 9, Understanding Query Plans*
- *Chapter 10, Understanding the Impact of Indexes on Your Query Design*

Understanding Query Plan

In the first part of this book, we went through refining and querying the database to get the desired result. In the second part, we learned about solving complex business and data problems and how to query to get the needed result. This part is about optimizing queries to improve query performance.

We now understand how to query and fetch the desired result for complex business problems. In this chapter, we will learn about query plans, and how the SQL Server query optimizer works to generate a query plan and select the appropriate query plan to fetch the desired result.

By the end of this chapter, you will have a basic understanding of query optimization techniques, and an understanding of the query optimizer and what it does. You will also have an understanding of the query execution plan, how it helps to optimize the query, whether the query is efficient or not, and how we can improve or optimize the query for optimal performance. You will also learn about the different types of execution plans, and how to view, save, compare, and analyze query execution plans.

In this chapter, we will be covering the following main topics:

- Understanding query optimization techniques
- Understanding the query optimizer
- Understanding and exploring query execution plans

Technical requirements

To work with the examples and illustrations in this chapter, you will need to have SSMS installed. We will be working with the `WideWorldImporters` database on SQL Server. Please refer to the *Appendix* for tool installation and database restoration guidance.

You will find the code for this on GitHub here: `https://github.com/PacktPublishing/SQL-Query-Design-Best-Practices/tree/main/Chapter09`

ptimization techniques

'o not perform as expected, and users and businesses complain
w. Over time, queries start running slower as the load grows
d techniques to find the root cause of poorly performing
' on the findings.

icrosoft that we can use to diagnose and improve the
es. *Chapter 1* showed one such technique, which we
her techniques involve adding proper indexes and
apter 10.

nance improvement technique that we can use to diagnose
ance queries is query plans. Query plans are a roadmap, generated and
nizer to fetch the desired result set.

ne question arises, *what is the query optimizer?* We will discuss the query optimizer and its
workings now.

Understanding the Query Optimizer

The query optimizer is an important part of the SQL Server database engine that generates the
execution plan for a query based on the query operators, the schema, tables, hints, load on the SQL
Server, the database statistics, and so on. The SQL Server database engine then decides and picks
the optimal plan to execute the query. This optimal query execution plan might not be the best of
all execution plans for the query but will be the best for the time when the query is getting executed.
The query optimizer generation is a CPU-intensive operation and hence, Microsoft has designed it
to store execution plans in a buffer called a **plan cache**. The optimizer first checks the existing query
plans for the query and generates a plan if it doesn't find suitable plan in the plan cache; otherwise, it
picks the best suitable plan from the plan cache.

The query optimizer uses parsing, binding, optimization, and execution steps to complete the query
execution and return the result:

- **Parsing**: Parsing is the process of analyzing the SQL syntax of the query. During this step, the
  query optimizer validates the keywords used in the query and T-SQL rules are followed. It
  checks the spellings of keywords, tables and columns, functions, and other database objects.

- **Binding**: Binding is the process of checking for the validity of database objects referenced in
  queries against the system catalogs, such as constraints, data types, and so on. Binding provides
  a basic list of processes required to complete the query execution.

- **Optimization**: Optimization is the process of choosing the best possible plan to execute the
  query from the plan cache, based on the query cost. The query cost is the sum of the cost of
  each step in the query execution plan.

- **Execution**: Execution is when the query execution plan selected by the query optimizer is executed and generates the final result set.

As we now have understood how the query optimizer generates and chooses a query plan, let's discuss the query execution plan.

Understanding and exploring the Query Execution Plan

Sometimes, we get questions from business users about queries or reports running slowly, and we struggle to understand the root cause and how to fix it. The **Query Execution Plan** is the answer to that question. Now, you must be wondering what the query execution plan is, right?

There are multiple steps that SQL Server takes to execute the query. The graphical representation of these steps is called the Query Execution Plan. It displays the details of each step, such as the number of actual rows, estimated rows, I/O and CPU cost, percentage of the cost of each step, and so on. Each step in the execution plan is called a **node**.

Are you wondering what a query execution plan looks like? Here is an example of a query execution plan for the SELECT TOP (1000) * FROM [WideWorldImporters].[Sales]. [Customers]; query displaying the nodes of the execution plan:

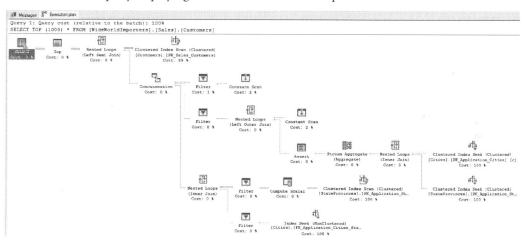

Figure 9.1 – A sample query execution plan

Let us look at this in more detail in the next section.

Query Plan types

There are three types of execution plans available in **SQL Server**: estimated execution plan, actual execution plan, and live query statistics. Let's understand each of these with examples.

The estimated execution plan

These are compiled plans produced by the Query optimizer, based on the estimates that SQL Server would most probably use to execute the query. To display the estimated execution plan, open an existing SQL query or write a new query. Let's take a simple query to see its execution plan:

```
SELECT TOP (1000) [CityID]
      ,[CityName]
      ,[StateProvinceID]
      ,[Location]
      ,[LatestRecordedPopulation]
      ,[LastEditedBy]
  FROM [WideWorldImporters].[Application].[Cities];
```

Use the *Ctrl* + *L* key combination or click on the **Display Estimated Execution Plan** button on the toolbar, as shown in the following screenshot:

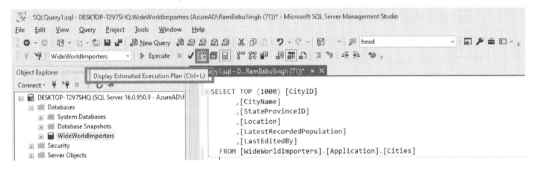

Figure 9.2 – The Display Estimated Execution Plan option on the toolbar

Here is how an estimated execution plan looks for this query:

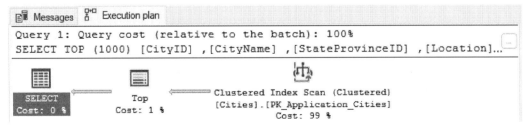

Figure 9.3 – The estimated execution plan of the query in the query pane

The Actual Execution Plan

The actual execution plan is generated after the query execution, and hence displays the actual information that the SQL Server database engine uses to execute the query. Here is how we do it:

To display the Actual Execution Plan for the same query, use the previous query, and use the *Ctrl + M* key combination or click on **Include Actual Execution Plan**, as shown in the figure here:

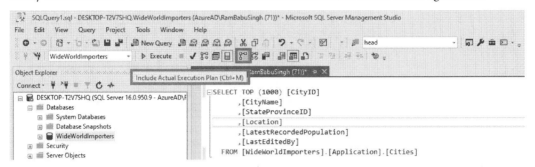

Figure 9.4 – The Include Actual Execution Plan option on the toolbar

Now, click on the **Execute** button or use the *Alt + X* key combination to execute the query, which will display an additional **Execution plan** tab in the result pane shown as follows:

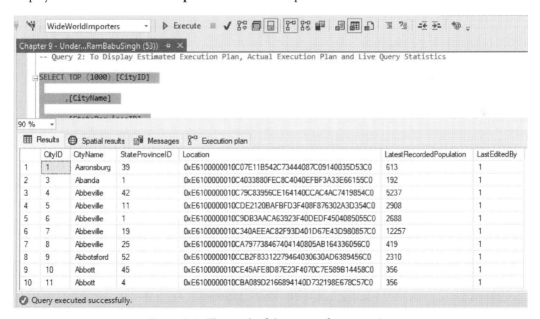

Figure 9.5 – The result of the query after execution

Click on the **Execution plan** tab to view the Actual Execution Plan, which will look as follows:

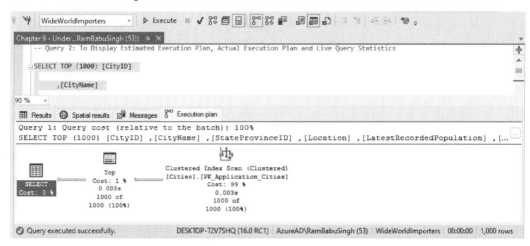

Figure 9.6 – Displays the Actual Execution Plan of the query in query pane

Live Query Statistics

Live Query Statistics is a compiled execution plan that displays the live statistics of the query as the query is executing. The statistics keep changing every second during the query execution. This live query plan displays the query progress as the query steps are executing, and hence displays operator-level live execution statistics such as the number of rows, operator progress, elapsed time, and so on. As the data statistics are available in real time, we do not need to wait to finish the execution; we can find whether there is any issue on the node in real time and cancel the query to address the issue later. This option is only available starting from SQL Server 2016.

To display the live query statistics, perform the following steps:

1. Click on the **Include Live Query Statistics** button on the toolbar, as shown in the following screenshot:

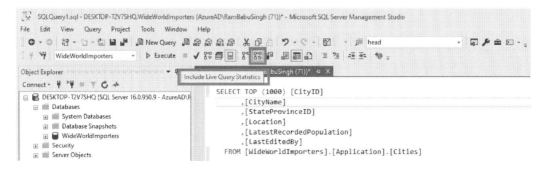

Figure 9.7 – The Include live query statistics option on the toolbar

2. Now, click on the **Execute** button or use the *Alt + X* key combination to execute the query. You will notice an additional tab, **Live Query Statistics**, in the result pane, as shown in the preceding screenshot:

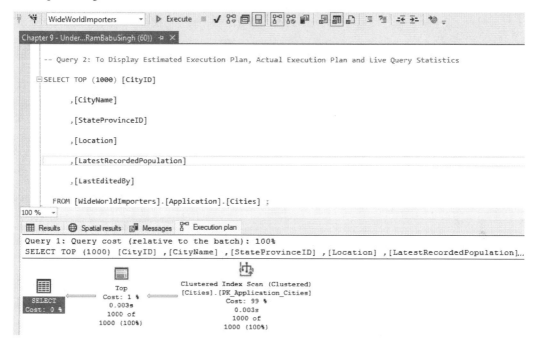

Figure 9.8 – The result of the query after query execution in the result pane

Live Query Statistics is also called the Live Execution Plan, and these names will be used interchangeably.

We have to save these query execution plans for investigation. For example, to compare two execution plans, we need to at least save one execution plan and then compare it with either another saved plan for the query or generate an execution plan for the same query using the methods we learned about earlier.

To save the execution plan in XML format, there are two methods: using SHOWPLAN_XML while running the query in the query editor, or using the execution plan in a graphical interface.

To save a query plan using the XML showplan SET option, try the following:

1. Open SSMS and connect to the WideWorldImporters database.

2. Turn SHOWPLAN_XML on, as referenced here:

```
SET SHOWPLAN_XML ON;
GO
```

This command will then generate an estimated query plan in XML format. It contains the information generated during the compilation of the query, not the execution of the query, hence it does not execute the query itself.

3. To get the actual execution plan in XML format, use the STATISTICS XML option, as referenced here:

```
SET  STATISTICS XML ON;
GO
```

4. This command will then generate the actual query plan in XML format. It contains the information during the execution of the query and executes the query.

Execute the referenced query here to get the estimated query plan:

```
SET SHOWPLAN_XML ON;
GO


SELECT TOP (1000) [CityID]
      ,[CityName]
      ,[StateProvinceID]
      ,[Location]
      ,[LatestRecordedPopulation]
      ,[LastEditedBy]
   FROM [WideWorldImporters].[Application].[Cities] ;
GO


SET SHOWPLAN_XML OFF;
GO
```

Here is how the query is executed:

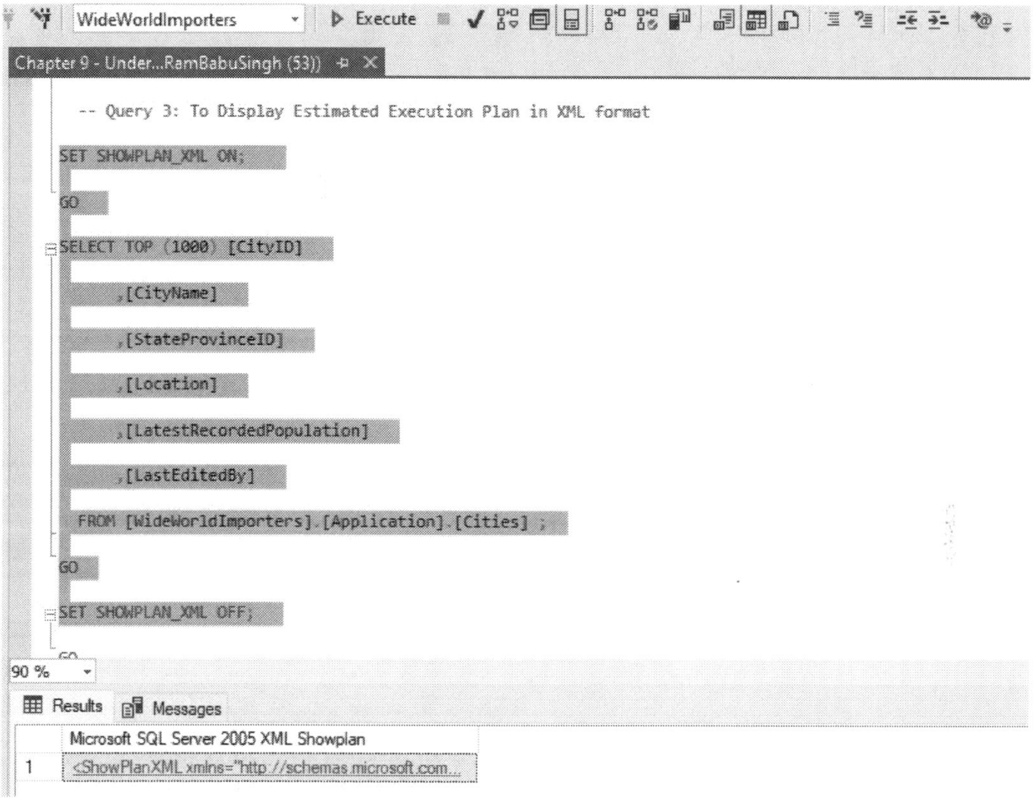

Figure 9.9 – The XML plan of the query in the query result pane

5.   In the **Results** pane, right-click the result and select the **Save Results As…** option, as referenced here:

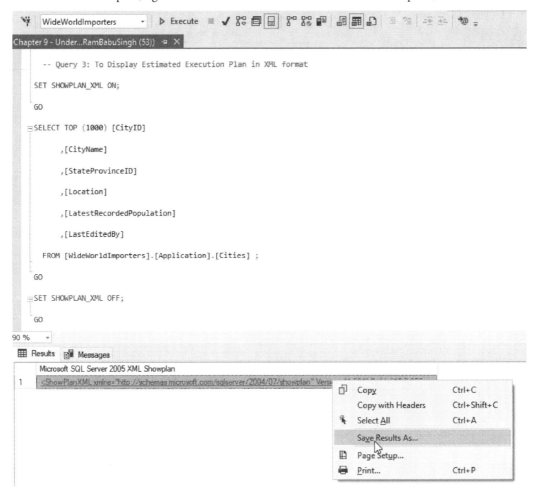

Figure 9.10 – The Save Result ts As... option to save the XML query plan

Select the location where you want to save the query plan, name the query plan with the `.sqlplan` extension, set the **Save as type:** option to **All files** (*.*), and click the **Save** button, as shown here:

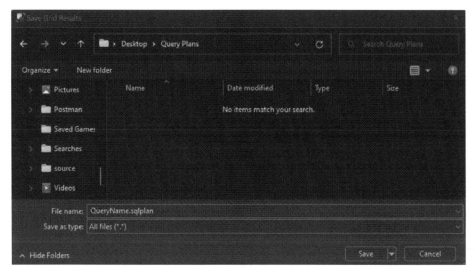

Figure 9.11 – Displays where you can save the plan

To save a query plan using SSMS, perform the following steps:

1. Generate the execution plan as per your requirements; we discussed how to generate all three types of the execution plan in this chapter.

2. Right-click on the **Execution plan** tab of the **Results** pane as shown:

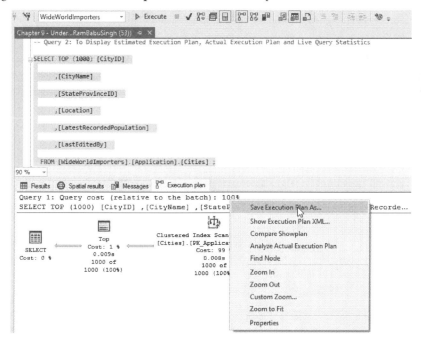

Figure 9.12 – The Save Execution Plan As... option

3. Select the location where you want to save the query plan, name the query plan with the
    `.sqlplan` extension, set the **Save as type:** option to **All files (*.*)**, and click on the **Save**
    button, as referenced here:

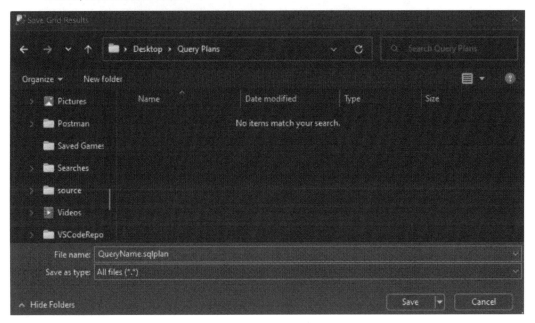

Figure 9.13 – How to save the query execution plan

To open the saved XML plan using SSMS, perform the following steps:

1. Go to **File | Open | File option**, or use the *Ctrl + O* key combination to open the **Open File**
    dialog box.

2. Navigate to the file location where you have saved the XML execution plan in the XML format.

3. Select the desired file and click **Open**, as referenced here:

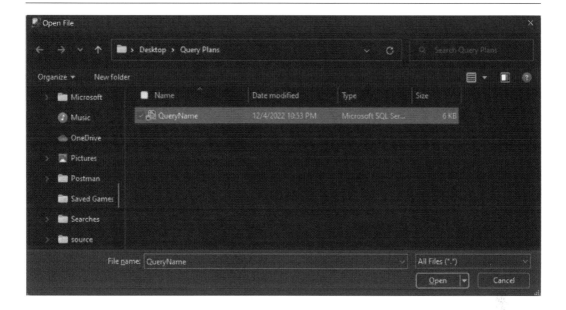

Figure 9.14 – How to open a saved execution plan

4. You will see the execution plan as referenced here:

Figure 9.15 – The saved execution plan

As we now understand how to save execution plans, let's look at how to compare two executions to see which one is better.

Comparing execution plans

As we discussed in this chapter, an optimizer can store multiple plans for a query and uses the best possible plan. However, sometimes, we observe slowness in the query. This could be because the query optimizer has generated a new plan and used it instead of the old plan. We can compare the existing plan with the new plan to find the best one and force the SQL Server to use the plan of our choice.

To compare query execution plans, follow these steps:

1. Open the query execution plan or drag and drop a plan file into SSMS, or you can execute the executing query and generate the estimated/actual execution plan.

2. Right-click anywhere in **Execution plan** and select **Analyze Actual Execution Plan**, as shown here:

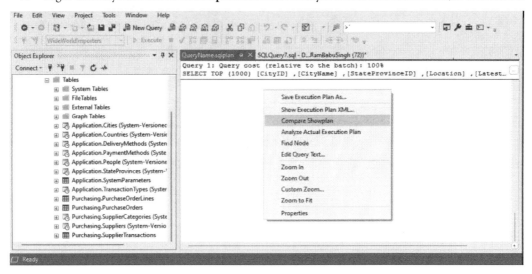

Figure 9.16 – How to get the Compare Showplan option to compare the execution plans

3. Select and open the second query plan file that you want to compare with the newly generated execution plan or open the Execution plan file.

4. The comparison of two query execution plans looks like the following:

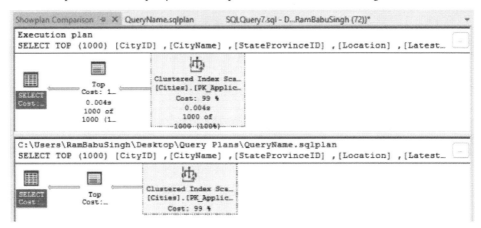

Figure 9.17 – The comparison of two execution plans

5. Look at the **Properties** window on the right side of the screen; you will notice the *not equal* sign highlighted, which lets you know the differences between the two query plans. Refer to the following screenshot:

Figure 9.18 – The Properties comparison of two execution plans

Notice the **Showplan Analysis** window at the bottom, which has three tabs:

- **Statement Options**: This tab shows the highlighted similar operations and the same highlighted operators or the nodes of two execution plans compared. You can browse through the similar compared plans or choose the highlighted differences in the plans instead of similarities, or both. Refer to the following screenshot:

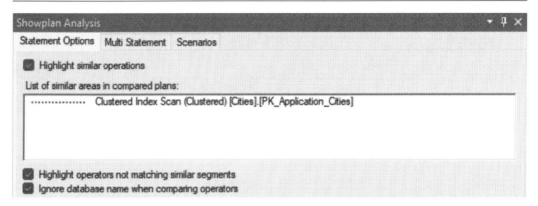

Figure 9.19 – The options to get the similarities of two execution plans

- **Multi Statement**: This tab is used when we compare plans with multiple statements to allow the right statement pair to be compared, as shown here:

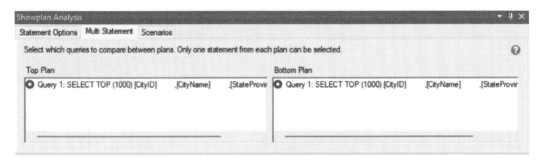

Figure 9.20 – The comparison of statements of both plans

- **Scenarios**: In this tab, we can find an automated analysis or relevant aspects to get cardinality estimation differences between two plans. You can see that, for each operator in the left window, the right window shows the details and the links you can refer to:

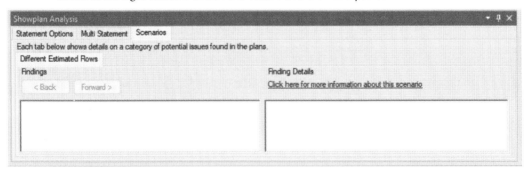

Figure 9.21 – The findings and details from the comparison of two execution plans

We discussed how we can compare two plans to identify which one is best. Besides comparing the two plans, we will analyze each plan to understand them in detail next.

Analyzing the query plan

To diagnose, optimize, and fine-tune a SQL query, we must have a deeper understanding of the query process and the execution plan. For that, SSMS is loaded with a functionality to analyze the query execution plan, especially for complex and large execution plans. It would help us to find the inaccurate cardinality estimation and get possible mitigation recommendations.

Here are the steps to analyze the execution plan:

1. Open a saved XML execution plan or use the newly generated execution plan using SSMS.

2. Right-click anywhere in **Execution plan** and select **Analyze Actual Execution Plan**, as shown here:

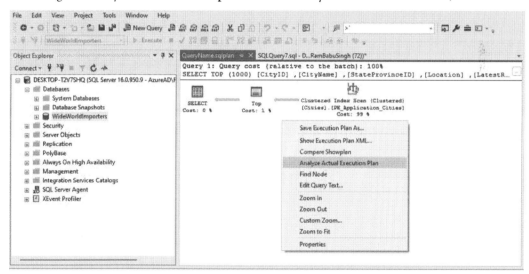

Figure 9.22 – How to get the Analyze Actual Execution Plan option

3. **Showplan Analysis** displays the actual execution plan, the properties of execution plans, and the showplan analysis. The **Showplan Analysis** window contains two tabs: **Multi Statement** and **Scenarios**. Please refer to the following screenshot:

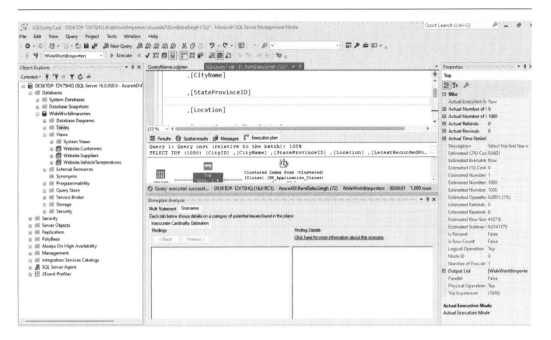

Figure 9.23 – The result of Showplan Analysis

And with this, we have learned about the **Multi Statement** and **Scenarios** tabs for comparing query plans.

So, now we can view, compare, and analyze actual execution plans, understand the properties of each node of an execution plan for deeper understanding, and troubleshoot the query performance issues of poor performing queries using query execution plans.

With all this new information, what do we get? How can we use this information to diagnose and improve the performance of our query?

Let's understand it with the help of a simple example. Use the query and generate the actual execution plan to see whether the query's performance can be improved by adding an index:

```
SELECT
     [CityName]
FROM [WideWorldImporters]. [Application].[Cities]
WHERE CityName='Abbeville'
```

The execution plan shows that the performance of the query can be improved by 99.0992% if we add the suggested index. Notice the highlighted text in the figure, which shows the index is being scanned to get the desired row:

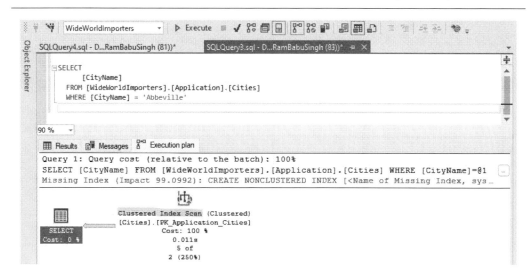

Figure 9.24 – The actual execution plan using an clustered index scan and recommending an index

Right-click on the missing index statement in green and select **Missing Index Details...** as referenced here:

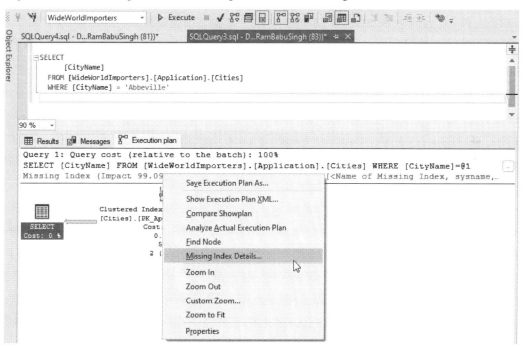

Figure 9.25 – Missing index details to get recommended index code

You will get the code referenced in the figure here:

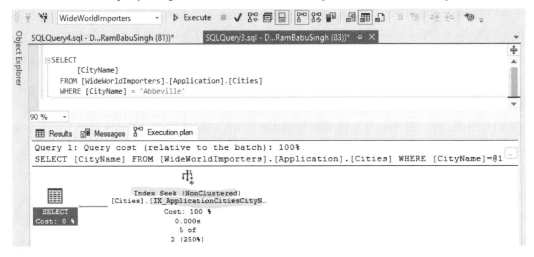

Figure 9.26 – The index definition

Indexes are covered in details in *Chapter 10*. Let's now give a meaningful name to the index and create it with the code shown here:

```
USE [WideWorldImporters]
GO
CREATE NONCLUSTERED INDEX [IX_ApplicationCitiesCityName]
ON [Application].[Cities] ([CityName])
GO
```

Now, let's rerun the query and generate the actual execution plan, as shown in this figure:

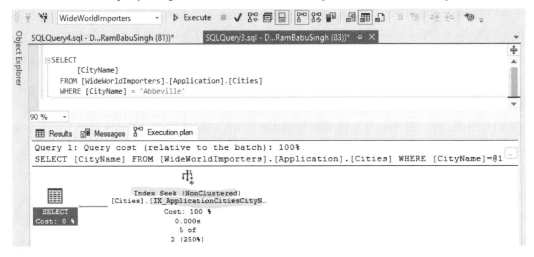

Figure 9.27 – The result of Showplan Analysis

Notice that, now, the new index is being used and it's using `Index Seek` instead of a clustered index scan. An index scan is an expensive operation with respect to `Index Seek`. Hence the performance of the query will be improved after we create this query.

The index recommendation for query plans is not always good and proper testing must be performed before implementing it into the production environment.

Summary

In this chapter, we gained an understanding of query optimization techniques, the query optimizer, and query execution plans.

We then learned about various types of execution plans, namely an Estimated Execution Plan, actual execution plan, and live query statistics. We learned how to generate the Estimated Execution Plan, actual execution plan, and live query statistics with the help of a sample of a query. We learned how to save the query plan in XML format so we can use it later. We learned, with an example, how to compare two execution plans and how to analyze an actual execution query plan for a deeper understanding of the query execution and query plan to troubleshoot the poorly performing queries and address their slowness.

In the next chapter, we will expand our knowledge and understand indexes, index types, and how indexes help to improve the query performance and faster data retrieval.

10

Understanding the Impact of Indexes on Query Design

In the previous chapter, we discussed the query optimization techniques—query execution plan. We discussed the Query Optimization Techniques, Query Optimizer, various query execution plans such as Estimated Execution Plan, Actual Execution Plan and Live Query Statistics. We discussed how to display execution plans, how to save execution plan in XML format, how to compare two execution plans and analyze an execution plan and how to use the execution plan to diagnose performance issue and fix them. With this, we added another tool to our toolkit of query optimization techniques to improve the performance of our queries to gain optimal performance.

In this chapter, we will learn about another optimization and performance improvement technique called **indexes**. We will discuss index types with examples and how indexes can impact the query design. We will then go through an example to improve the performance of the query.

In this chapter, we will be cover the following main topics:

- Understanding indexing and index types
- How indexes impact query design
- The impact of indexes on query performance

Technical requirements

To work with the examples and illustrations in this chapter, you will need to have SQL Server Management Studio installed. We will be working with the `WideWorldImportersDW` database on SQL Server. Please refer to the *Appendix* for tool installation and database restoration guidance.

You will find the code from this chapter on GitHub here: `https://github.com/PacktPublishing/SQL-Query-Design-Best-Practices/tree/main/Chapter10`

Understanding index and index types

An index is a reference list for users to make their search process easier and faster from the database table. Indexes maintain data in ordered tables or maintain a separate list of the pointers to data to improve the read efficiency of query processing. To search for a value in an unindexed table, SQL has to go through every row and column until the value is found, whereas if the table is indexed, SQL can reference the index and can directly go to the record and column where the value is located. Therefore, indexing becomes the most efficient option for data retrieval and searching.

Formally, indexes are an invaluable tool in relational databases, such as SQL Server. There are many types of indexes available in SQL Server, each of which can be used to increase the overall performance of a database. Clustered indexes are the most popular of these index types and organize data in pages sorted by the clustered index column(s) value. Non-clustered indexes are created outside the existing table and store a copy of all columns specified in the index with a pointer to the data in table. Indexes help to read data faster, especially if we have indexes on columns participating in filters (the WHERE and JOIN instances and the HAVING clause and data sorts, such as the ORDER BY clause.

Next, let's work on indexes and create, drop, rename, and alter indexes with examples.

Using CREATE to create an index

Now we have a basic understanding of the index and how it can impact the query performance, let us take an example. The [Customer Key] column on the [Fact].[Sale] table is the column that uniquely identifies each row in the table; hence adding an index to this column would optimize the query performance.

Let's create an [IX_Fact_Sale_CustomerKey] index on [Fact].[Sale] table at the [Customer Key] column. Here is the code example of creating it:

```
CREATE INDEX [IX_Fact_Sale_CustomerKey] ON [Fact].[Sale]
(
[Customer Key] ASC
);
```

The dynamic management view, sys.indexes, provides the lists of the index info created in the database. Use the query and look at the results to familiarize yourself with them:

```
select * from sys.indexes where name='IX_Fact_Sale_
CustomerKey';
```

The result provides the index name, with other details, such as the object_id type as the index type, type_desc as the index type description, index_id, and so on. We can also view the index created using SSMS, as shown in the following screenshot:

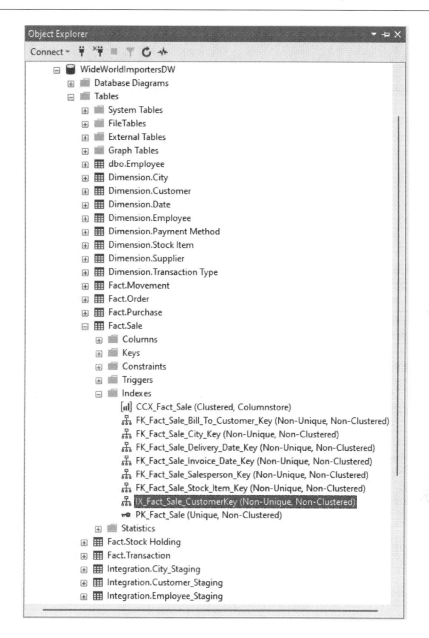

Figure 10.1 – Displays the IX_Fact_Sale_CustomerKey index created on the dbo.Employee table

If you do not specify an index type, such as CLUSTERED, NONCLUSTERED, or UNIQUE, by default, SQL server creates a NONCLUSTERED index on the specified column. So, the preceding statement creates a non-clustered index.

You might have noticed the [IX_Fact_Sale_CustomerKey] index name starts with IX, which represents that it's a non-clustered index. In the database world, we use prefixes on the name of the index to denote the index type, so we can identify the type of index without looking at the index definition/code.

Here are the prefixes used for the type of indexes:

- PK_: Primary keys
- UK_: Unique keys
- IX_: Non clustered non-unique indexes
- UX_: Unique indexes

We will see these later in this chapter.

The DROP index

Over time, we observe that some indexes are not being used in queries for operations such as index *seek*/index *scan*. Indexes are an overhead for write operations as SQL server has to keep indexes updated during write operations, such as INSERT, UPDATE, and DELETE. Hence we should drop such indexes to keep SQL Server performance optimal.

So, how to check whether the index is unused? The sys.dm_db_index_usage_stats **dynamic management view** (**DMV**) provides a list of indexes that have been used since the last server restart, and hence any indexes not listed in this DMV have not been used.

We created the [IX_Fact_Sale_CustomerKey] index on the [Fact].[Sale] table in the earlier section. Because we know we haven't run any queries on the table, it's not been used. You can go ahead and check whether the index is listed in the sys.dm_db_index_usage_stats DMV using a select statement. So, we can go ahead and drop the index. To drop the [IX_Fact_Sale_CustomerKey] index on the [Fact].[Sale] table, use the following statement:

```
DROP INDEX [IX_Fact_Sale_CustomerKey] ON [Fact].[Sale];
```

We dropped this index just to demonstrate a DROP INDEX statement. Because we will need this index later in the chapter, let's recreate it:

```
CREATE INDEX [IX_Fact_Sale_CustomerKey] ON [Fact].[Sale]
(
[Customer Key] ASC
);
```

Using RENAME to rename an index

There might be scenarios where some developers have not followed the naming conventions defined by your organization. There are two options for renaming an index:

- Use DROP to drop the index you want to rename and recreate the index with a new name. We have already learned how to create and drop an index, so go ahead and practice this by renaming the index but don't forget to revert it as we will need the index in the next step, just in case you are practicing. Drop the [IX_Fact_Sale_CustomerKey] index and create the [IX_Fact_Sale_Customer_KeY] index. To revert it, drop the [IX_Fact_Sale_Customer_KeY] index and recreate the [IX_Fact_Sale_CustomerKey] index.

- Use the sp_rename inbuilt stored procedure to rename an index.

    So, let's rename an index using sp_rename. For example, to change the name of the index we created from [IX_Fact_Sale_CustomerKey] to [IX_Fact_Sale_Customer_Key], execute the following code:

    ```
    EXEC sp_rename N'[Fact].[Sale].[IX_Fact_Sale_
    CustomerKey]', N'IX_Fact_Sale_Customer_Key', N'INDEX';
    ```

    You will get the message as shown here instead of "Commands completed successfully."

    ```
    Caution: Changing any part of an onrombject name could break
    scripts and stored procedures.
    ```

Because we will use this index name later in the chapter, let's rename it to its original name, IX_Fact_Sale_CustomerKey:

```
EXEC sp_rename  N'[Fact].[Sale].[IX_Fact_Sale_Customer_Key]',
N'IX_Fact_Sale_CustomerKey', N'INDEX';
```

Modifying indexes

To modify an existing index, such as adding, dropping, and changing the position of a column in the index, we should drop the existing index and recreate it with the desired changes. For example, if you want to add the [Bill To Customer Key] column to the [IX_Fact_Sale_CustomerKey] index on the ON [Fact].[Sale] table, we will first drop the index with the DROP statement, as shown here:

```
DROP INDEX [IX_Fact_Sale_CustomerKey] ON [Fact].[Sale]
```

And now, we will create it with the [Bill To Customer Key] column. The statement to create the [IX_Fact_Sale_CustomerKey] index with the [Bill To Customer Key] column is as follows:

```
CREATE INDEX [IX_Fact_Sale_CustomerKey] ON [Fact].[Sale]
(
[Bill To Customer Key] ASC,
[Customer Key] ASC
);
```

A scenario is discussed later in the chapter in *The covering index* section to better understand the scenario where we might need this in real time.

The ALTER index

The ALTER index statement is used to alter the properties and to maintain the index. For example, if you need to change the property to allow page locks while the index is being rebuilt, then set the ALLOW_PAGE_LOCKS property to ON, as by default, it's OFF. If you want the statistics to be recomputed during the index operations, then set the STATISTICS_NORECOMPUTE property to ON, as by default, it's OFF. Similarly, when IGNORE_DUP_KEY is ON, a warning message appears when a duplicate key value is inserted into a unique index. Only the rows violating the uniqueness constraint fail. So, if you do not want the entire insert statement to fail, you should set IGNORE_DUP_KEY to ON.

Here is the example to set the ALLOW_PAGE_LOCKS, STATISTICS_NORECOMPUTE, and IGNORE_DUP_KEY properties to ON on the [IX_Fact_Sale_CustomerKey] ON [Fact].[Sale] index table:

```
ALTER INDEX [IX_Fact_Sale_CustomerKey] ON [Fact].[Sale]
SET ( ALLOW_PAGE_LOCKS = ON,
STATISTICS_NORECOMPUTE = ON,
IGNORE_DUP_KEY = OFF
);
```

The ALTER index statement is also used to maintain/rebuild/reorganize the index to get the optimal read performance, which is discussed later in this chapter. Refer to the following Microsoft link for a detailed understanding of the ALTER index and the index properties we saw earlier:

https://learn.microsoft.com/en-us/sql/t-sql/statements/alter-index-transact-sql?view=sql-server-ver16

Now we understand working with indexes, let's explore the types of indexes that we can work with in SQL Server.

Exploring the types of indexes

Based on storage type, the index structure is different for each data storage type; these can be disk-based row store indexes, column store indexes, and memory-optimized indexes. Let's discuss the most important indexes along with some examples.

We will review the types of indexes next.

Clustered indexes

These are an integral part of SQL Server and are used to organize data based on the clustered index value. This type of index allows for the pages of data to be ordered in a specific way, allowing for faster reads and queries. The clustered index then stores the actual data rows in the table, so each table can only have one clustered index. When creating a clustered index, it is important to choose a column or columns that will be used frequently in searches and queries, as this will improve the performance of the database.

Clustered indexes are created using the CLUSTERED keyword in the CREATE statement.

Because the database tables already have clustered indexes on each table, we cannot create another clustered index on it. We will create a table called Employee to demonstrate how to create a clustered index.

Please refer to the example here to create the dbo.Employee table:

```
CREATE TABLE dbo.[Employee]
(
    EmployeeID INT NOT NULL IDENTITY(1,1) ,
    Name VARCHAR(25) NOT NULL,
    Manager INT NOT NULL,
    Job TEXT NOT NULL,
    Salary INT NOT NULL,
    Commission INT,
    HireDate DATE NOT NULL,
    DeptID INT NOT NULL,
);
```

Now let's create the PK_Employee_EmployeeID clustered index on the dbo.Employee table:

```
CREATE CLUSTERED INDEX [PK_Employee_EmployeeID] ON dbo.
[Employee]
(
EmployeeID ASC
);
```

Validate the index has been created by expanding the table and index similar to what's shown in *Figure 10.1*. If a clustered index already exists on the table and you try to create another one, you will get a warning message stating, `Cannot create more than one clustered index on view 'table/view name'. Drop the existing clustered index 'index name' before creating another one.` For example, try to run the CREATE CLUSTERED statement to create the clustered index again:

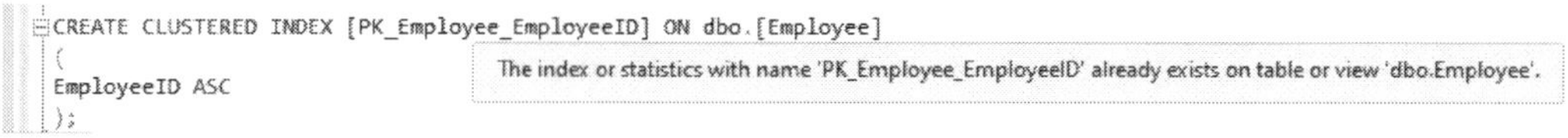

```
CREATE CLUSTERED INDEX [PK_Employee_EmployeeID] ON dbo.[Employee]
(
    EmployeeID ASC          The index or statistics with name 'PK_Employee_EmployeeID' already exists on table or view 'dbo.Employee'.
);
```

Figure 10.2 – A warning is displayed when you try to create more than
one clustered index on a table in the query editor pane

If you try to execute this statement, because a clustered index already exists on the [Fact].[Sale] table, it will throw an error stating, `The operation failed because an index or statistics with name PK_Employee_EmployeeID already exists on table dbo.Employee.` Please refer to the screenshot here:

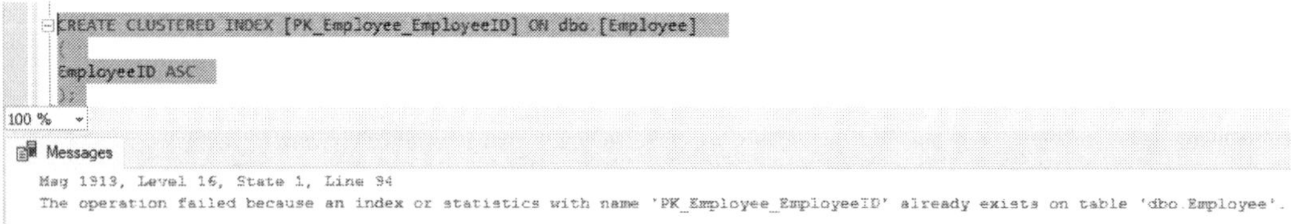

```
CREATE CLUSTERED INDEX [PK_Employee_EmployeeID] ON dbo.[Employee]
    EmployeeID ASC
    );
100 %
Messages
    Msg 1913, Level 16, State 1, Line 94
    The operation failed because an index or statistics with name 'PK_Employee_EmployeeID' already exists on table 'dbo.Employee'.
```

Figure 10.3 – An error is displayed when executing the command to create
an additional clustered index on a table which already has one

Generally, the clustered index gets created when we create a table with a primary key or when we create a primary key on an existing table that doesn't have any clustered indexes. For example, if we create the same table with the following code, a primary key and a clustered index will be created on the table:

```
DROP TABLE dbo.[Employee]
CREATE TABLE dbo.[Employee]
(
    EmployeeID INT NOT NULL IDENTITY(1,1) PRIMARY KEY,
    Name VARCHAR(25) NOT NULL,
    Manager INT NOT NULL,
    Job TEXT NOT NULL,
    Salary INT NOT NULL,
    Commission INT,
    HireDate DATE NOT NULL,
    DeptID INT NOT NULL,
)
```

Here is a screenshot displaying both the primary key and the clustered index that have been created:

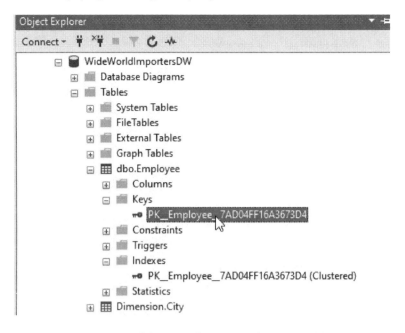

Figure 10.4 – Validating and viewing indexes using SSMS

The NONCLUSTERED index

Non-clustered indexes are another type of index used in SQL Server. Unlike clustered indexes, non-clustered indexes store copies of all columns specified in the index outside the table. This allows for faster searches because the data does not have to be sorted through as in the clustered index. Non-clustered indexes are also less expensive than clustered indexes because they do not require as much space or memory as clustered indexes.

To create a non-clustered index, use the NONCLUSTERED keyword; however, its optional as, by default, it creates a non-clustered index. Here is an example of creating a non-clustered index for [IX_Fact_Sale_InvoiceDateKey] ON [Fact].[Sale]:

```
CREATE NONCLUSTERED INDEX [IX_Fact_Sale_InvoiceDateKey] ON
[Fact].[Sale]
(
[Invoice Date Key] ASC
);
```

Validate the index has been created by expanding the table and index. We have already discussed how to validate an index on a table.

You can create up to 999 non-clustered indexes on a table, including any indexes created by PRIMARY KEY or by UNIQUE KEY. Just because you can create up to 999 indexes, you probably should not do so because of the overhead of maintaining that many indexes, and most of the indexes won't be used because either they are redundant or not needed for queries on that table. You can create non-clustered indexes after a unique clustered index has been created on a view.

The UNIQUE index

A UNIQUE index is a type of index used in SQL Server to ensure that each row of data is unique. This is accomplished by setting a constraint on the indexed columns so that if two rows have the same value, an error will occur. This can be especially useful when ensuring that certain columns, such as IDs, are not duplicated in the data. Unique indexes can also be combined with other types of indexes to provide a more robust way to query and retrieve data from the database. A unique index can be clustered or non-clustered index type.

To create the unique index, use the UNIQUE keyword. For example, to create a unique key on the [Dimension].[City] at [City Key] column, use the following statement:

```
CREATE UNIQUE INDEX [UK_DimensionCity_CityKey] ON [Dimension].
[City]
(
[City Key] ASC
);
```

This creates a non-clustered unique index. Validate the index has been created as described earlier.

The filtered index

Filtered indexes are optimized, non-clustered indexes created for a targeted set of data in a table to improve the query performance and the reduce index maintenance because we need to maintain the smaller dataset and smaller index. Because these are created on a subset of data of a table, filtered indexes take a smaller amount of disk space. Filtered indexes use the WHERE clause to filter the targeted dataset.

Here is how we create a filtered index on [Fact].[Order] at [WWI Order ID] for YEAR([Order Date Key]) = 2016:

```
CREATE NONCLUSTERED INDEX [FI_Integration_Order_WWI_Order_ID]
ON [Fact].[Order]
(
[WWI Order ID] ASC
)
WHERE [Order Date Key] >= '2016-01-01'
AND [Order Date Key] <= '2016-12-31';
```

Validate the index has been created as described earlier.

The covering index

Covering indexes are non-clustered indexes with the INCLUDE clause, which allows you to have non-key columns used in the SELECT statement to be included in the leaf pages of the non-clustered index to improve the performance of the query. The key columns you used to created indexes are the factor that affects the storage of pages in the B-tree structure. In a B-tree structure, there is a root and a minimum of two leaf levels. It might contain intermediate leaves as well, depending on the records. With SQL Server 2005, Microsoft added this new feature for non-clustered indexes. These columns are not part of the index; instead, they are included in the leaf pages of the index. You can include up to 1,023 columns in the leaf node; however, be careful, as it will also be an overhead to maintain the index. The larger the index, the more space it takes up on disk and impacts the write performance of the database.

To create a covering index, use the INCLUDE keyword. For example, you create the covering index to cover the following query:

```
SELECT [City Key]
       , [Customer Key]
       , [Salesperson Key]
       ,AVG([Quantity]) [Avg Quantity]
       , AVG([Unit Price]) [Avg Unit Price]
       , SUM([Profit]) [TotalProfit]
FROM [Fact].[Sale]
WHERE [Invoice Date Key] BETWEEN '2013-01-01' AND '2016-01-03'
GROUP BY [City Key]
       , [Customer Key]
       , [Salesperson Key];
```

Here, the [City Key], [Customer Key], [Salesperson Key], [Quantity], [Unit Price], and [Profit] columns need to be included to create a covering index for this query.

Here is the statement to create the covering index for this query:

```
CREATE NONCLUSTERED INDEX [IX_Fact_Sale_InvoiceDateKey] ON
[Fact].[Sale]
  (
   [Invoice Date Key] ASC
  )
INCLUDE ([City Key]
```

```
        ,[Customer Key]
        ,[Salesperson Key]
        ,[Quantity]
        ,[Unit Price]
        ,[Profit]
    );
```

If you already created an index using a particular name, you'll get this error and then have them drop IX_Fact_Sale_InvoiceDateKey and recreate it. We created the index in the *The NONCLUSTERED index* section, but now we realize that a covering index will work better, so we have to drop and recreate the index:

```
DROP INDEX [IX_Fact_Sale_InvoiceDateKey] ON [Fact].[Sale];
```

Now rerun the CREATE INDEX statement to create the covering index and validate that the index has been created.

Now that we understand the index types and have worked with different types of indexes, let's explore how an index can impact the query design.

The impact of indexes on query design

As we know, indexes improve the read performance of queries, so we should always keep in mind the columns that participate in the JOIN, WHERE, GROUP BY, HAVING, and ORDER BY clauses must have an index. This is because columns participating in the JOIN and WHERE clauses are the deciding factor and are read/accessed first from the raw data. Then all other filters are applied, such as GROUP BY, HAVING, and ORDER BY, based on the result set and the functions used in the queries.

If you write a query that has an index on the column being used in the WHERE clause for filtering the data, its performance will be drastically better after we run the same query after creating the index on that column. This applies to the columns participating in the JOIN, GROUP BY, HAVING, and ORDER BY clauses.

To further improve performance, you should include the columns participating in the SELECT statement, and if you are going to create a report for a particular year or a department, you can create a filtered index with the WHERE clause. This was discussed in *The filtered index* section and *The covering index* section.

The impact of indexes on query performance

Indexes improve the performance of complex queries that involve large sets of data. Without an index, a query might take forever to return a few hundred records, whereas, with indexes, it can return the same result in a few seconds or minutes.

Lets prepare data to examine the performance of a **common table expression** (**CTE**) query used in *Chapter 5*:

```sql
CREATE TABLE [dbo].[Sale](
[Sale Key] [bigint] IDENTITY(1,1) NOT NULL,
[City Key] [int] NOT NULL,
[Customer Key] [int] NOT NULL,
[Bill To Customer Key] [int] NOT NULL,
[Stock Item Key] [int] NOT NULL,
[Invoice Date Key] [date] NOT NULL,
[Delivery Date Key] [date] NULL,
[Salesperson Key] [int] NOT NULL,
[WWI Invoice ID] [int] NOT NULL,
[Description] [nvarchar](100) NOT NULL,
[Package] [nvarchar](50) NOT NULL,
[Quantity] [int] NOT NULL,
[Unit Price] [decimal](18, 2) NOT NULL,
[Tax Rate] [decimal](18, 3) NOT NULL,
[Total Excluding Tax] [decimal](18, 2) NOT NULL,
[Tax Amount] [decimal](18, 2) NOT NULL,
[Profit] [decimal](18, 2) NOT NULL,
[Total Including Tax] [decimal](18, 2) NOT NULL,
[Total Dry Items] [int] NOT NULL,
[Total Chiller Items] [int] NOT NULL,
[Lineage Key] [int] NOT NULL
) ;

DECLARE @times_records INT
SET @times_records = 0
WHILE @times_records <= 100
BEGIN
INSERT INTO [dbo].[Sale]
            ([City Key]
            ,[Customer Key]
            ,[Bill To Customer Key]
            ,[Stock Item Key]
            ,[Invoice Date Key]
            ,[Delivery Date Key]
            ,[Salesperson Key]
```

```
            ,[WWI Invoice ID]
            ,[Description]
            ,[Package]
            ,[Quantity]
            ,[Unit Price]
            ,[Tax Rate]
            ,[Total Excluding Tax]
            ,[Tax Amount]
            ,[Profit]
            ,[Total Including Tax]
            ,[Total Dry Items]
            ,[Total Chiller Items]
            ,[Lineage Key])
    SELECT
        [City Key]
        ,[Customer Key]
        ,[Bill To Customer Key]
        ,[Stock Item Key]
        ,[Invoice Date Key]
        ,[Delivery Date Key]
        ,[Salesperson Key]
        ,[WWI Invoice ID]
        ,[Description]
        ,[Package]
        ,[Quantity]
        ,[Unit Price]
        ,[Tax Rate]
        ,[Total Excluding Tax]
        ,[Tax Amount]
        ,[Profit]
        ,[Total Including Tax]
        ,[Total Dry Items]
        ,[Total Chiller Items]
        ,[Lineage Key]
      FROM [WideWorldImportersDW].[Fact].[Sale]
      SET @times_records = @times_records + 1
    END;
```

Now run the CTE query and note the execution time. It took five seconds on the machine used to test it:

```
--start of CTE queries
;with
ISODates as (
SELECT distinct [Date],[ISO Week Number] as [ISOWeekNumber]
  FROM [Dimension].[Date])
--separate multiple CTEs with comma
,DryTotalQuery as (
SELECT [Invoice Date Key] as DryInvoiceDateKey
      ,Sum([Total Dry Items]) as DailyTotalDry
  FROM [dbo].[Sale]
  WHERE [Invoice Date Key] between '2013-01-01' and '2016-01-
03' and [Total Dry Items] <> 0
  GROUP BY [Invoice Date Key])
  --separate multiple CTEs with comma
,ChillerTotalQuery as (
SELECT [Invoice Date Key] as ChillerInvoiceDateKey
      ,Sum([Total Chiller Items]) as DailyTotalChiller
  FROM [dbo].[Sale]
  WHERE [Invoice Date Key] between '2013-01-01' and '2016-01-
03' and [Total Chiller Items] = 0
  GROUP BY [Invoice Date Key])
  --end of CTEs
  --Query selecting from CTEs:
  SELECT
   [Date]
  ,[ISOWeekNumber]
  ,ISNULL(DailyTotalDry,0) as DailyTotalDry
  ,ISNULL(DailyTotalChiller,0) as DailyTotalChiller
  ,ISNULL(DailyTotalDry,0) + ISNULL(DailyTotalChiller,0) as
TotalDailyItems
  FROM ISODates d
  LEFT OUTER JOIN DryTotalQuery dtq on d.[Date] = dtq.
DryInvoiceDateKey
 LEFT OUTER JOIN ChillerTotalQuery ctq on d.[Date] = ctq.
ChillerInvoiceDateKey
  WHERE d.[Date] between '2013-01-01' and '2016-01-03'
  ORDER BY [Date];
```

Now let's create an index here and check whether it improves the performance and the time to return the result or not:

```
CREATE NONCLUSTERED INDEX [IX_Fact_Sale_Invoice_Date_Key]  ON
[dbo].[Sale] ([Invoice Date Key],[Total Dry Items]);
```

Now run the CTE query again and note the time. It took four seconds on the first run and three seconds on the second run on the machine used to test. You might observe different execution times to return the result depending on the dataset size, RAM, CPU, I/O, load on the SQL server, and so on.

Well, we now understand how an index can change the performance of a query; however, it comes with the overhead of maintaining these indexes for the overall optimal performance of the system. Let's understand why indexes need maintenance and what is required to maintain these indexes in good health.

Understanding index maintenance

Over time, indexes get fragmented due to write (UPDATE, DELETE, and INSERT) operations on the table on which indexes exist, which causes read operations to slow down as the SQL server now must scan a greater number of pages in the index due to the fragmentation. Therefore, we must keep track of the indexes used and the fragmentation in the indexes and should address the fragmentation to keep indexes healthy.

Now, this brings us to the topic of identifying fragmentation in indexes and to address fragmentation in indexes to keep them healthy. So, let's discuss index health and defragmenting the index next.

Index health

To identify fragmented indexes, we must check all the indexes where the average fragmentation is more than zero. To get the list of fragmented indexes, use the following standard query, which uses the catalog views to read the system data:

```
SELECT OBJECT_NAME(IND.OBJECT_ID) AS [Table Name],
IND.NAME AS [Index Name], PS.INDEX_TYPE_DESC AS [Index Type],
PS.AVG_FRAGMENTATION_IN_PERCENT [Avg Fragmentation]
FROM SYS.DM_DB_INDEX_PHYSICAL_STATS(DB_ID(), NULL, NULL, NULL,
NULL) PS
INNER JOIN SYS.INDEXES IND
ON IND.OBJECT_ID = PS.OBJECT_ID
AND IND.INDEX_ID = PS.INDEX_ID
WHERE PS.AVG_FRAGMENTATION_IN_PERCENT > 0
ORDER BY PS.AVG_FRAGMENTATION_IN_PERCENT DESC;
```

Here is the result of the query:

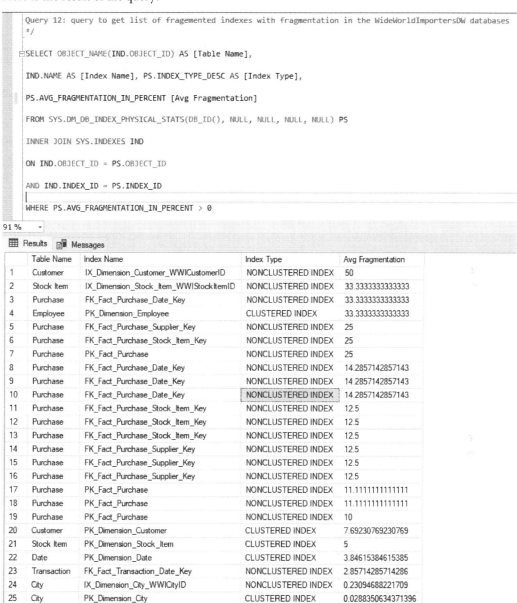

```
Query 12: query to get list of fragemented indexes with fragmentation in the WideWorldImportersDW databases
*/

SELECT OBJECT_NAME(IND.OBJECT_ID) AS [Table Name],

IND.NAME AS [Index Name], PS.INDEX_TYPE_DESC AS [Index Type],

PS.AVG_FRAGMENTATION_IN_PERCENT [Avg Fragmentation]

FROM SYS.DM_DB_INDEX_PHYSICAL_STATS(DB_ID(), NULL, NULL, NULL, NULL) PS

INNER JOIN SYS.INDEXES IND

ON IND.OBJECT_ID = PS.OBJECT_ID

AND IND.INDEX_ID = PS.INDEX_ID

WHERE PS.AVG_FRAGMENTATION_IN_PERCENT > 0
```

91 %

Results | Messages

	Table Name	Index Name	Index Type	Avg Fragmentation
1	Customer	IX_Dimension_Customer_WWICustomerID	NONCLUSTERED INDEX	50
2	Stock Item	IX_Dimension_Stock_Item_WWIStockItemID	NONCLUSTERED INDEX	33.3333333333333
3	Purchase	FK_Fact_Purchase_Date_Key	NONCLUSTERED INDEX	33.3333333333333
4	Employee	PK_Dimension_Employee	CLUSTERED INDEX	33.3333333333333
5	Purchase	FK_Fact_Purchase_Supplier_Key	NONCLUSTERED INDEX	25
6	Purchase	FK_Fact_Purchase_Stock_Item_Key	NONCLUSTERED INDEX	25
7	Purchase	PK_Fact_Purchase	NONCLUSTERED INDEX	25
8	Purchase	FK_Fact_Purchase_Date_Key	NONCLUSTERED INDEX	14.2857142857143
9	Purchase	FK_Fact_Purchase_Date_Key	NONCLUSTERED INDEX	14.2857142857143
10	Purchase	FK_Fact_Purchase_Date_Key	NONCLUSTERED INDEX	14.2857142857143
11	Purchase	FK_Fact_Purchase_Stock_Item_Key	NONCLUSTERED INDEX	12.5
12	Purchase	FK_Fact_Purchase_Stock_Item_Key	NONCLUSTERED INDEX	12.5
13	Purchase	FK_Fact_Purchase_Stock_Item_Key	NONCLUSTERED INDEX	12.5
14	Purchase	FK_Fact_Purchase_Supplier_Key	NONCLUSTERED INDEX	12.5
15	Purchase	FK_Fact_Purchase_Supplier_Key	NONCLUSTERED INDEX	12.5
16	Purchase	FK_Fact_Purchase_Supplier_Key	NONCLUSTERED INDEX	12.5
17	Purchase	PK_Fact_Purchase	NONCLUSTERED INDEX	11.1111111111111
18	Purchase	PK_Fact_Purchase	NONCLUSTERED INDEX	11.1111111111111
19	Purchase	PK_Fact_Purchase	NONCLUSTERED INDEX	10
20	Customer	PK_Dimension_Customer	CLUSTERED INDEX	7.69230769230769
21	Stock Item	PK_Dimension_Stock_Item	CLUSTERED INDEX	5
22	Date	PK_Dimension_Date	CLUSTERED INDEX	3.84615384615385
23	Transaction	FK_Fact_Transaction_Date_Key	NONCLUSTERED INDEX	2.85714285714286
24	City	IX_Dimension_City_WWICityID	NONCLUSTERED INDEX	0.23094688221709
25	City	PK_Dimension_City	CLUSTERED INDEX	0.0288350634371396

Figure 10.5 – Displays the list of the fragmented indexes with average fragmentation in each index

Based on the fragmentation, we can reorganize or rebuild the indexes to address fragmentation. We will discuss REBUILD to defragment the index here and REORGANIZE next.

The REBUILD index

The REBUILD index is the operation of dropping and recreating the index. However when we use the REBUILD operation, SQL Server takes care of all operations for us, and hence we do not need to issue DROP and CREATE statements to rebuild the indexes. To rebuild the index, use the ALTER INDEX statement. If the fragmentation percentage is above 25%, we should rebuild the indexes. Here is the example to rebuild the FK_Fact_Sale_City_Key index on the [Fact].[Sale] table:

```
ALTER INDEX FK_Fact_Sale_City_Key ON [Fact].[Sale] REBUILD;
```

To rebuild all indexes on the [Fact].[Sale] table, use the following statement:

```
ALTER INDEX ALL ON [Fact].[Sale] REBUILD;
```

REBUILD is an I/O-intensive operation, and hence we should not execute during peak business hour; instead, we should run it in off-peak hours to avoid system slowness during business hours.

The REBUILD index locks the table, and hence there is an option to REBUILD indexes ONLINE. The ONLINE REBUILD index has slower functions; however, it doesn't lock the tables for other operations for a noticeable amount of time. For example, here is the statement to rebuild all indexes on the [Fact].[Sale] table:

```
ALTER INDEX ALL ON [Fact].[Sale] REBUILD WITH (ONLINE = ON);
```

The REORGANIZE index

The REORGANIZE index is the other method to defragment indexes. It's less I/O intensive than REBUILD, but slower. Hence, we reorganize indexes where fragmentation is less than or equal to 25%. There is no such rule to stick with 25%, but it should be decided based on your system requirement.

To reorganize the index, use the ALTER INDEX statement, as we did for the REBUILD indexes. Here is the example of reorganizing the FK_Fact_Purchase_Date_Key index:

```
ALTER INDEX FK_Fact_Purchase_Date_Key ON [Fact].[Purchase]
REORGANIZE;
```

To reorganize all indexes on the [Fact].[Purchase] table, use the following statement:

```
ALTER INDEX ALL ON [Fact].[Purchase] REORGANIZE;
```

Indexes are good, but they also have downsides for write operations specifically; hence, we must weigh the net performance before implementing them in production. So, you must be cautious when it comes to indexes.

Caution

Index defragmentation is a routine job of any DBA who creates SQL Server agent jobs and schedules to run during off-peak business hours. In general, these jobs run on a nightly basis; however, for some systems, the requirement might be to run more frequently, such as every few hours.

Creating indexes on production during business hours should never be done as it might cause performance issues. If your tables are large and contain millions of records, it may take hours and hang the system. We should not create indexes directly in production; instead, they should be created in a development environment and thoroughly tested to ensure they do not negatively impact the performance of the system. While an index improves the performance of read operations, it degrades the write performance as now it needs to maintain the index, and in the case of clustered indexes, it has to make the space for new rows to be inserted by splitting the page(s).

So, now we understand indexes, index types, and how we can keep our indexes healthy for optimal performance of queries and the system.

Summary

In this chapter, we covered a basic understanding of indexes, how to create, drop, alter, or modify an index, and how to rename an index. Then we learned about index types based on the storage, a basic understanding of clustered, non-clustered, covering, unique, and filtered indexes, and how to create these with examples. Then we learned about the impact of indexes on query design and the impact of indexes on query performance.

We learned about how an index improves performance, along with how it can degrade the system's performance. We learned we should always be cautious before creating indexes in production.

In the next chapter, we will expand our knowledge of and understand the basics of the JSON file format and how SQL Server handles JSON data.

Further reading

Indexes are an advanced topic and should be created carefully as these may impact the system's performance negatively and drastically. I would suggest further reading for a deeper understanding, and that you should first create these in dev and test and observe how they impact the performance of the query and the system overall.

For a deeper understanding, take a look at the Microsoft book here: `https://learn.microsoft.com/en-us/sql/relational-databases/indexes/indexes?view=sql-server-ver16`.

Part 4:
Working with Your Data
on the Modern Data Platform

No book today on SQL design patterns would be complete without delving into the complexities that the modern data platform has introduced. In this part, we cover **JSON** and data lake integration into your queries. We wrap up the book and support you as you move forward:

- *Chapter 11, Handling JSON Data in SQL Server*

- *Chapter 12, Integrating File Data and Data Lake Content with SQL*

- *Chapter 13, Organizing and Sharing Your Queries with Jupyter Notebooks*

- *Appendix, Preparing Your Environment*

11

Handling JSON Data in SQL Server

JSON data has been around for a long time. It is the preferred format for mobile and application data. Application developers love JSON because of its flexibility and overall ease of use. Application tools such as .NET have a significant amount of built-in functionality to support this technology.

It is this very flexibility that brings us to handling JSON data in SQL Server. By its very nature, JSON is not relational nor is it tabular. This means typical SQL support for working with JSON does not exist as we normally view it. In this chapter, we will be introducing you to the functionality within SQL Server that supports the production and consumption of JSON.

The following topics will be covered in this chapter:

- Introducing the JSON functionality built into SQL Server (and some of its limitations)
- Using JSON SQL functionality to build JSON-formatted results from our database
- Using JSON SQL functionality to shape JSON data into tabular data
- Combining JSON data and tabular data into a singular set of results

Technical requirements

To work with the examples and illustrations in this chapter, you will need to have **Azure Data Studio** installed. We will be working with the `WideWorldImporters` database on **SQL Server** or **Azure SQL Database**. Please refer to the *Appendix* for tool installation and database restoration guidance.

You can find the code for this chapter on GitHub: `https://github.com/PacktPublishing/SQL-Query-Design-Best-Practices/tree/main/Chapter11`

In this chapter, we will also be looking at some of the latest JSON functions available in **SQL Server 2022** and **Azure SQL Database**. To get the most value out of this chapter, it is recommended that you use SQL Server 2022 or Azure SQL Database to run the examples. The remaining JSON functions work with SQL Server 2016 and above.

Introducing JSON functionality built into SQL Server

JSON functions were first released in SQL Server 2016. This is not the first NoSQL data supported inside of the SQL Server engine. Before this, XML was supported in SQL Server with similar functions but with one key difference. Unlike XML, which is supported as a native data type inside of SQL Server, JSON is only supported with functions that work with JSON data but not a data type. Before we discuss the functions available in SQL Server, let's briefly review JSON formatting.

The basics of JSON

JSON is a flexible data storage solution. As noted in the introduction to this chapter, it is often used to support mobile and web applications. One key aspect of JSON is that it does not support a schema and is prone to schema drift through development life cycles. This means that the data within it and the construction or organization of that data can change over time. Another key aspect to understand about JSON is that it is case-sensitive. While most of the work that we do in SQL Server is not subject to case sensitivity, you will need to pay attention to case sensitivity in this chapter as it could be the reason a query or function does not work as expected.

JSON objects are primarily composed of two key constructions:

- **Objects**
- **Arrays**

JSON objects are primarily built out as one or more key-value pairs. Curly braces are used to encapsulate each object and an object itself can have nested objects within it. The following is an example of the construction used for JSON objects:

```
{"key":"value"}
```

JSON **arrays** are collections of objects within a document. These collections are enclosed with square brackets. The following code demonstrates a typical JSON construction using arrays:

```
{"key":
 [
    {"key":"value"},
    {"key":"value"}
 ]
}
```

Here is an example using actual data in this format:

```
"Restaurant": {
    "Restaurant ID": 1,
```

```
        "RestaurantName": "Sensational Servings MSP",
        "City": "Minneapolis",
        "Seats": [
            {
                "TableType": "Bar",
                "Seat Number": 1
            },
            {
                "TableType": "Bar",
                "Seat Number": 2
            }
        ]
    }
}
```

Hopefully, this gives you a good understanding or introduction to the JSON data format. Next, we will look at how SQL Server handles JSON with functions and as data.

JSON functions in SQL Server

Now that we have seen examples of how JSON is formatted, let's dig into the various functions supported within SQL Server. We have two lists of functions – those that were supported during the initial release of JSON functionality in SQL Server 2016, followed by the list of new functionality introduced in SQL Server 2022. If you're using a version of SQL Server before 2022, this will help you understand which functions are not currently available to you.

The following functions were released with SQL Server 2016:

- ISJSON: This function is used to determine whether the text is properly formatted JSON.

- JSON_VALUE: This function returns scalar values from JSON documents or snippets.

- JSON_QUERY: This function returns JSON-formatted arrays or objects from JSON documents or snippets.

- JSON_MODIFY: This function is used to modify JSON objects and arrays.

- OPENJSON: This command is used to convert JSON data into a tabular format, allowing you to work with it in combination with relational data.

- FOR JSON: This function, along with various options, allows you to build JSON results from relational queries. We will be using this command to build JSON that we will use throughout the rest of this chapter.

The following functions were released with SQL Server 2022:

- `JSON_PATH_EXISTS`: This new function can interrogate a JSON document to determine whether the path you are looking for exists
- `JSON_OBJECT`: This function creates JSON-formatted objects
- `JSON_ARRAY`: This function creates JSON-formatted arrays

One other change that you should be aware of in SQL Server 2022 is that `ISJSON` has been expanded with an optional parameter for specifying the scope of the investigation from the function. Because this parameter is optional, it has no impact on SQL Server 2016 and above, but can be used to do a more precise investigation of a part of a JSON snippet, such as an array or object.

We will be using the latest functionality throughout this chapter, and we will reference specific SQL Server 2022 functionality when used. Before we dig into the examples and details around the functions and code, there are a few other things you should be aware of about how SQL Server handles JSON data.

JSON as data in SQL Server

As we noted in the opening paragraph, JSON is not supported as a native data type in SQL Server. The reason this is important to understand is that JSON data is stored in a `VARCHAR ()` or `NVARCHAR ()` data type in most situations. This means that it is nearly impossible to build a meaningful index on the data to support optimized queries natively on those JSON fields. This is also one of the reasons why, in many cases, we may store JSON data, but we will also extract data we want to use in reporting or to optimize query operations in SQL Server. It is possible to use normal tabular data extracted from JSON into proper fields as indexes to support more complex query scenarios.

While it is not natively supported as a data type inside SQL Server, there are plenty of functions that allow us to use JSON in many different scenarios. In the next section, we will build out a foundational understanding of the JSON path in SQL Server. This expands on the overall structure of JSON and how it works in the context of the SQL Server engine.

JSON path in SQL Server

As you saw from the list of new functions in SQL Server 2022, there is a specific function related to the JSON path. So, what is the JSON path? In essence, the JSON path involves mapping the key-value pairs and arrays through a known construction that is commonly used in JSON and implemented in SQL Server. Because a JSON document can be nested indefinitely and inconsistently, it is important to understand how to refer to various objects and arrays within the document that you are working with.

In SQL Server, the following format is commonly used to interrogate a JSON document. It starts with a root and then uses curly braces and dots to fully describe the path:

```
'$.Restaurant.Name'
```

The dollar sign ($) represents the context or starting point for the path. Depending on how you're interfacing with the JSON document, this could be a field in a table or a parameter being sent into your stored procedure, for example. It is effectively the starting point or the outside boundary for the path.

From this point forward, whenever you're using a dot or a period, you are effectively drilling into the next level of the document. So, for the first level, you have a dollar sign followed by a dot then an object enclosed in curly braces, or an array enclosed in square brackets.

If you are working with an array, you will need to specify which object in the array you intend to work with. This is done by specifying the numbered position of the object within the array. JSON arrays are zero-based, unlike most functions within SQL Server. So, in the following example, we are going for the second nested object, which is an array, and the first object within the array:

```
'$.Restaurant.Seats[0].Seat'
```

Understanding this methodology is important for understanding how you can return relational results in a properly formatted and understandable JSON document. This methodology is also important for understanding how to retrieve results from a JSON document. From this building block, we will explore how to create JSON documents from our example database and then how to work with that data in queries for reporting.

In the next section, we'll start by creating JSON documents, which we will store in a new table in our database so that we can use them for later queries.

Formatting results as JSON in SQL Server

To demonstrate how we want JSON and its usage within SQL, we will be creating a table and inserting JSON into it for use throughout the rest of this chapter. In this section, we will build a query that will generate JSON that can be stored and a couple of tables for illustration and demonstration purposes for extracting JSON data. We will be using FOR JSON and its related options to generate JSON data to be stored in our table.

Throughout the rest of this chapter, we will be working with data from the WideWorldImporters database. If you want to follow along step by step, now is the time to open SQL Server Management Studio or Azure Data Studio, depending on the platform you have decided to use. We recommend that you use *Azure Data Studio* as it works best with JSON data results. If you only have SQL Server Management Studio available, the results will still be available to you but will be formatted in an XML format as opposed to a JSON format. Open the tool and connect to your database. Then, open a blank query window connected to your database – you are ready to go.

As we go through the next few sections in this chapter, we will build a customer table where all the order information is stored in a JSON column. This is a common format that allows for order information to be updated with a single customer reference point.

Here is the logical schema for the new table we will be creating, followed by the code used to create that table:

- CustomerID
- CustomerName
- CustomerOrderHistory

We will use the following SQL to create the new table. Keep in mind that there is no native data type for JSON, so we will be using VARCHAR(MAX) to hold the JSON data for the orders:

```
CREATE TABLE dbo.CustomerOrders
    (CustomerID INT NOT NULL,
        CustomerName VARCHAR (200) NOT NULL,
        CustomerOrderHistory VARCHAR (MAX)NOT NULL
    );
```

Now that we have the table ready to go, we will begin working with the FOR JSON query syntax to build out our customer order history information.

Using FOR JSON

This functionality was introduced in SQL Server 2016 to support the ability to extract data stored in tables as JSON documents. FOR JSON has two primary ways of formatting the results in the JSON document. As its name suggests, AUTO lets the SQL Server engine handle the formatting automatically. PATH gives the query designer a certain set of options to manage the nesting of the JSON document. PATH is a method we will be using to load our table. Next, we will demonstrate how to use AUTO so that you understand the difference between the two options.

FOR JSON AUTO

The AUTO keyword lets the SQL Server engine manage the formatting for the JSON output. SQL Server will format results as a JSON array containing the results as objects in that array by default.

Here is an example of a query that extracts the order information for a customer and any snippet of the results generated:

```
SELECT TOP (3) OrderID , CustomerID, OrderDate
FROM Sales.Orders
WHERE CustomerID = 2 AND YEAR((OrderDate) = 2016
FOR JSON AUTO;
```

When you execute the preceding query in Azure Data Studio, a single record result is returned, as shown here:

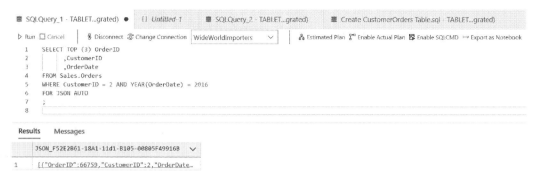

Figure 11.1 – Azure Data Studio query results with FOR JSON AUTO

This record is a clickable link that will open a new tab in Azure Data Studio containing properly formatted JSON data. We limited the earlier query to three records to show the complete JSON results here:

```
[
    {
        "OrderID": 66759,
        "CustomerID": 2,
        "OrderDate": "2016-02-17"
    },
    {
        "OrderID": 71147,
        "CustomerID": 2,
        "OrderDate": "2016-04-26"
    },
    {
        "OrderID": 69482,
        "CustomerID": 2,
        "OrderDate": "2016-03-30"
    }
]
```

If you remove the filters, the JSON document will contain all the orders within the specified filters as a part of the array, with each object in the array representing one row of the query results.

In the following example, we are adding a `JOIN` clause to our SQL query. SQL Server will use the join information to organize the results into nested arrays. In our example, we are adding the `Customers` table to the query, which will then generate the orders organized underneath the customer as a separate array. We will continue to use the filters that we applied earlier to reduce the size of the results for demonstration purposes:

```
SELECT TOP (3)
    c.CustomerID,
    c.CustomerName,
    o.OrderDate          , o.OrderID
FROM Sales.Customers c
INNER JOIN Sales.Orders o ON c.CustomerID = o.CustomerID
WHERE o.CustomerID = 2 AND YEAR(o.OrderDate) = 2016
FOR JSON AUTO;
```

When the preceding query is executed, it returns the results formatted as arrays.

You can continue to explore `FOR JSON AUTO` to see the variety of ways that the SQL Server engine formats the JSON output. For example, if you were to rearrange the preceding query by putting the order information first, you would get an object containing an array with the customer information for each order. The SQL Server engine will use the order of the columns and the join information to build a JSON document with minimal formatting from the query writer.

While this is the simplest way to generate results, in the next section, we will explore how to explicitly build a JSON-formatted result that will likely better serve our needs.

FOR JSON PATH

While `AUTO` relied on the SQL Server engine to manage the array nesting in the results, `PATH` allows a query writer more control over the nesting format. The `PATH` keyword lets the query writer define the path in a dot-separated format. You may recall from the results as shown earlier that the query engine used the alias of the table as part of the structure of the array. By using a dot-separated path, we can specify the name of the object and its associated array in the SQL query.

The data we plan to load into our table will contain some order information and order detail information.

The following list shows the overall structure we are trying to build for our JSON results that we will save to the table:

- Customer
  - Order:
    - Order lines

As you can see, we need to nest ordered details within each order within `Customer`. The following query will generate those results using the dot-separated pattern, as described earlier:

> **Be aware!**
>
> JSON documents are case-sensitive. It is important to understand how you want your results to be formatted to make sure that they meet your requirements. In most cases, we recommend lowercase when building paths. This is one of the most common issues you will experience when working with JSON.

```
SELECT TOP (3)
    c.CustomerID AS 'customer.id',
     c.CustomerName AS 'customer.name',
     o.OrderID AS 'customer.order.id',
     o.OrderDate AS 'customer.order.orderdate',
    d.OrderLineID AS 'customer.order.orderline.id',
    d.StockItemID AS 'customer.order.orderline.stockitemid',
    d.Description AS 'customer.order.orderline.description',
    d.Quantity AS 'customer.order.orderline.quantity',
    d.UnitPrice AS 'customer.order.orderline.unitprice'
FROM Sales.Customers c
INNER JOIN Sales.Orders o ON c.CustomerID = o.CustomerID
INNER JOIN Sales.OrderLines d on d.OrderID = o.OrderID
WHERE o.CustomerID = 2 AND YEAR(o.OrderDate) = 2016
FOR JSON PATH;
```

A sample of the results is shown here:

```
[
    {
        "customer": {
        "id": 2,
        "name": "Tailspin Toys (Sylvanite, MT)",
        "order": {
            "id": 66759,
            "orderdate": "2016-02-17",
            "orderline": {
                "id": 210152,
                "stockitemid": 201,
```

```json
                    "description": "Red and white urgent despatch
                                    tape 48mmx75m",
                    "quantity": 72,
                    "unitprice": 3.70
                    }
                }
            }
        },
        {

            "customer": {
                "id": 2,
                "name": "Tailspin Toys (Sylvanite, MT)",
                "order": {
                    "id": 66759,
                    "orderdate": "2016-02-17",
                    "orderline": {
                        "id": 210151,
                        "stockitemid": 120,
                        "description": "Dinosaur battery-powered
                                        slippers (Green) L",
                        "quantity": 3,
                        "unitprice": 3.20
                    }
                }
            }
        },
```

As you can see, by specifying the sequence in the order in which we want the results, the order of the columns in the table does not matter as we have explicitly laid out the path for those results. You may have also noticed that the results come back at the row level, even though we specified paths that we would typically want together. This is a common issue when working with the path structure on complex results. Before we can insert this into the table, we will need to build the structure differently.

New functionality is available in SQL Server 2022 and Azure SQL Database that allows us to have even more control over the formatting of the results in JSON queries. We will delve into using those functions next.

JSON_OBJECT

Where the previous functionality specifically built out query results from the results of a SELECT statement, we are now going to explore new functionality available to us in SQL Server 2022 that will allow us to explicitly define the object we would like returned. In this scenario, we may not be able to cleanly select the data in a format that can be used by FOR JSON. This added functionality allows us to define how we want the object to be set up and created.

Simply put, JSON_OBJECT returns a set of key-value pairs as an object formatted properly for JSON. Here is a simple example to illustrate the function and the resulting values:

```
SELECT JSON_OBJECT ('name': 'Steve', 'role': 'author');
```

Here are the formatted results:

```
{
    "name": "Steve","role": "author"
}
```

As we can see, we were able to return multiple attributes as key-value pairs describing the object we are working with. There is an optional attribute to the function that allows you to handle null. When working with **NULL**, you can determine whether or not you retain the value or are allowed to be absent when null. Due to the flexible nature of JSON, null values are typically removed from the JSON document as opposed to being stored. In relational databases, we must store missing values as null and columns due to the tabular nature of the structure.

The two options for handling null are as follows:

- **NULL ON NULL**: This option adds a NULL value to the key-value pair when null is present
- **ABSENT ON NULL**: This option will remove any key-value pair that has a null value

In the following query, we are creating a set of customer objects to demonstrate the JSON_OBJECT function in a query context. In this query, we know that there are some customers we do not have an alternate contact person for. If that value does not exist, we will ignore it and not include an attribute for that missing element:

```
SELECT TOP (3) JSON_OBJECT ('id':c.CustomerID , 'name':c.
CustomerName , 'alt':AlternateContactPersonID ABSENT ON NULL)
FROM Sales.Customers c
WHERE c.CustomerID in (2, 150, 801);
```

As you can see from the results, for each row, we get a JSON object:

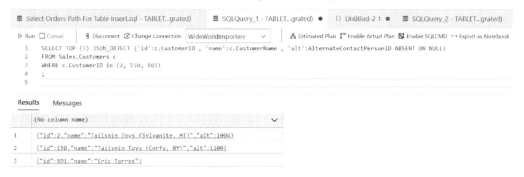

Figure 11.2 – Multiple row results after using JSON_OBJECT

As before, you can click on the result link to see the formatted values being returned from this function.

JSON_ARRAY

Like the `JSON_OBJECT` function in the previous section, `JSON_ARRAY` is also a new function that was added in SQL Server 2022. Whereas the previous function created objects, this function will create JSON arrays. Once again, this is a way to create arrays that are not easily generated from the `FOR JSON` functionality that was described earlier.

This function will return a properly formatted JSON array of attributes, objects, and other items that can be stored. Be aware that this functionality does not support the creation of object-based arrays from a table. Like `JSON_OBJECT`, this will return one array for each result in the `SELECT` statement. The primary difference in the construction is that square brackets will be used to enclose your array as opposed to curly braces.

This allows you to create arrays for each row in a result set; however, it does not allow you to create an array of objects from that set. This results in similar construction as the `FOR JSON PATH` functionality. The primary difference between the two options is that `PATH` returns a single JSON document containing all the results, whereas `JSON_ARRAY` returns a row for each row returned from the query. Depending on what you need to do to support your specific use case, you can choose the proper functions to get the results you need, as well as the required JSON. We have a few more options to cover regarding formatting JSON results from SQL Server. We will cover these next.

Additional parameters for FOR JSON

There are a few additional parameters that you can use when working with `FOR JSON`. In this section, we will briefly describe those functions and their purpose as they may provide additional value for you as you create formatted JSON results from your SQL queries.

The ROOT option adds a root name to either your object or your array when working with FOR JSON. Without this option in place, you will get the results we showed earlier, which is a collection of objects without a top-level attribute:

```sql
SELECT TOP (2)
    c.CustomerID AS 'customer.id'
    , c.CustomerName AS 'customer.name'
    , o.OrderID AS 'customer.order.id'
    , o.OrderDate AS 'customer.order.orderdate'
FROM Sales.Customers c
INNER JOIN Sales.Orders o ON c.CustomerID = o.CustomerID
WHERE o.CustomerID = 2 AND YEAR(o.OrderDate) = 2016
FOR JSON PATH, ROOT('orders');
```

Here's what the resulting JSON document looks like with the new root highlighted:

```
{
    «orders»: [
        {
            "customer": {
                "id": 2,
                "name": "Tailspin Toys (Sylvanite, MT)",
                "order": {
                    "orderdate": "2016-02-17"
                                        },...
```

The next option we want to discuss is the INCLUDE_ NULL_VALUES function, which will include null values in your results. This functionality, when added to the FOR JSON clause (for example, FOR JSON AUTO, INCLUDE_NULL_VALUES), will create null values in the results of your queries. As noted previously, null values are typically not included in most JSON results. JSON is flexible and designed to not include null values in most cases.

The final parameter that we want to call out is WITHOUT_ARRAY_WRAPPER. Like the previous two functions, adding this after your FOR JSON clause will remove the square brackets used with the results in your JSON output. You may need to use this format if the consuming application requires no arrays.

With that, we have covered how to format JSON results in SQL Server and Azure SQL Database. The focus of this opening section has been on generating JSON documents or snippets to be used by consuming applications. Once we've loaded our table with the queries in the next section, we will begin working with JSON as part of the data and formatting it for ease of use for reporting and storage purposes.

Filling the table

We will wrap up this section by inserting a few hundred values into the table we created earlier in this chapter. We will be using this table with the order information stored as JSON later in this chapter when we work with JSON functions that work explicitly with JSON documents.

Run the following code to update the table:

```
INSERT INTO dbo.CustomerOrders
    (CustomerID, CustomerName, CustomerOrderHistory)
(
SELECT c.CustomerID
, c.CustomerName
, (SELECT o.OrderID AS 'order.id'
    , o.OrderDate AS 'order.orderdate'
    , o.CustomerID AS 'order.customerid'
    ,(SELECT d.OrderLineID AS 'orderline.id'
        , d.OrderID AS 'orderline.orderid'
        , d.StockItemID AS 'orderline.stockitemid'
        , d.Description AS 'orderline.description'
        , d.Quantity AS 'orderline.quantity'
        , d.UnitPrice AS 'orderline.unitprice'
        FROM Sales.OrderLines d
        WHERE d.OrderID = o.OrderID
        FOR JSON PATH
    ) as 'order.lines'
    FROM Sales.Orders o
    WHERE c.CustomerID = o.CustomerID AND YEAR(o.OrderDate) =
2016
    FOR JSON PATH, ROOT('orders')
  ) AS Orders
FROM Sales.Customers c);
```

Before we move on to working with the data we just loaded into the table, we would like to point out a couple of items in the preceding query. The primary syntax to call out is the use of subqueries to structure the JSON document the way we would like to have it stored. By using subqueries as fields with the FOR JSON PATH statement, we were able to structure the resulting document with the order line detail as an array within the order object. We chose to use the ROOT function in this scenario as it was needed for the document we were creating. While this new functionality in SQL Server 2022 allows a certain level of precise control in the formatting, it was not well suited for building the document the way we have described here.

Now that we have the JSON stored in the database in our new table, let's start interrogating and shaping that data back into tabular structures. Next, we will use JSON functions to determine the validity of the JSON we have stored.

Working with JSON data in SQL queries

So far, we have focused on how to build JSON-formatted results from the queries we have been creating. In this section, we are going to explore how to work with JSON data in our queries. We will look at how to discover and validate our JSON data, followed by extracting and modifying that information. We will wrap this section up by building out a query to convert JSON data into tabular data with a relationship to relational data as well.

Discovering JSON data in SQL Server

There are two primary functions we will work with within SQL Server to discover and validate JSON data. These functions confirm that we are working with JSON data and that the data we are looking at exists in the JSON document.

ISJSON

ISJSON is used to evaluate a variable, expression, or field in a SQL query to determine that the structure of that data is properly formatted JSON. In our example, we will investigate the `CustomerOrderHistory` field in our `CustomerOrders` table to make sure that the JSON that we inserted previously in this chapter has been formatted properly. This function will return `1` (true) or `0` (false), depending on what it finds. Our expectation in this exercise is that it will return true when used to interrogate our column:

```
SELECT TOP (1) ISJSON(CustomerOrderHistory) FROM dbo.
CustomerOrders;
```

This query should result in a single value, which is `1`. This function also allows an additional parameter to be used to determine the type of test you want to conduct. We effectively use the default parameter, which is `VALUE`. Here is a list of other options that can be used:

- `OBJECT`: This option will determine whether the expression being evaluated is a valid JSON object.

- `ARRAY`: This option will determine whether the expression is being evaluated as a valid JSON array.

- `SCALAR`: This option is used to determine whether a top-level JSON value has been properly formatted as a scalar value in JSON. For example, an string enclosed in single quotation marks would be invalid as JSON requires double quotation marks to enclose a string expression.

Now that we know how to identify a valid JSON expression, the next step is to find out whether a specific path exists.

JSON_PATH_EXISTS

Earlier in this chapter, we discussed the importance of JSON PATH in SQL Server. This dot formatting is used to describe the location and depth of nested JSON in a document. This function was just introduced in SQL Server 2022 and Azure SQL Database. It allows you to input a path to determine whether that path exists in the JSON document you're investigating.

This function is only available in SQL Server 2022 and Azure SQL Database.

This function has three potential return values. It will return NULL if the input value is also NULL. This is most likely to happen if you're using this in the context of a stored procedure and a parameter is not passed to the function. The other values are as expected: 1 = path found and 0 = path not found. This function does not return errors because if a path is not found, it will always return 0.

The following query will determine if orderline.id exists in the JSON stored in our CustomerOrderHistory field on the CustomerOrders table. As you can see, we designate the full path down to the level we are looking for:

```
SELECT TOP (1) JSON_PATH_EXISTS(CustomerOrderHistory,
'$.orders[0].order.lines[0].orderline.id') FROM dbo.
CustomerOrders;
```

This query results in a returned value of 1. This means that the id attribute in the order line object has been found and the overall path is valid.

In this query, we will determine whether we used customerid in the orderline object in our CustomerOrderHistory JSON document:

```
SELECT TOP (1) JSON_PATH_EXISTS(CustomerOrderHistory,
'$.orders[0].order.lines[0].orderline.customerid') FROM dbo.
CustomerOrders;
```

Because this attribute did not exist in the path as specified, the query returns a result of 0.

One limitation you need to account for is that the path structure requires that an array position be specified when an array is used in the path. Our CustomerOrderHistory field stores a JSON document in an order array and each order has an array of *order lines*. If you need to evaluate more than the first or a specific position, you will need to have a way to determine which position in the array you wish to evaluate. For example, you could build a loop to evaluate each member of an array for the path you are looking for and evaluate those results to determine whether the JSON is structured as needed.

Now that we have validated and confirmed the structure of our JSON, next, we want to retrieve values from it that we can use in query results.

Extracting JSON data in SQL Server

When working with JSON data in SQL Server, one of the most common functions you will find yourself using is JSON_VALUE. This function allows you to return scalar values from the JSON document that can be easily used in reporting and other relational scenarios. JSON_QUERY allows you to return JSON snippets from documents or other result sets. This is most valuable when working with applications.

> **JSON path with lax and strict**
>
> Earlier in this chapter, we described the functionality of using JSON PATH in SQL Server to find data within a JSON document. There are two ways the path resolution can be handled. The default option is lax. This option will return a null value if the path is not found. If you specify strict by adding the strict keyword at the beginning of the path before the dollar sign, functions using PATH will result in an error when the path is not found. An example of this format is 'strict $. name'. In this scenario, if the name object does not exist, an error will be returned.

JSON_VALUE

JSON_VALUE is a function that returns the scalar value from a JSON object that was found at the location of the path. This function takes two parameters – the JSON expression and the JSON path.

In this example, we want to retrieve the product name on the first line of the first order in our table. This is a simple example and uses the first array position in both cases:

```
SELECT TOP (1) JSON_VALUE(CustomerOrderHistory, '$.orders[0].
order.lines[0].orderline.description') FROM dbo.CustomerOrders;
```

Depending on the order of your table, you should have received Dinosaur battery-powered slippers (Green) M as your result.

While we have shown the JSON_VALUE function in the context of a table and a query, you can also pass a properly formatted JSON string or variable into the expression and retrieve the value from that as well. This is a common use case when working with applications that send JSON values as part of the data to be entered into a table.

In the next function, we will look at how to retrieve JSON-formatted results.

JSON_QUERY

JSON_QUERY will return the JSON document when executed against a parameter or field. Using the default path or the dollar sign, the following simple query will return the entire result, properly formatted from our table:

```
SELECT TOP (1) JSON_QUERY(CustomerOrderHistory) FROM dbo.
CustomerOrders;
```

The `JSON_QUERY` function has been modified since its introduction in SQL Server 2016. We are mentioning this here in case you're using that version. In **SQL Server 2017**, the `PATH` parameter was added to this function. In SQL Server 2016, this function was primarily used to return a clean JSON snippet and did not use any parameters.

When working with `JSON_QUERY` and the path expression, be aware that you cannot return values but only valid objects or arrays in the results.

Let's compare two queries here related to order lines. In our first query, we will return the order line array from the first order in the array:

```
SELECT TOP (1) JSON_QUERY(CustomerOrderHistory, '$.orders[0].
order.lines') FROM dbo.CustomerOrders;
```

This query works because we specified the entirety of the array as the target in the path. The next query will try to retrieve the order line ID. Because the order line ID is a value, it will either return null when using `lax`, which is the default, or it will error when using `strict` in the path expression. Both queries are shown here with the path expression parameter explicitly used:

```
SELECT TOP (1) JSON_QUERY(CustomerOrderHistory,'lax
$.orders[0].order.lines[0].orderline.id') FROM dbo.
CustomerOrders;
```

When you run this first query, you will get a return value of `NULL` because you specified `lax` in the path. You will get the same result if you choose to use the default setting and not include `lax` in the path:

```
SELECT TOP (1) JSON_QUERY(CustomerOrderHistory,'strict
$.orders[0].order.lines[0].orderline.id') FROM dbo.
CustomerOrders;
```

When running this query with the `strict` parameter, SQL Server will return an error. One thing to keep in mind is that JSON is very flexible and does not have an enforced schema. As a result, if you choose to use `strict` in your queries, you should also plan to handle this error as it will likely occur.

`JSON_QUERY` can be used to exchange results with applications that rely on JSON-formatted values. Used in combination with the `JSON_OBJECT` and `JSON_ARRAY` functions, effective application integration can be achieved with SQL Server.

Modifying JSON data in SQL Server

In some cases, we may be required to update data in the JSON document with SQL. While this functionality is supported in SQL Server, it is not the most efficient pattern for updating large volumes of JSON data and should be used sparingly. You will run into issues when working with larger JSON documents or expressions.

JSON_MODIFY

JSON_MODIFY is used to modify a JSON string and then return the modified string. What is important to understand about this function is that it does not modify the value in place but instead returns a new string that can be used as the replacement document. One thing of note about this function is that it will error if the JSON string you are attempting to modify is not valid. When working with this function in the context of a stored procedure or similar long complex SQL, we recommend that you evaluate the expression being passed with the ISJSON function and handle that issue before it errors. If you are using the latest version of SQL Server or Azure SQL Database, it would likely be a good idea to verify the path exists, as well as to use the JSON_PATH_EXISTS function.

> **Note**
>
> In SQL Server 2017 and above, you can use a variable as the value of the path. That functionality is not supported in SQL Server 2016.

In our first example, we are going to pull the order date from one of our orders and update the date. As you will see, this will return the updated value in the JSON. In our example, the JSON_MODIFY statement will return the entire JSON document stored in the field in the first row of our table. However, it will not change the underlying table:

```
SELECT TOP (1) JSON_MODIFY(CustomerOrderHistory, '$.orders[0].
order.orderdate', '2017-01-01') FROM dbo.CustomerOrders;
```

In this example, we will run the same update as shown in the preceding query but we will modify the data in the table using an update statement. We will be filtering for a specific customer to make the change against rather than using the TOP (1) construction:

```
UPDATE dbo.CustomerOrders SET CustomerOrderHistory = JSON_
MODIFY(CustomerOrderHistory, '$.orders[0].order.orderdate',
'2017-01-01') WHERE CustomerID = 100;
```

After you have run the update, you can review the change that's been made by running a standard SQL statement with a filter applied. You will notice that only the first order in CustomerOrderHistory has been updated for that customer.

As you can see, there are a lot of options for working with JSON data in SQL Server, including the ability to update the JSON document.

In the final part of this section, we will explore how to make complex queries, including the ability to return tabular data in our results.

Building tabular results from JSON data in SQL Server

A common requirement in reporting is to flatten the JSON data so that it can be easily used in reporting or by analytics tools such as Power BI. While some of these tools can interrogate and explore JSON documents, they tend to work better with tabular formatted data. One common use case we have seen is creating views using some of the techniques we are about to demonstrate to have tabular versions of JSON data ready for reporting and analytics tools to use. Our final example will create such a view for you to have as a reference.

When creating these views, our primary function of choice is OPENJSON. By using this, combined with the CROSS APPLY operator, we can return rows of data from JSON documents joined with relational data for ease of use.

In our example, we are going to create a set of queries and bring them together into a single view that will contain the customer information from the table combined with some order information.

We will start with a basic SQL statement that returns any specific customer with all three fields from our customer orders table:

```
SELECT CustomerID, CustomerName, CustomerOrderHistory
FROM dbo.CustomerOrders
WHERE CustomerID between 1 and 10;
```

Using OPENJSON and CROSS APPLY, we will expand our results so that they include a row for each order for this customer from the JSON document in the customer order history field. OPENJSON converts the requested JSON content into a tabular format, which can then be joined to other relational data using the CROSS APPLY operator. The result of combining these commands is that each matching row from the JSON document will be matched to the one related in the outer query. Here is how that query is built:

```
SELECT o.CustomerID, o.CustomerName ,r.OrderID, r.OrderDate
FROM dbo.CustomerOrders o
CROSS APPLY OPENJSON (o.CustomerOrderHistory, '$.orders')
WITH (OrderID INT '$.order.id'
,OrderDate DATE '$.order.orderdate') AS r
WHERE o.CustomerID BETWEEN 1 AND 10;
```

As you can see, the OPENJSON function pivots an array and applies all the matching records from the field as new rows in the resulting table. This is effectively a cross-join between the related field, CustomerOrderHistory, in the parent row.

In our example, the uniqueness of the row is defined by `CustomerID` from the relational table and `OrderID` from the JSON document. If we continue to expand to the order line level in the JSON document, the granularity of the results will be at `OrderLineID`.

To further expand our query, we are going to add a `CustomerSince` field, which will be generated from the first order date from the JSON document. The primary difference between using `JSON_VALUE` to collect data from the JSON document and using `OPENJSON` is that when working with an array, we need to specify the position in the array we want to use.

In the following example, we are specifying the first order in the array and assuming that it is the first order the customer has done with us:

```
SELECT o.CustomerID, o.CustomerName ,r.OrderID, r.OrderDate,
cast (JSON_VALUE (CustomerOrderHistory, '$.orders[0].order.
orderdate')as date) as CustomerSince
FROM dbo.CustomerOrders o
CROSS APPLY OPENJSON (o.CustomerOrderHistory, '$.orders')
WITH (OrderID INT '$.order.id'
,OrderDate DATE '$.order.orderdate') AS r
WHERE o.CustomerID BETWEEN 1 AND 10;
```

This is straightforward in many cases as JSON is appended quite often but not usually updated out of order. However, there is no guarantee that that is going to work as expected. If you need more precise control over the values being returned, you will likely need to use `OPENJSON` to pivot the array and then use standard SQL techniques to interrogate the array for the latest value.

As you can see, using the functions we have available, we were able to generate tabular results from our JSON documents. By adding this to a view, we can share a tabular result in SQL Server that can be used in multiple reporting and analytics tools easily.

Use the following `CREATE VIEW` syntax to create the view:

```
CREATE VIEW dbo.V_CustomerOrderHistory AS (
SELECT o.CustomerID, o.CustomerName ,r.OrderID, r.OrderDate,
cast (JSON_VALUE (CustomerOrderHistory, '$.orders[0].order.
orderdate')as date) as CustomerSince
FROM dbo.CustomerOrders o
CROSS APPLY OPENJSON (o.CustomerOrderHistory, '$.orders')
WITH (OrderID INT '$.order.id'
,OrderDate DATE '$.order.orderdate') AS r
WHERE o.CustomerID BETWEEN 1 AND 10);
```

Using the functions shown in this section, you can effectively work with JSON data in your SQL queries. These functions, combined with standard SQL operators such as APPLY, give you a significant amount of functionality and flexibility when creating these queries.

Summary

In this chapter, you learned how SQL Server supports JSON as incoming data as well as how to build JSON documents from relational data. By understanding the functions that were included in this chapter, you will be able to navigate JSON data and build tabular results that can be easily used in reporting. You should now understand how to create JSON documents from relational databases that can be used by applications and developers to exchange data with SQL Server. By using these functions and techniques, you are better prepared to handle the modern data estate, which includes streaming and web-based data that is commonly formatted as JSON.

In the next chapter, we will be discussing how to work with data in your data lake or files. If that data is stored in JSON, you'll be able to use the functions from this chapter directly with the data coming from those files or data lakes.

12

Integrating File Data and Data Lake Content with SQL

As we come close to wrapping up our book, we would like to cover a very powerful function called `OPENROWSET()`, which makes data accessible to different Azure data services, such as Azure SQL, Azure SQL Managed Instance, and Synapse Analytics.

In this chapter, we will focus on accessing data from Azure File Storage and learn about the different options available with the `OPENROWSET(BULK..)` function, used mainly with files and Synapse Analytics.

We will cover the following topics in this chapter:

- Understanding the `OPENROWSET(BULK..)` function
- Different options using `OPENROWSET(BULK..)` with Synapse Analytics
- Required security and storage permissions
- Understanding external tables with Synapse Analytics

Technical requirements

To work with the examples and illustrations in this chapter, you will need access to an Azure subscription and to provision Azure Storage (Data Lake Storage Gen2) and the Azure Synapse Analytics service inside a resource group. The Data Lake service container can also be provisioned while creating the Synapse Analytics service.

This chapter uses two CSV files, which are available at the following GitHub URL:

`https://github.com/PacktPublishing/SQL-Query-Design-Best-Practices/tree/main/Chapter12`

Along with the CSV files, we have a SQL script file available at the same GitHub URL, which should be used from the Synapse Studio to execute SQL examples listed in this chapter. Please refer to the *Appendix* for tool installation and database restoration guidance.

Understanding the OPENROWSET (BULK..) function

The OPENROWSET(BULK..) function is used to access remote data from a data source (for example, connect to a file stored in Data Lake Gen 2). It can be directly referenced in the FROM clause, similar to calling a table name and pulling data from it as a set of rows.

OPENROWSET(BULK..) can read different types of file structures – PARQUET, DELTA, or delimited text (CSV), and access can be controlled with different login options – Azure AD logins or SQL logins (publicly available files can be accessed by just the web data path).

There is a slight difference in using the OPENROWSET(BULK..) syntax while reading Parquet/Delta files or a CSV file.

Let's look at the syntaxes used for the OPENROWSET(BULK..) function.

This is OPENROWSET(BULK..) for reading Parquet or Delta files:

```
--OPENROWSET syntax for Parquet/Delta Lake files
OPENROWSET
( { BULK 'storage path to Parquet file' , [DATA_SOURCE = <data
source name>, ]
    FORMAT= ['PARQUET' | 'DELTA'] }
)
[WITH ( {'column_name' 'column_type' }) ]
[AS] table_alias(column_alias,...n)
```

This is OPENROWSET(BULK..) for reading CSV files :

```
--OPENROWSET syntax for delimited files (CSV)
OPENROWSET
( { BULK ' storage path to Parquet file ' , [DATA_SOURCE =
<data source name>, ]
    FORMAT = 'CSV'
    [ <bulk_options> ]
    [ , <reject_options> ] }
)
WITH ( {'column_name' 'column_type' [ 'column_ordinal' | 'json_
path'] })
[AS] table_alias(column_alias,...n)
<bulk_options> ::=
[ , FIELDTERMINATOR = 'char' ]
[ , ROWTERMINATOR = 'char' ]
```

```
[ , ESCAPECHAR = 'char' ]
[ , FIRSTROW = 'first_row' ]
[ , HEADER_ROW = { TRUE | FALSE } ]


<reject_options> ::=
{
    | MAXERRORS = reject_value,
    | ERRORFILE_DATA_SOURCE = <data source name>,
    | ERRORFILE_LOCATION = '/REJECT_Directory'
}
```

The BULK option in OPENROWSET() in Synapse SQL reads data from a file and converts it into rows. Data can be read directly without storing it in a table using a simple SELECT statement. Isn't that pretty cool?

> **Important**
>
> The OPENROWSET() function is not supported in a Synapse dedicated SQL pool and can be only used for serverless SQL pools.

To run our example scripts, we have created two sample CSV files – Suppliers.csv and PurchaseOrders.csv – with data extracted from our WideWorldImporters database. These two files are available in our chapter's Git repository listed in the *Technical requirements* section:

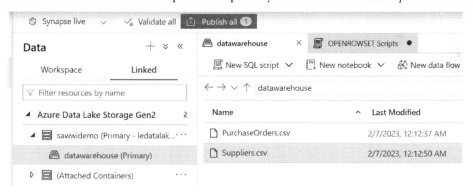

Figure 12.1 – Azure Storage with two CSV files uploaded

The two files, PurchaseOrders.csv and Suppliers.csv, are uploaded to the datawarehouse container in Azure Storage services connected with Synapse Analytics.

Now, to access the preceding CSV data using OPENROWSET (), have a look at the following script. This is a simple SELECT query using the BULK option with OPENROWSET () and pulling data as a table from the Suppliers.csv file:

```
SELECT *
FROM
OPENROWSET (
    BULK 'https://<STORAGE SERVICE NAME >.dfs.core.windows.net/
datawarehouse/Suppliers.csv'


) AS [SuppliersCSV]
```

The query needs to provide the full CSV file path to the BULK operator, define the file format (in our case, it's a CSV file), and add PARSER_VERSION.

Replace <STORAGE SERVICE NAME> with your Azure Storage service name.

After updating the Storage service name, when you run the preceding query in Synapse Studio, you will get the following output:

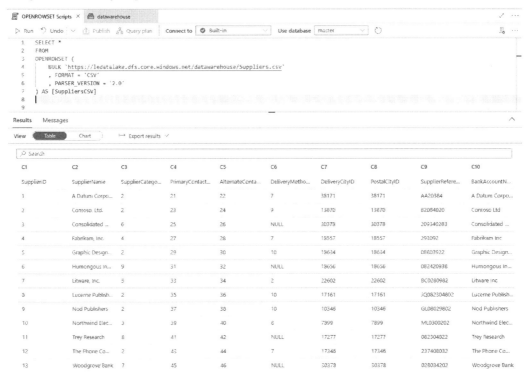

Figure 12.2 – Azure Synapse Analytics supplier data pulled using OPENROWSET()

When you closely look at the data, the row shows the column name as part of the data. Row 1 is supposed to be the file header and we need to define that under the BULK option using the HEADER_ROW = TRUE option:

```
SELECT *
FROM
OPENROWSET (
    BULK 'https://ledatalake.dfs.core.windows.net/
datawarehouse/Suppliers.csv'
    , FORMAT = 'CSV'
    , PARSER_VERSION = '2.0'
    , HEADER_ROW = TRUE
) AS [SuppliersCSV]
```

This is the output we get:

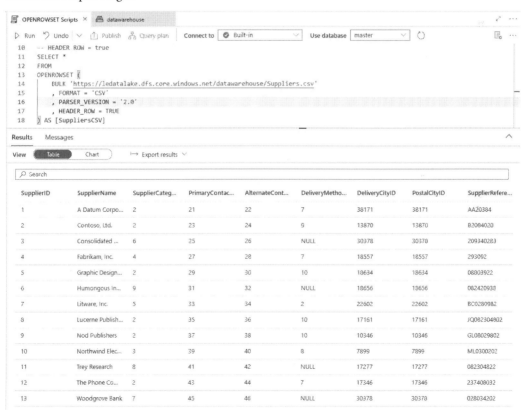

Figure 12.3 – Supplier data with the HEADER_ROW option

Now, say we need to pull a few specific columns from the `Supplier` table, we can use the `WITH` option and predefine columns we need to extract out of the files. The following is the script for it:

```sql
SELECT *
FROM
OPENROWSET (
    BULK 'https://ledatalake.dfs.core.windows.net/
datawarehouse/Suppliers.csv'
    , FORMAT = 'CSV'
    , PARSER_VERSION = '2.0'
    , HEADER_ROW = TRUE
)
WITH (
    [SupplierID] INT
    , [SupplierName] VARCHAR (100)
    , [DeliveryCityID] INT
    , [PostalCityID] INT
)
AS [SuppliersCSV]
```

The following shows its output:

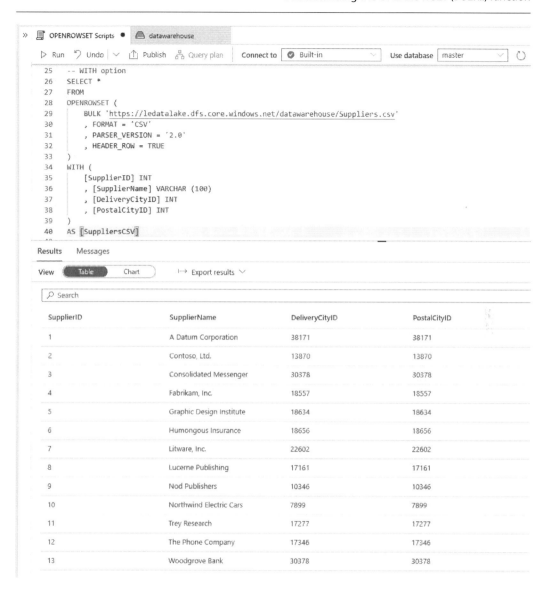

Figure 12.4 – Supplier data with the WITH option

You will see we have four columns – **SupplierID**, **SupplierName**, **DeliveryCityID**, and **PostalCityID** – in the **Results** pane for the Suppliers.csv file.

You can also use other T-SQL functions with OPENROWSET() to combine tables and retrieve content. Let's explore this with an example.

We will use the same `Suppliers.csv` file and join it with `PurchaseOrders.csv`, which has `SupplierID` as a reference column:

```
SELECT
    [SuppliersCSV].SupplierID
    , [SuppliersCSV].SupplierName
    , [PurchaseOrdersCSV].OrderDate
    , [PurchaseOrdersCSV].LastEditedBy
FROM
    OPENROWSET (
        BULK 'https://ledatalake.dfs.core.windows.net/
datawarehouse/Suppliers.csv'
        , FORMAT = 'CSV'
        , PARSER_VERSION = '2.0'
        , HEADER_ROW = TRUE
    ) AS [SuppliersCSV]
    INNER JOIN
        (SELECT *
        FROM
        OPENROWSET (
            BULK 'https://ledatalake.blob.core.windows.net/
datawarehouse/PurchaseOrders.csv'
            , FORMAT = 'CSV'
            , PARSER_VERSION = '2.0'
            , HEADER_ROW = TRUE
        ) AS [PurchaseOrdersCSV]) AS [PurchaseOrdersCSV]
    ON [SuppliersCSV].SupplierID = [PurchaseOrdersCSV].
SupplierID
WHERE [SuppliersCSV].SupplierID = '10';
```

Here is the output for it:

```
30    SELECT
31        [SuppliersCSV].SupplierID
32        , [SuppliersCSV].SupplierName
33        , [PurchaseOrdersCSV].OrderDate
34        , [PurchaseOrdersCSV].LastEditedBy
35    FROM
36        OPENROWSET (
37            BULK 'https://ledatalake.dfs.core.windows.net/datawarehouse/Suppliers.csv'
38            , FORMAT = 'CSV'
39            , PARSER_VERSION = '2.0'
40            , HEADER_ROW = TRUE
41        ) AS [SuppliersCSV]
42        INNER JOIN
43            (SELECT *
44            FROM
45            OPENROWSET (
46                BULK 'https://ledatalake.blob.core.windows.net/datawarehouse/PurchaseOrders.csv'
47                , FORMAT = 'CSV'
48                , PARSER_VERSION = '2.0'
49                , HEADER_ROW = TRUE
50            ) AS [PurchaseOrdersCSV]) AS [PurchaseOrdersCSV]
51        ON [SuppliersCSV].SupplierID = [PurchaseOrdersCSV].SupplierID
52    WHERE [SuppliersCSV].SupplierID = '10';
```

Results   Messages

View   Table   Chart   ↦ Export results ∨

🔎 Search

SupplierID	SupplierName	OrderDate	LastEditedBy
10	Northwind Electric Cars	2013-01-01T00:00:00.0000000	6
10	Northwind Electric Cars	2013-01-02T00:00:00.0000000	5
10	Northwind Electric Cars	2013-01-03T00:00:00.0000000	3
10	Northwind Electric Cars	2013-01-04T00:00:00.0000000	14
10	Northwind Electric Cars	2013-01-05T00:00:00.0000000	14
10	Northwind Electric Cars	2013-01-07T00:00:00.0000000	17
10	Northwind Electric Cars	2013-01-09T00:00:00.0000000	7
10	Northwind Electric Cars	2013-01-14T00:00:00.0000000	15
10	Northwind Electric Cars	2013-01-15T00:00:00.0000000	6

Figure 12.5 – Using INNER JOIN with the OPENROWSET function

We get a result set with four columns – **SupplierID**, **SupplierName**, **OrderDate**, and **LastEditedBy** – two from each file, into one result set. This capability of using T-SQL makes the OPENROWSET function very powerful.

Here, I have listed a few additional commonly used bulk options with `OPENROWSET(BULK..)`:

Option Syntax	Description
`ROWTERMINATOR = 'row_terminator'`	This option is used to specify any row terminator character(s). If nothing is specified, the default row terminator will be used, which executes. Default terminators for `PARSER_VERSION = '1.0'` are `\r\n`, `\n`, and `\r`. Default terminators for `PARSER_VERSION = '2.0'` are `\r\n` and `\n`.
`FIELDTERMINATOR = 'field_ terminator'`	This option is used to specify any field terminator character(s), such as "`|`". The default value is "`,`" (a comma character).

Table 13.1 – List of common bulk options

So, by now, you should have a good understanding of the `OPENROWSET(BULK..)` function, and given a few examples that we walked through, you should be able to write SQL queries to read files from Azure Storage and pull data into Synapse serverless SQL pools.

Next, we will look at the security and storage permissions that are necessary to make sure we have access to files and don't get an error while running SQL queries.

Required security and storage permissions

The big question that comes to mind while accessing files stored in Azure Storage services is, do we have enough privilege to read the content from the files? This section explains this in detail and walks through a scenario on how to enable this.

There are the following three methods for enabling access:

- **Role-based access control (RBAC)** (short for **role-based access control**): This assigns a role to an Azure AD user on Azure Storage where files are stored and need to be read by using the `OPENROWSET ()` function. The user must have the `Storage Blob Data Reader`, `Storage Blob Data Contributor`, or `Storage Blob Data Owner` RBAC role to the Storage account, but if you are trying to write back on the Storage service, you need the `Storage Blob Data Contributor` or `Storage Blob Data Owner` role.

- An **access control list (ACL)**: This assigns a more granular `Read`, `Write`, and `Execute` permission on the files and directories in the Storage service. If this is for reading files only, we need `Execute` ACL on all folders and `Read` ACL on the files that are going to be read.

- A **shared access signature (SAS)**: This is a time-limited token to access files on the Storage services and contains permission granted to the reader and the period for which the token is valid.

For the first option with RBAC, when you create a Synapse Analytics service and if your files to be accessed are stored in the primary Storage service, you can grant RBAC roles during the service creation itself. Refer to the following screenshot for this:

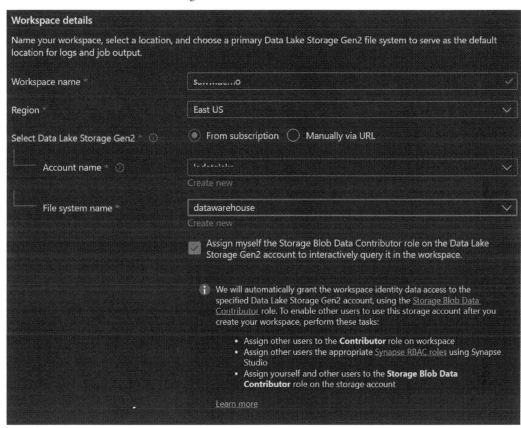

Figure 12.6 – RBAC assigned during Synapse Analytics creation

Here, you will see we have a checkbox to enable access by granting a `Storage Blob Data Contributor` role to the same user account provisioning the Synapse Analytics service.

For the Storage service already created (or not assigned as primary to the Synapse service), you can assign roles from the **Access Control (IAM)** options for that Azure Storage service, as shown here:

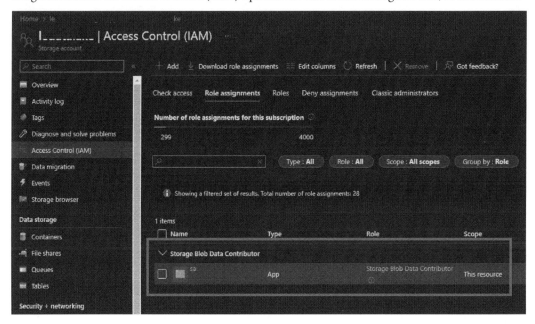

Figure 12.7 – RBAC assigned to a Storage service to access files

So, based on company security requirements, different options are available to grant access to files that will be used by the OPENROWSET Bulk function. The commonly used and recommended option is the RBAC option.

Understanding external tables

Similar to what we learned about OPENROWSET, we have a different option to read files from Storage using external tables. The big difference to an OPENROWSET bulk function is that with Synapse Analytics, we can use external tables to read remote file content to a dedicated SQL pool or a serverless SQL pool.

We have two types of external tables – Hadoop and native external tables – and the focus for this chapter will be on native external tables. We can read and export data in various formats, such as CSV, Parquet, and ORC, using native external tables, which is very similar to what we learned about earlier in the chapter with the OPENROWSET function.

> **Note**
> Native external tables are available in a serverless SQL pool, and the option for this in a dedicated SQL pool is in public preview at the time of writing.

You can create an external table using the following three steps:

1. Establish a connection to the source (along with credentials to access storage) via `CREATE EXTERNAL DATA SOURCE`.

   Here is the syntax for it:

   ```
   CREATE EXTERNAL DATA SOURCE <data_source_name>
   WITH (
   LOCATION = '<prefix>://<path>'
   [, CREDENTIAL = <database scoped credential> ]
    )
   [;]
   ```

   Here, `<data_source_name>` is the user-defined name and must be unique within the Synapse database. `LOCATION` is the path to the remote data source and will connect to the Azure Storage service, and finally, `CREDENTIAL` (which is optional) is the credential that is used to authenticate and read content from storage.

   Here is an example of it:

   ```
   CREATE DATABASE ExternalTableDBDemo;
   CREATE MASTER KEY ENCRYPTION BY  PASSWORD='<please insert
   your own password>';
   CREATE DATABASE SCOPED CREDENTIAL ExternalTblsCred
   WITH IDENTITY = 'SHARED ACCESS SIGNATURE',
   SECRET =  '<please insert your own secret>';
   CREATE EXTERNAL DATA SOURCE ExternalTblsDS WITH (
   LOCATION = 'https://ledatalake.dfs.core.windows.net/
   datawarehouse/Suppliers.csv',
       CREDENTIAL = ExternalTblsCred
   );
   ```

   In the preceding example, you will notice that for `CREATE EXTERNAL DATA SOURCE`, we have three scripts to successfully establish a connection:

   - Create a master key (if it doesn't exist from before)

   - Create a database scope credential, `ExternalTblsCred`

   - Create an external data source connection, `ExternalTblsDS`, using the database scope credential established in the preceding step

   Once we have executed all three scripts, we will create a new external data source connection to `Suppliers.csv`.

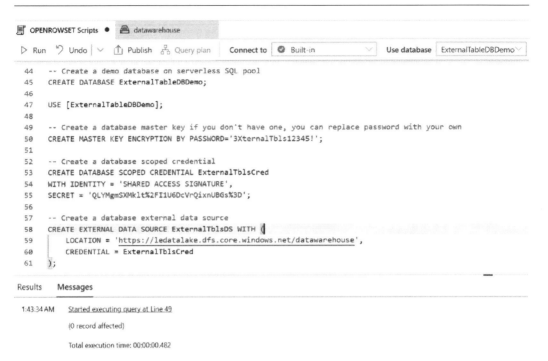

Figure 12.8 – Script out of CREATE EXTERNAL DATA SOURCE

2.   Describe the file format using CREATE EXTERNAL FILE FORMAT.

Here is the syntax for it:

```
-- Create an external file format for PARQUET files
CREATE EXTERNAL FILE FORMAT et_file_format_name
WITH(
    FORMAT_TYPE=PARQUET
    [,DATA_COMPRESSION={<compression binary class>}
    ]);


--Create an external file format for DELIMITED TEXT files
CREATE EXTERNAL FILE FORMAT et_file_format_name
WITH(
    FORMAT_TYPE=DELIMITEDTEXT
    [,DATA_COMPRESSION=<compression binary class>]
    [,FORMAT_OPTIONS(<format_options>[ ,...n  ])]
    );
<format_options> :
```

```
{
    FIELD_TERMINATOR=field_terminator
    | STRING_DELIMITER=string_delimiter
    | FIRST_ROW=integer
    | USE_TYPE_DEFAULT={ TRUE|FALSE}
    | ENCODING={'UTF8'|'UTF16'}
    | PARSER_VERSION={'parser_version'}
}
```

Here, we have two different syntaxes for file format: PARQUET and DELIMITEDTEXT (for example, a comma-delimited CSV file). The DELIMITEDTEXT option has a few additional <format_options> to provide details on the delimited file structure.

Here is an example:

```
-- Create file format for Suppliers.csv
CREATE EXTERNAL FILE FORMAT SuppliersFF
WITH
(
    FORMAT_TYPE = DELIMITEDTEXT,
    FORMAT_OPTIONS (
        FIELD_TERMINATOR = ','
        , STRING_DELIMITER = '"'
        , PARSER_VERSION = '2.0'
        , FIRST_ROW = 2
    )
);
```

Here, we are going to read content from the Suppliers.csv file, which is comma-delimited, and since it contains the first row as a header, we have specified FIRST_ROW = 2. This is how it looks:

Figure 12.9 – Script out of CREATE EXTERNAL FILE FORMAT

3. We then pull content from the file via CREATE EXTERNAL TABLE.

    Here is the syntax for it:

    ```
    CREATE EXTERNAL TABLE { external_table_name }
        (<table_column_definition> [ ,...n ] )
        WITH (
            LOCATION='folder_or_filepath',
            DATA_SOURCE=external_data_source_name,
            FILE_FORMAT=external_file_format_name
            [,TABLE_OPTIONS=N'{"READ_OPTIONS":["ALLOW_
    INCONSISTENT_READS"]}' ]
            )
    [;]
    <table_column_definition> :
    column_name <data_type>
        [ COLLATE collation_name ]
    ```

In the final script, to create an external table, you can use a one- to three-part name to create external_table_name. Keep in mind that the external table is not going to load data into the external table, and it's going to contain metadata (the table definition) only.

LOCATION specifies the file path to the Storage service and will be a full path including the folder and filename. You will reference DATA_SOURCE and FILE_FORMAT from *steps 1* and *2*.

You can define <column_definition>, which includes the column name and data type. This should match the data content in the remote file.

Here is an example of it:

```
CREATE EXTERNAL TABLE SuppliersExternalTbl
(
    [SupplierID] INT
    , [SupplierName] VARCHAR (100)
    , [DeliveryCityID] INT
    , [PostalCityID] INT
)
WITH (
    LOCATION = 'Suppliers.csv',
    DATA_SOURCE = ExternalTblsDS,
    FILE_FORMAT = SuppliersFF
)
GO


SELECT TOP 10 * FROM SuppliersExternalTbl;
```

Here, create `SuppliersExternalTbl` with four columns and map `DATA_SOURCE` and `FILE_FORMAT` to the data source and file format created in *steps 1* and *2*, respectively.

The last script queries the top 10 records from the external table:

Figure 12.10 – SQL script for CREATE EXTERNAL TABLE

So, in this section, we learned about external tables and walked through three steps on how to establish connectivity to the source file(s), defined the correct file format, and then created an external table to read content from the remote file(s) stored in Azure Storage services.

For each step, we explained the syntax and followed it with an example. The scripts for the examples are available in the chapter's GitHub repository. Please refer to the *Technical requirements* section at the start of this chapter to get the link to the GitHub location.

Summary

In this chapter, we learned what the OPENROWSET (BULK...) function is and how to use this function to pull data from the Storage service directly into the Synapse Analytics tabular structure without having to load it into a table. After the OPENROWSET bulk function, we looked at external tables and detailed three steps to create an external table on a serverless SQL pool with a similar functionality of pulling content from remote files in storage.

Both the OPENROWSET bulk function and external tables are very powerful tools to connect directly to Azure Storage services and don't need to be converted into tables or build pipelines to make data available for further engineering/analytics work.

In our next chapter, we will move our work to Jupyter Notebook, and look at how to create notebooks, write queries, create documentation from inside the notebook, and share them with team members.

Organizing and Sharing Your Queries with Jupyter Notebooks

As you continue to work in modern applications and with modern database solutions, you will no doubt encounter Jupyter notebooks. Jupyter notebooks have been in use in various technology stacks including Databricks and Synapse. What you may not realize is that Jupyter notebooks are also available in Azure Data Studio to support better documentation and easier sharing of your SQL queries. Jupyter notebooks provide a more elegant documentation solution for your SQL scripts. They also enable you to easily execute scripts within the context of a larger set of scripts and share the results of those executions if needed.

In this chapter, we will give an introduction to how Jupyter notebooks are supported in Azure Data Studio and how you can use them to organize and share your queries with your peers.

In this chapter, we are going to cover the following primary topics:

- Creating Jupyter notebooks in Azure Data Studio
- Adding queries in your Jupyter notebook
- Documenting your code with markdown in your notebooks
- Managing and sharing your queries with Jupyter notebooks

Technical requirements

To work with the examples and illustrations in this chapter, you will need to have Azure Data Studio installed. We will be working with the `WideWorldImporters` database on SQL Server or Azure SQL Database. Please refer to the *Appendix* for tool installation and database restoration guidance. You will find the completed notebook for this chapter on GitHub here: `https://github.com/PacktPublishing/SQL-Query-Design-Best-Practices/tree/main/Chapter13/Notebooks/My%20Analytics`

Creating Jupyter notebooks in Azure Data Studio

Most data professionals who specialize in SQL are not familiar with notebooks. Jupyter notebooks have typically been in the domain of data science and data lakes. When working with data lakes, it is common to use code such as **Python** and deploy it using notebooks with tools such as **Databricks**. If you have not used Databricks or other notebook-supported tools, this will be your first exposure to one. If you're familiar with notebooks already, keep reading; you may find they are implemented in Azure Data Studio a bit differently from the tools that you are familiar with.

Understanding notebooks in Azure Data Studio

Azure Data Studio natively supports both Jupyter books and Jupyter notebooks. When starting to use notebooks inside of Azure Data Studio, the instinctive way to interact with them is by using the **NOTEBOOKS** option in the side menu, as shown here:

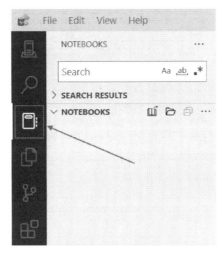

Figure 13.1 – The NOTEBOOKS option on the Azure Data Studio sidebar

When you select this option, you will see the preceding screen. The key thing that is missing from this option is the ability to create a notebook. From here, you can create a Jupyter book within which you can create notebooks, but you cannot create notebooks from this menu option. Before we move on to creating a Jupyter book with notebooks and other files stored within it, let's explore the easy way to create a notebook initially inside Azure Data Studio.

Creating a notebook in Azure Data Studio

There are a couple of paths you can take to create a new notebook in Azure Data Studio. When you initially open Azure Data Studio, it is available on the welcome screen as a button. You can also use the **File | New Notebook** option in the menu to create a new notebook. Using either of these options, go ahead and create a new notebook.

This will open a new notebook file with the default name shown, as follows:

Figure 13.2 – New notebook in Azure Data Studio

We will delve into adding code and text to your notebook in a later section. Now that you've created your first notebook, save it to the location of your choice, as we will use this later to show how to import a notebook into your Jupyter book.

Let's begin the process of creating a Jupyter book that you can use to organize and store your notebooks and other markdown files.

Creating the Jupyter book

Azure Data Studio supports the organization of Jupyter notebooks in a Jupyter book. A Jupyter book is effectively a folder structure with some metadata attached to allow Azure Data Studio to know how the book is organized. Before we create our new Jupyter book, let's describe what we're going to create and then add that content to the book.

Throughout the rest of the exercises and examples in this chapter, we will be creating a Jupyter book with some basic SQL queries with the WideWorldImportersDW database. We will be taking on the role of a data analyst who is trying to discover and share discoveries using the notebook as part of the process.

Let us begin the process of creating the book. We will take a step-by-step approach and walk you through the creation and organization of the book as we make it.

First of all, we will need to create the overall book. Here is how we do it:

1. In Azure Data Studio, click on the **NOTEBOOKS** option in the left panel.
2. In the **NOTEBOOKS** section, click on ….

3. Choose **Create Jupyter Book**, as shown in the following screenshot:

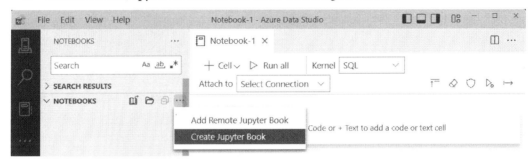

Figure 13.3 – Menu option to create a Jupyter book

4. Give your new Jupyter book a name, such as My Analytics.

5. Specify a location to store the book in. The optional Content folder can be used to add a folder with existing content to your Jupyter book or store your content in a different location. We will not be using this option in our chapter.

6. Click on **Create** to create the book.

Once you've completed these steps, you should see your Jupyter book with a README.md file in Azure Data Studio. At this point, you have yet to create a notebook in your Jupyter book.

Azure Data Studio should look similar to what you see here in *Figure 13.4*:

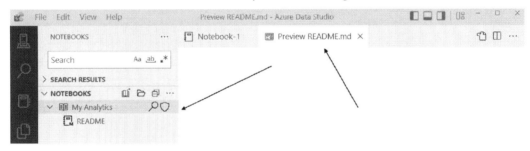

Figure 13.4 – Newly created Jupyter book

Before we continue much further, it's important to understand what an md or **markdown** file is. If you've been working with software for a while, you are familiar with the concept of a README file. That is like what we have created here by default when creating our Jupyter book. The purpose of this file is to provide an explanation of what we would find in the contents of our book, including information about the various notebooks we may include.

Go ahead and add some content about what you've been doing in the README file to get a feel for how it works. To add content to the README document, double-click anywhere in the document to open a new tab for editing. It also creates a preview tab with the formatted text that you can view. Be sure to save your file when you have completed your edits.

Now that we have created our Jupyter book and have a file in it, let's have a look at what was created in the backend. As data professionals, we always like to know how things are stored so, in this case, it is good to understand the structure of a Jupyter book. Browse to the location where you saved your Jupyter book in **File Explorer**. You will see that your Jupyter book has been created as a folder. If you open that folder, you will see that two files have been added to it that allow Azure Data Studio to understand the structure of the content contained within your Jupyter book.

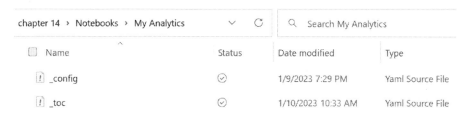

Figure 13.5 – Jupyter book folder structure with files

We will not dig into the contents of those files at this point. However, you may find it useful when troubleshooting to know that those files exist and that they are editable.

Now that we have our Jupyter book created with a README file, we will add a new notebook to our Jupyter book.

Adding a notebook to your Jupyter book

Adding a notebook to your Jupyter book is straightforward. The easiest way to add a notebook to your Jupyter book is to right-click on the Jupyter book in Azure Data Studio and choose **Add Notebook** from the menu, as shown here:

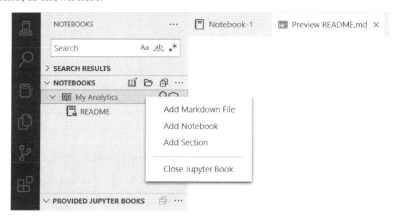

Figure 13.6 – Jupyter book menu

As you can see from the menu, we have a few options that we can add to our Jupyter book. Let's take them in order:

- A **markdown** file is just like the README file we created at the beginning. Use this file type in your Jupyter book when only text is being used.

- A **notebook** is like the file we created at the beginning of the chapter. This file supports both text and code and can execute code as well.

- A **section** is not a file at all. If you add a section, you are effectively adding a subfolder to your Jupyter book, which is important if you have a lot of content to add to a book.

For our purposes here, choose **Add Notebook** and give your notebook a meaningful name, such as `Analyzing Customers`. We will use this notebook to add queries and content around our customers from the database. Now, you should see two files in your Jupyter book. Notice in the following screenshot that the icons are slightly different, with a markdown file with a small **M** on the icon:

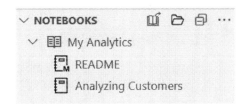

Figure 13.7 – The My Analytics notebook with both files added

Earlier in the chapter, we created a notebook. In Azure Data Studio, notebooks do not show up in the view as shown in the preceding screenshot unless they are included in a Jupyter book. There is also no simple way to add an existing notebook to a Jupyter book currently. We call this out because you can create notebooks quite simply in Azure Data Studio but not have them show up in the **NOTEBOOKS** pane. You can create notebooks from SQL query windows, the file menu, and the opening splash screen. However, none of those notebooks are part of a Jupyter book and will not show up in the **NOTEBOOKS** section in Azure Data Studio.

Here are the steps required to add our previously created notebook to our Jupyter book:

1. Move your previously created notebook to the Jupyter book folder, which will be the same as your Jupyter book name.

2. In the Jupyter book folder, open the `_toc` file, which is a YAML file with the structure of your Jupyter book stored in it. This file can be opened up in any text editor. It should look similar to the following code:

```
- title: README
  file: /README
- title: Analyzing Customers
  file: /AnalyzingCustomers
```

As you can see, the file is structured to show the title, which is the part shown in your Jupyter book in Azure Data Studio, and the actual filename. Now that we have the new notebook copied into our Jupyter book folder, let's continue with the next step.

3. Add the title and file line to the `_toc` file. You can give the title any name you would like, but the file needs to be the name of the file without the extension. Your updated YAML file should look like the following with the names you chose:

```
- title: README
  file: /README
- title: Analyzing Customers
  file: /AnalyzingCustomers
- title: Notebook 1
  file: /Notebook-1
```

4. Save the file and you should see the new notebook in your Jupyter book in Azure Data Studio.

Now that we have our Jupyter book created with our first notebook, let's add content to our new notebook.

Adding queries in your Jupyter notebooks

Now that you've created your notebook, it is time to add code. Jupyter notebooks in Azure Data Studio support a variety of code languages, including SQL, Python, and R. It is beyond the scope of this book to delve into languages beyond SQL. However, you should be aware that notebooks support a variety of workloads throughout the Azure data ecosystem, particularly in Synapse Analytics.

There are a few steps to go through to get our SQL working as code in our notebooks.

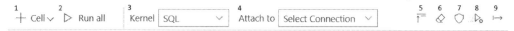

Figure 13.8 – Notebook toolbar

Before we delve into adding code specifically, let's do a quick review of the options available in the header of your notebook as shown in the previous screenshot:

1. **Cell** provides the option to add a text or code cell to your notebook.

2. The **Run all** option will run all the code in sequence in your notebook.

3. **Kernel** specifies which language is the primary language of your notebook. In our case, we will leave it as **SQL**.

4. The **Attach to** option lets you choose the connection you will use with your notebook to run your code.

5. The **Collapse Cells** button will hide the text and contents in each of your cells.

6. The **Clear Results** button will do exactly that and clear the results from running code in your notebook.

7. By default, notebooks created in Azure Data Studio are **Trusted**. If you open a notebook from another source, it is marked as **Not Trusted** and can be changed by using this button.

8. The **Run with parameters** button will allow you to execute the code in your notebook using parameters. However, this functionality is currently not supported with SQL notebooks.

9. **Export as SQL** exports your notebook as a SQL file, converting text cells into comments where possible.

Now that we've done a run-through of what's available in the notebook menu, we are ready to add and run code in our notebook.

Creating connections in your notebook

If you have already connected to your database through the server connection available in Azure Data Studio, simply choose the connection you created from the **Connections** dropdown and move to the next section of the chapter.

> **Note**
> Make sure that your connection is connected to the right database. If you have not created a connection to the database or are using the default setting in Azure Data Studio, you will need to complete the following steps to properly execute the code in the notebook.

If you have not already created a connection in Azure Studio, follow the steps ahead to connect to your server and then select that server from the list once you've created it:

1. On the **CONNECTIONS** tab, click on the **New Connection** button, which looks like a server with a plus sign.

Figure 13.9 – Creating a new connection

2. Complete the connection information to connect to your copy of `WideWorldImportersDW`. It does not matter where you have the database created if you can connect to it from Azure Data Studio. *Be sure to select the database when creating this connection.*

3. You can now attach your notebook to the connection you have created by using the **Attach to** dropdown and choosing **Change Connection**. Once again confirm that you are connecting to the *connection with the database specified*.

Now that your notebook is attached to the database, we can begin building code blocks.

Creating and executing SQL code in your notebook

Now that we are attached to a database, we will create some SQL that we will insert into a code block. We will not completely fill out our notebook with code in the context of this chapter but you are welcome to expand by adding additional SQL code to the notebook to practice using it.

We are going to create and execute code cells related to the customer data and the customer dimension in the `WideWorldImporters` Data Warehouse. We are going to work through adding code and executing code in a data analyst fashion. Our plan is to start simple and build more complex code as we go along in a data discovery-type mode.

Let us begin:

1. To add SQL code to our notebook, click on the + **Cell** button and choose **Code cell**.

2. Insert the following code into this cell:

```
SELECT COUNT(*) FROM Dimension.Customer;
```

3. To execute the code, click the **Run** button on the code cell, which looks like a right arrow or a play button. You can also press *F5* to execute the code in the cell.

This simple code gets us the count of customers we have in our database. Once executed, the results are as shown in the following code cell in *Figure 13.10*:

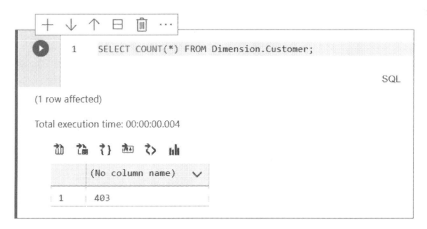

Figure 13.10 – Executed code cell with results

As you can see, not only are the results contained within the cell and the notebook but the performance metrics are also included as well.

Now that we know the count of customers, we can work on discovering what content we have related to customers. Let us see how:

1. Add a new code cell for the code we noted in *step 2* earlier in this subsection. You can do this by clicking the **+ Cell** button at the top of the notebook or hitting the plus symbol on the code cell we just created in the last exercise.

2. Place the following code into our cell:

```
SELECT TOP(10) * FROM Dimension.Customer;
```

3. Use the **Run** button or click *F5* to execute that code.

In this case, the results are wider than the width of the notebook. When the results are wider or longer than are easily visible within the cell area, you can use scroll bars to see all the results.

As you can see from the first few rows that were returned in the results in the cell after executing the query, the head office of Tailspin Toys is typically the billing customer for each of the stores that we sell to. We can use the following code cells to figure out how many stores are handled by each `Bill To Customer` instance.

The goal in these next steps is to demonstrate how to use a notebook for data discovery a step at a time and keep track of all your steps:

1. Add a new code cell. Insert and execute the code here into the cell to discover the number of unique `Bill To Customer` instances:

```
SELECT DISTINCT [Bill To Customer]
FROM Dimension.Customer.
```

2. Next, let's change the query to find out how many customers belong to each `Bill To Customer` instance. Add a new code cell. Insert and execute the following code to get that information:

```
SELECT [Bill To Customer]
, COUNT(*) AS [Customer Count]
FROM Dimension.Customer
GROUP BY [Bill To Customer]
```

3. In this final code cell, we are going to add the pretax sales data for our customers. Add a new code cell. Insert and execute the following code to add the sales data to our query:

```
SELECT customer.[Bill To Customer]
, COUNT(DISTINCT customer.[Customer Key]) AS [Customer
```

```
Count]
, SUM (orders.[Total Excluding Tax]) AS [Total Pretax
Sales]
FROM Dimension.Customer customer
INNER JOIN Fact.Order orders ON customer.[Customer Key] =
orders.[Customer Key]
GROUP BY [Bill To Customer]
```

Now that we have created a number of queries in cells in our notebook, let us look at a couple of options for formatting our results in the next section.

Formatting results

Using notebooks gives you some advantages over using SQL Server Management Studio. In particular, in this case, you were able to format the results in order to do some quick analysis and potentially share those formatted results with others. If you go back to the previous cell that we just ran that had Total Pretax Sales by Bill To Customer, we can visualize it as a bar chart.

Refresh the results if you need to in the last cell that we created. The results are currently presented in a table. As shown in the following table, select the **Show chart** button at the far right of the available buttons above the results:

	Bill To Customer		Customer Count		Total Pretax Sales	
1	Tailspin Toys (Head Office)		201		56171644.00	
2	N/A		1		65545913.60	
3	Wingtip Toys (Head Office)		201		55916718.80	

Figure 13.11 – Results window with a toolbar

When you click the **Show chart** button, you should see a bar chart created with the content as noted in the results. While not an ideal representation of the data we have here, this demonstrates that you can chart any content that you create. You should see a chart like *Figure 13.12*:

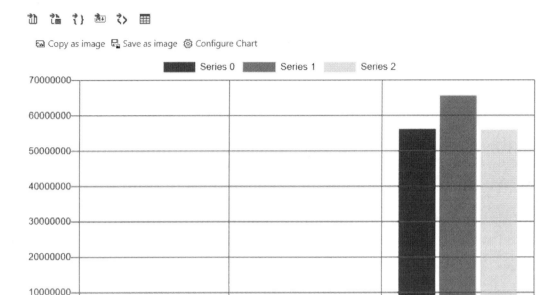

Figure 13.12 – Default results when clicking the Show chart button

Now, we will create a new code cell that will return results that are more easily charted. In this case, we will look at sales by date by customer:

1. Create a new code cell and add the following code to that cell call:

```
SELECT [Order Date Key]
, SUM ([Total Excluding Tax]) AS [Total Pretax Sales]
FROM Fact.[Order]
WHERE [Order Date Key] BETWEEN '1/1/2015' AND '1/31/2015'
GROUP BY [Order Date Key]
```

2. Execute the code cell.

3. Use the **Show chart** button to format the results. Once again, it creates a bar chart.

4. Now, we will customize results and use a line chart to represent our date range. Click on the **Configure Chart** button, which looks like a gear, and it will open a dialog box to change the options.

5. Take a moment and explore the options in front of you to see what you can do depending on what type of chart you would like to create.

6. We want to create a chart to support a better visualization of dates. In our case, we are using a line chart. Here are the three settings used to create the chart we want to use to visualize our data (be aware, the chart will update as you make changes):

- **Chart Type**: **Line**

- **Data Direction**: **Vertical**

- **Use column names as labels**: Checked

Figure 13.13 shows all the settings, including defaults that we left in place:

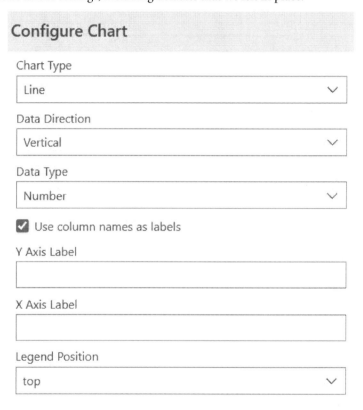

Figure 13.13 – Configure Chart dialog

Once you have configured those settings, you should see a line chart like the one displayed in *Figure 13.14*:

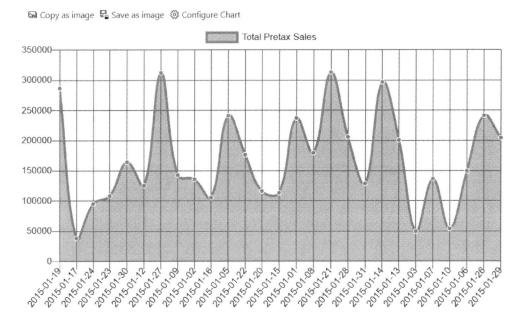

Figure 13.14 – Line chart visualization in your notebook

Once you have created visuals that you like, you have the option to save those visuals as an image to be used elsewhere if needed. While this is not an exhaustive tool to use for data visualization, it does help if you are working with the data as an analyst to understand the shape of the data or identify outliers and patterns.

Now that we have looked at a few ways to visualize our data, let's look at some of the options we have to export our results.

Exporting results

Another unique thing about notebooks is that you can *export* your results in a variety of formats. In *Figure 13.11*, you can see five additional buttons before the chart option. Each of these buttons represents a different type of export format to be used, as listed here in order from left to right:

- **CSV**
- **Excel**
- **JSON**
- **Markdown**
- **XML**

As you can see, this is a nice way to generate a result set that can be used in a variety of ways. The markdown option will allow you to save the results in a markdown file that can be added to your Jupyter book. The other options can be used for data exportation or further exploration with other tools.

Now that we have generated all these results, let us review how to clear results or refresh them.

Resetting results

When working with your code, it is common to generate results cell by cell as needed during your analysis. Now that you have completed your analysis, what do you do next? In this case, we are going to clear our results by clicking the eraser button at the top of the notebook. This will clear all results from all the code cells in your notebook.

Next, if you want to reset the results, for example, this is common when the underlying dataset has been updated. You can click the **Run all** button at the top of the notebook. This will execute all the code cells in the notebook in order. All your results will be displayed once again with fresh results from the latest query.

Now that we have worked with the results from our code, our next step is to add documentation to our code.

In the next section, we will explore adding documentation and formatting that documentation in our notebook.

Documenting your code with markdown in your notebooks

Now that we've added some code to the notebook, it is time to add documentation to clarify or expand on what the code should do. This is done using the **markdown** language, or **MD**. As you saw with the README file, we can create entire documents using markdown to supplement our documentation.

In this section, we are going to explore markdown and use it to add documentation directly into our notebook to support the SQL we have created.

Adding a text block to your notebook

Adding text to your notebook is straightforward. Simply click the + **Cell** button and choose **Text cell**. This will create a new cell that is formatted for markdown and has several formatting buttons included with it to make code presentation easier.

You can also add text blocks by clicking the + **Cell** button underneath the current cell you are in. This is helpful when adding cells in between the cells you have already created.

In the next few sections, we will add cells for a variety of purposes into our notebook and discuss the formatting options.

Creating a header for your notebook

If you have not already added a text cell to the top of your notebook, do so now. We are going to use this cell to create a formatted header for our notebook.

> **Repositioning cells**
>
> If you have created a cell that is out of position or need to move it around, use the up or down arrows on each cell to reposition it within the notebook.

In that text cell, enter some text for the title of your notebook. For example, we used `Wide World Importers - Customer Analytics` for our title, as shown here in *Figure 13.15*:

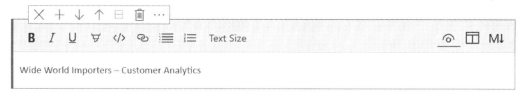

Figure 13.15 – Header text cell

Now that we have the text in the cell, highlight the text and choose **Text Size**. Change this to **Header 1**. Complete your header cell by adding a couple of sentences to describe the purpose of the notebook and add a bulleted list to cover some objectives. Your header should look like the example shown in *Figure 13.16*:

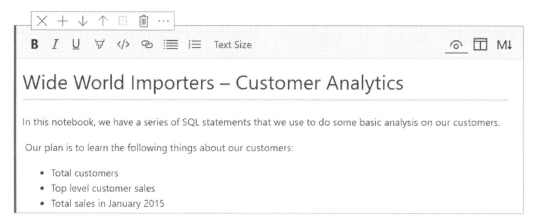

Figure 13.16 – Formatted header cell

As you can see, we have many formatting options that we can use to make the cell display text in a meaningful way. In the next section, we will add some documentation to our code cells and then dig into the markdown created as we did this.

Using basic markdown for documentation

Markdown is a language that supports simple formatting for documents that can be shared and displayed in a variety of technology tools. Open the header that we created in markdown and look at the formatting that was used in the native markdown to support our formats. Click the button with the capital **M** and a down arrow to open that cell in markdown. You should see a set of code that looks like that shown here:

Figure 13.17 – Header cell shown with markdown

As you can see, markdown is a simple formatting methodology. Because of its simplicity, it is easy to format content as needed that can be displayed properly in notebooks and other tools that support the markdown syntax.

The following shows a table of the most common markdown formatting used in markdown files today:

To create this format	Use this markdown
Header 1 (H1)	# header
Header 2 (H2)	## header
Header 3 (H3)	### header
Header 4 (H4)	#### header
Bold	**insert word here** __insert word here__
Italics	*insert word here* _insert word here_
Ordered list	1. Maple 2. Oak 3. Elm
Unordered list	* maple * oak * elm

Figure 13.18 – Common markdown formatting table

Change the markdown in your header by using a different header format, such as H2. Now, when you switch back to the normal view of your text cell by clicking the eye button, you will see that the header has changed in size. Depending on what you are more comfortable with when creating markdown, you may find some value in using the markdown editor as opposed to the ribbon-supported editor in Azure Data Studio.

If you want to see side-by-side changes as you make them, use the Split view option next to the markdown, which looks like a table, to see the immediate changes to markdown side by side with your regular view.

As you can see, you can use both editors to work with the markdown in your text cell. Whether you edit in the cell itself or in the markdown, the changes are immediately available and viewable in both locations. Before we move to the next section, the markdown in our cells is stored in the notebook natively as markdown and only formatted for ease of use in Azure Data Studio.

Adding images and links to your documentation

Before we move on to sharing and distributing notebooks, we will walk through adding more interesting items such as images and links to our documentation. Let us start by adding an image as follows:

1. Add a new text cell to the bottom of your notebook.

2. Select an image of your choice.

3. Copy and paste it into your notebook.

Voila! You have an image in your notebook.

Be aware that it is not possible to edit images in your notebook once you have added them. You will need to remove them and re-add them as necessary to get the size or cropping that you desire. If you look at the markdown of the image in your cell, you will see that it has created a fairly significant block of code to translate that image. If you plan to use a lot of images in your notebook, we would recommend that you put each image in its own cell in most cases so you can fully edit the text around it. While this is not always optimal, it will make it easier to work with the markdown if you need to make other edits.

Links can be added by simply copying and pasting them into your text cell in your notebook. Both images and links can be effective uses of adding additional documentation or support to the content in your notebook. For example, if you are matching a notebook to a presentation or have slides already created with relevant supporting information, you can copy and paste those slides into the appropriate cells as references for your end users or yourself to use.

Text cells with the markdown capability allow you to add rich documentation and support to the code you have created. Now that you have a rich set of documentation and your Jupyter book and its related notebooks, let us look at how to share that content with others.

Managing and sharing your queries with Jupyter notebooks

Congratulations on completing your first notebook in Azure Data Studio. As you can see, it is a great way to consolidate SQL code with related documentation. Now that you have a notebook to share, we will discuss how to share it.

Simple sharing of Jupyter books and notebooks

The reality is that sharing your notebook is as simple as sharing the Jupyter notebook file. You can send this via email or share for people to download. Sharing notebooks in this fashion is an easy way to distribute code with all the relevant documentation needed for others to use your code. Once another user has access to your notebook, they can use the **Open File** option in the **File** menu to open that notebook directly in Azure Data Studio. Once they have opened the notebook, they only need to connect to a compatible data source to work with the code in the notebook.

Sharing your entire Jupyter book involves sharing the folder and all of its related content. The recommendation to do this would be to zip the folder up and send it to others to share or use. Once they have unzipped the folder, they will be able to add all of the contents of the Jupyter book into the **NOTEBOOKS** section in Azure Data Studio. This is similar to the work we have been doing throughout the chapter.

Using GitHub to collaborate on your notebook

If you work in a team that can collaborate on these notebooks, the recommendation is to use a source control solution such as a GitHub repo. This will allow you to manage changes to the content and even use the branch and merge methodologies if needed. By using this functionality within Azure Data Studio and making it a part of your normal development practice, you will be able to share documentation and code in a complete set without having to do this with just SQL files, as has been done in the past.

Integrating third-party Jupyter books

In Azure Data Studio, it is possible to upload Jupyter books from GitHub. Microsoft has a couple of teams who are actively releasing content using this method. The key to working with content in this manner is to create release versions of your Jupyter book for others to consume.

> **Release versions of Jupyter books**
>
> Only Jupyter books that have been created as GitHub releases are available to integrate. It is outside of the scope of this book to fully describe the steps necessary to create a GitHub release. The key thing to remember is that it will create a zipped folder with your Jupyter book contents. Once you have created that release, you will be able to share it the same way that the Microsoft public repos have been shared.

You can use the following steps to connect to a Jupyter book that has been released via GitHub:

1. From the **NOTEBOOKS** section in Azure Data Studio, in the **...** menu, choose **Add Remote Jupyter Book**, as shown here:

Figure 13.19 – Add Remote Jupyter Book

2. This will open a dialog box on the right-hand side of Azure Data Studio. The default selection at the top is **GitHub**. Then, choose a repository to connect to. In our case, we will select this repository: `repos/microsoft/tigertoolbox`.

3. Click **Search** to populate the rest of the options in the dialog box. Now that you have the options populated, you can select the options as shown in *Figure 13.20*:

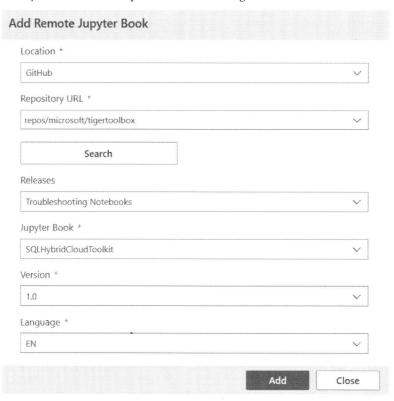

Figure 13.20 – Add Remote Jupyter Book dialog

4. Once you have all your options selected, click on **Add**. This will add the new Jupyter book to your **NOTEBOOK sections**, as shown here:

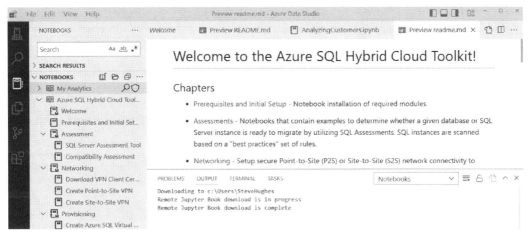

Figure 13.21 – Newly imported Jupyter book

As you can see, the ability to share notebooks and Jupyter books with peers and other developers changes how we distribute our SQL code. Whether sharing a simple notebook with some clear documentation or a more formal Jupyter book such as what Microsoft has provided, we now have the ability as SQL developers to effectively document and share our SQL code with others.

Summary

In this chapter, you have learned how to create a Jupyter book and its related content, such as Jupyter notebooks. You now have the ability to develop and execute code in notebooks and then follow that up with good documentation that you can share with others on your team. The completed notebook used in this chapter is available on the GitHub site as noted in the *Technical requirements* section at the beginning.

This chapter also wraps up this book on SQL. Throughout this book, you have learned many different techniques to improve both writing and tuning your SQL in common everyday practice. By combining those skills with the notebook skills learned in this final chapter, you are on your way to becoming a modern data developer with a broad range of skills for the marketplace.

Appendix
Preparing Your Environment

As part of the *Appendix*, we will be setting up the technical prerequisites for this book. This includes several tools that'll be used throughout this book to move data and explore queries. It is recommended that you install the following tools on the device as these will be used with the exercises in this book:

- **SQL Server Management Studio** (**SSMS**) and **Azure Data Studio**. You can find the installation instructions at `https://learn.microsoft.com/en-us/sql/ssms/download-sql-server-management-studio-ssms`. Be sure to install both SQL Server Management Studio and Azure Data Studio.

- **Microsoft Azure Storage Explorer** is used to move files in and out of Azure. You'll find the installation at `https://azure.microsoft.com/en-us/products/storage/storage-explorer/`. For more information about the product, please refer to the following documentation: `https://learn.microsoft.com/en-us/azure/vs-azure-tools-storage-manage-with-storage-explorer`.

- All the examples in this book will be using the **Wide World Importers** sample databases provided by Microsoft, which can be found here: `https://github.com/Microsoft/sql-server-samples/releases/tag/wide-world-importers-v1.0`. Instructions for which sample databases will be used for Azure and SQL Server can be found later in this *Appendix*. If you want to download them early or understand how to use these backups, we will be using the full backups for SQL Server and the standard backups for Azure SQL Database.

Prerequisites for running the exercises

This book covers many illustrations and examples of working with SQL and improving your overall writing and performance. To make this simple for all our users, we have chosen to use the `Wide World Importers` sample databases available from Microsoft. Depending on the nature of the query that we are constructing and providing examples for, one of the two databases provided by Microsoft will be used. There is a data warehouse sample as well as an operational database sample that we will be working on, as noted here:

- `WideWorldImporters`
- `WideWorldImportersDW`

There are two recommended ways to work through the examples in this book, depending on your access to Azure. We will walk through the installation path and plan for both patterns using the data warehouse database as our example. You will be able to follow the same instructions using the matching operational database. Bear in mind that this means you will have *two* databases in either location to be able to run the exercises as created within this book.

Now, we will walk you through the choices and help you choose a platform to build the examples on.

Choosing a platform

The two platform choices that we recommend are **Azure SQL Database** and **SQL Server 2022 Developer Edition**. Both options are low to no cost, depending on how you implement them. We encourage you to use the platform you are most comfortable with for the exercises.

The first approach is using Azure SQL Database with a standard size, such as S0. This is a low-cost option that does not require any environment setup on your local computer. Furthermore, Azure SQL Database is a no-version solution. Any of the work that we present in this book should be compatible with that environment. When using this option, we will be leveraging the bacpac option to restore the databases.

The other recommended approach is to use the developer edition of SQL Server. The current version of SQL Server at the time of writing is 2022. The only area where we are aware of a significant change is in the JSON functionality as new features become available.

If you have an existing copy of SQL Server 2016 or above installed in your environment, you should be able to use that for most of the examples in this book. Since we can't identify all the nuances and differences from 2016 forward if something does not function or appear as expected, refer to the release notes from the latest version of SQL Server to see if it is new. This book will be using the 2022 release of SQL Server as its baseline.

In the next two sections, we will walk through how to set up the environments and load up the appropriate backups into your databases. If you already have one of these environments set up, skip to the sections for each one where we discuss how to restore the database to your server or instance.

Setting up the Azure environment

The next few sections will walk you through the process of setting up your Azure environment. This will allow you to restore the database in Azure SQL Database. Keep in mind that Azure SQL Database is *always the latest version* available. The examples in this book work with SQL Server 2022 and the latest version of Azure SQL Database available at that time. While we do not expect any significant changes to the functionality, it is in your best interest to understand which version you are looking at if you have an issue.

The next section describes how to set up your subscription and resource group in Azure if you have never done so before. If you already have a subscription or are familiar with how to set up a subscription or resource group, you can proceed to the section after the next one.

Creating your subscription and resource group

This section will describe how to set up a subscription using a pay-as-you-go account. If you have never used a pay-as-you-go account, we recommend that you go to `https://azure.microsoft.com`. From there, you will see a button or multiple buttons that allow you to try Azure for free. Follow the instructions provided to create your first Azure subscription. It will likely require that you have a credit card, but you should not have to worry about spending related to the work here as you will get $200 in credit.

> **Note**
>
> Be aware that this is a true pay-as-you-go account and can incur expenses over and above the $200 credit, which you will then have to pay for. You will not be limited to the services you will use in this book, and it is possible to set up expensive services that may exceed your $200 credit. Keep this in mind and make sure you know the costs of services before you set them up, and do not leave unnecessary services running, as this can quickly use up your credit.

Once you have created your subscription, you can create a resource group. Give the resource group a name you will recognize. You will add all the components that support the exercises in this book to this resource group. This will allow you to manage expenses as well as remove all these assets when you are done with the exercises to prevent additional expenses later. It is not recommended that you split these resources across multiple resource groups.

If this is your first time creating a resource group, you can choose the region that sounds closest to you. There is a small chance you will not be able to use that region for all your resources, but that is rare. For example, if you are in Florida, you would typically choose East US 2. If you're curious about where they are located, you can see the regions on the Azure website at `https://azure.microsoft.com/en-us/global-infrastructure/geographies`.

Now that you have your subscription and resource group set up, the next section will walk you through creating an Azure SQL Server and restoring the database. While you may have set up Azure SQL Databases previously, if you have not restored a backup to Azure SQL Server, we recommend that you review the steps in the next section.

Creating an Azure SQL Server and restoring the database

Now that you have an Azure subscription and resource group created, the next step is to add the Azure SQL Server to your resource group. This is how we do it:

1. To start this process, click the **Create** button on your resource group page.

2. Search the **Marketplace** area for Azure SQL.

3. Select **Azure SQL** from the **Marketplace** area.

4. On the **Azure SQL** page, click **Create**.

5. On the **Select SQL deployment option** page, find the **SQL databases** section and change **Resource type** to **Database server**. Then, click **Create**, as shown in the following screenshot:

Figure 1 – Azure SQL deployment options

6. On the basics page for **Create SQL Database Server**, choose the **Subscription** and **Resource group** properties you will be using from the drop-down list.

7. Give your SQL Server a **Server name** and **Location**, as shown in the following screenshot:

Create SQL Database Server   ...
Microsoft

⚠ Changing Basic options may reset selections you have made. Review all options prior to creating the resource.

Basics   Networking   Additional settings   Tags   Review + create

SQL database server is a logical container for managing databases and elastic pools. Complete the Basic tab, then go to Review + Create to provision with smart defaults, or visit each tab to customize. Learn more ⎘

Project details

Select the subscription to manage deployed resources and costs. Use resource groups like folders to organize and manage all your resources.

Subscription * ⓘ	Pay-As-You-Go ⌄
Resource group * ⓘ	sqlbook-rg ⌄
	Create new

Server details

Enter required settings for this server, including providing a name and location.

Server name *	dow-sqlbook ✓
	.database.windows.net

Location *	(US) East US ⌄

Authentication

Select your preferred authentication methods for accessing this server. Create a server admin login and password to access your server with SQL authentication, select only Azure AD authentication Learn more ⎘ using an existing Azure AD user, group, or application as Azure AD admin Learn more ⎘ , or select both SQL and Azure AD authentication.

Authentication method	◯ Use only Azure Active Directory (Azure AD) authentication
	◯ Use both SQL and Azure AD authentication
	⦿ Use SQL authentication
Server admin login *	Enter server admin login

Figure 2 – Create SQL Database Server basics page

8. In the **Authentication method** section of the page, choose the **Use SQL authentication** option, as shown in the preceding screenshot.

9. In the available text boxes, add a SQL **Server admin login** name to use and provide a password.

> **Note**
>
> This is a development environment. Using SQL authentication is not a best practice for production environments. However, it is outside the scope of the work we are doing to include the setup and implementation of Azure Active Directory to support the best authentication method. If you have this option available to you, you are welcome to use it. Throughout this book, we will assume you are using SQL authentication when working with an Azure SQL Database.

10. Once you have made all the necessary selections, click **Review + Create**, then click **Create** to add your SQL database server to your resource group.

While your server is being deployed, you can download the backup files you will use. We will be using what is called a `bacpac` file to restore the database. Browse to the `Wide World Importers` sample database page at `https://github.com/Microsoft/sql-server-samples/releases/tag/wide-world-importers-v1.0`. For the exercises that we are doing, choose the two files under the **Azure SQL Database Standard tier** section, as shown in the following screenshot. Once you have downloaded both files, we will upload those to Azure storage using **Microsoft Azure Storage Explorer**:

Figure 3 – Wide World Importers sample database for Azure SQL Database

To restore the database in Azure, you will need to create a storage account in your resource group and move the file into BLOB storage. In the next set of steps, you will add a storage account to your resource group:

1. Open the Azure portal and go to your subscription and resource group.

2.   From the resource group page, click the **Create** button.

3.   Search for `storage` in the **Marketplace** area and click **Create** for the **Storage account** option.

4.   On the **Create a storage account** page, select your **Subscription** and **Resource group** and give your account a name.

5.   To keep costs low, choose **Standard** and **Local redundant storage** or **LRS**.

6.   Click **Review**, then **Create** to add this storage account to your resource group.

Now that you have a storage account, you need to move the backups to the **Blob** storage in that account. If you have not already done so, download and install **Microsoft Azure Storage Explorer** from the link provided in the *Technical requirements* section. We will use Storage Explorer to move the files in the next set of steps:

1.   Open **Microsoft Azure Storage Explorer**.

2.   Connect to your Azure subscription and storage account. If you are unfamiliar with working with Azure Storage Explorer, please refer to the following documentation to connect to your subscription and storage account: `https://learn.microsoft.com/en-us/azure/ vs-azure-tools-storage-manage-with-storage-explorer`.

3.   Expand the storage account you just created.

4.   Right-click on the **Blob Containers** option and select **Create Blob Container**, as shown in the following screenshot:

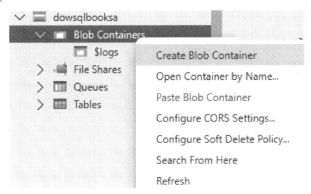

Figure 4 – Creating a Blob container

5.   Give your new container a name, such as `backups`.

6.   Open the container, click on the **Upload** button, and choose **Upload files**.

7.   From the **Upload** dialog box, select the files that we downloaded from **Wide World Importers** and upload them to the container that you created.

Now, everything has been set up to restore those databases to your Azure SQL Server. This last set of steps for the Azure section will walk you through how to restore one of the databases to the server. Repeat these steps with the other backup to restore the other database as well:

1. Open the Azure portal and browse your resource group. Select the SQL Server you created there.

2. From the **Options** list located at the top of that page, choose **Import database**.

3. On the **Import database** page, click **Select backup**.

4. Choose the storage account you created and added the backups to it.

5. Browse to your blob storage container and select the backup you wish to restore.

6. In the **Pricing tier** options, you need to choose how you want to configure your Azure SQL Database.

    Our recommendation is to choose the **S0** configuration, which has a monthly cost but is manageable. This option is not the default option when setting up your database. You'll find this option located under **DTU-based** in the **Standard** group on the list. You can upgrade as needed but the cost will be consistent for the month and the storage will be more than enough for what you need. The other option is to use **serverless** and select a size that fits your needs. Serverless is a **v-Core**-based option and gives you more options when tuning your database. It does have a short window for startup and you should set it to shut down when you want it to. Depending on the amount of usage you have, it may or may not cost more than an S0 or S1 subscription. For this set of instructions, we will be choosing **S0**.

7. Once you have chosen your subscription level, add your credentials and restore the database.

If you choose to restore both databases, remember that both databases incur separate costs inside Azure. You will want to manage your costs as you move forward and work with the exercises in this book.

Congratulations! You've successfully restored a database in Azure and are ready to move forward with the exercises in this book.

Setting up the SQL Server developer environment

In this section, we will guide you through the basics of the SQL Server setup used to support the exercises and demos in this book. We will be using the SQL Server 2022 Developer Edition installed locally. We will walk you through the steps required to install SQL Server and restore the `WideWorldImporters` database. Let's check it out in the next section.

Installing SQL Server 2022 Developer Edition

The Developer Edition of SQL Server is free to download. You will need to open a web browser to `https://www.microsoft.com/en-us/sql-server/sql-server-downloads`. From this location, scroll down until you see the SQL Server **Developer** download option, as shown in the following screenshot:

Developer

SQL Server 2022 Developer is a full-featured free edition, licensed for use as a development and test database in a non-production environment.

Figure 5 – SQL Server 2022 Developer Edition download

Once you have downloaded the installation from this site, follow these steps to complete the installation process:

1. Open the installer from your download location. You will see a dialog box, as shown here:

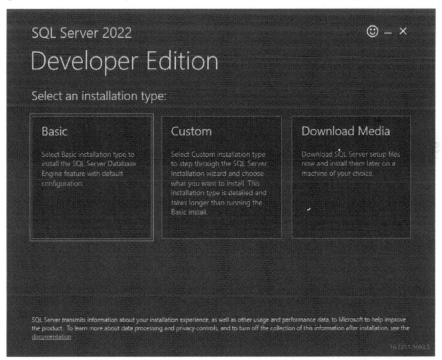

Figure 6 – Installing SQL Server 2022 Developer Edition

2. To keep this simple, we will be using the **Basic** installation option.

3. Accept the licensing option and continue.

    We recommend keeping the default location. However, if you have installed SQL Server in the past, you may need to change the location of the installation to suit your needs.

4. Click **Install** to continue. Once the installation is complete, as shown in the following dialog box, take note of the instance name as you will need to use it for connecting. The exception to this is that if the instance name is **MSSQLSERVER** in your installation, then it is a default instance and will not require an instance name when connecting:

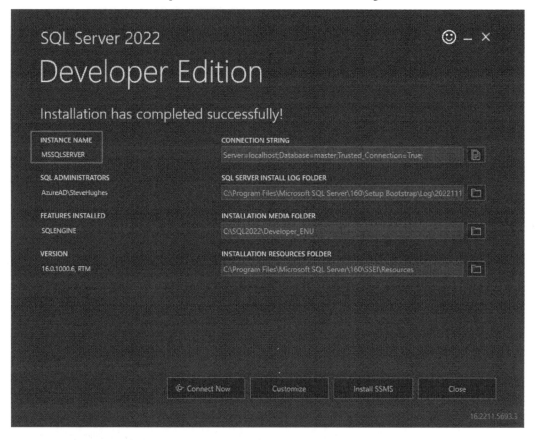

Figure 7 – Completed SQL Server 2022 Developer Edition installation

5. If you have not already installed SSMS, you can click **Install SMSS**, as shown in the preceding screenshot, to open a web page where you can download and install **SQL Server Management Studio** and **Azure Data Studio**.

6. Open **SQL Server Management Studio** to begin the process of restoring the backup.

7. Connect to the server instance that you have installed.

8. Next, you need to retrieve the database backup of `Wide World Importers` from Microsoft's GitHub repository: `https://github.com/Microsoft/sql-server-samples/releases/tag/wide-world-importers-v1.0`.

9. As shown in the following screenshot, click the link for **WideWorldImporters-FULL.bak**:

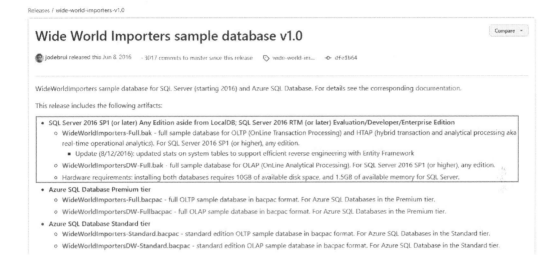

Figure 8 – Wide World Importers sample database for SQL Server

10. This will download the database that we will use for some of our examples. We will also be using the **DW** database, and you can choose to download that now as well. We recommend that you save these download files in a directory such as `C:\Temp` to make sure that they can be easily found when restoring the database.

    Return to SQL Server Management Studio.

11. Right-click on the **Databases** folder in the server where you want to restore the database to the server and choose **Restore database**.

12. In the **Restore Database** dialog, choose **Device** and use the ellipsis (…) button to select your backup file. If the file does not appear as an option in the window, click **Add** to select the backup file. Once you have selected your backup file, the **Restore Database** dialog should look like the one shown in the following figure:

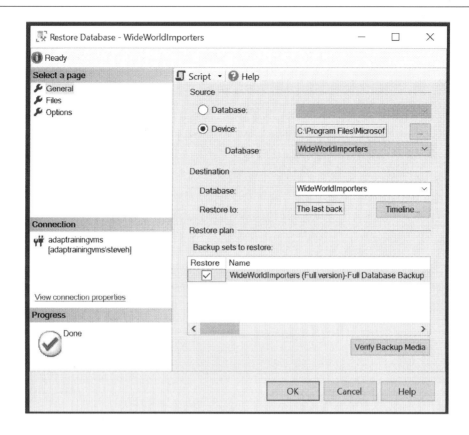

Figure 9 – Restore Database in SQL Server

13. Click **OK** to restore the database to your server.

Congratulations! Your database is ready for the exercises in this book.

Index

V

W

Packtpub.com

Subscribe to our online digital library for full access to over 7,000 books and videos, as well as industry leading tools to help you plan your personal development and advance your career. For more information, please visit our website.

Why subscribe?

- Spend less time learning and more time coding with practical eBooks and Videos from over 4,000 industry professionals

- Improve your learning with Skill Plans built especially for you

- Get a free eBook or video every month

- Fully searchable for easy access to vital information

- Copy and paste, print, and bookmark content

Did you know that Packt offers eBook versions of every book published, with PDF and ePub files available? You can upgrade to the eBook version at packtpub.com and as a print book customer, you are entitled to a discount on the eBook copy. Get in touch with us at customercare@packtpub.com for more details.

At www.packtpub.com, you can also read a collection of free technical articles, sign up for a range of free newsletters, and receive exclusive discounts and offers on Packt books and eBooks.

Other Books You May Enjoy

If you enjoyed this book, you may be interested in these other books by Packt:

SQL Server Query Tuning and Optimization

Benjamin Nevarez

ISBN: 978-1-80324-262-0

- Troubleshoot queries using methods including extended events, SQL Trace, and dynamic management views

- Understand how the execution engine and query operators work

- Speed up queries and improve app performance by creating the right indexes

- Detect and fix cardinality estimation errors by examining query optimizer statistics

- Monitor and promote both plan caching and plan reuse to improve app performance

- Troubleshoot and improve query performance by using the Query Store

- Improve the performance of data warehouse queries by using columnstore indexes

- Handle query processor limitations with hints and other methods

Business Intelligence with Databricks SQL

Vihag Gupta

ISBN: 978-1-80323-533-2

- Understand how Databricks SQL fits into the Databricks Lakehouse Platform
- Perform everyday analytics with Databricks SQL Workbench and business intelligence tools
- Organize and catalog your data assets
- Program the data security model to protect and govern your data
- Tune SQL warehouses (computing clusters) for optimal query experience
- Tune the Delta Lake storage format for maximum query performance
- Deliver extreme performance with the Photon query execution engine
- Implement advanced data ingestion patterns with Databricks SQL

Packt is searching for authors like you

If you're interested in becoming an author for Packt, please visit `authors.packtpub.com` and apply today. We have worked with thousands of developers and tech professionals, just like you, to help them share their insight with the global tech community. You can make a general application, apply for a specific hot topic that we are recruiting an author for, or submit your own idea.

Share Your Thoughts

Now you've finished *SQL Query Design Pattern Best Practices*, we'd love to hear your thoughts! Scan the QR code below to go straight to the Amazon review page for this book and share your feedback or leave a review on the site that you purchased it from.

`https://packt.link/r/1-837-63328-2`

Your review is important to us and the tech community and will help us make sure we're delivering excellent quality content.

Download a free PDF copy of this book

Thanks for purchasing this book!

Do you like to read on the go but are unable to carry your print books everywhere? Is your eBook purchase not compatible with the device of your choice?

Don't worry, now with every Packt book you get a DRM-free PDF version of that book at no cost.

Read anywhere, any place, on any device. Search, copy, and paste code from your favorite technical books directly into your application.

The perks don't stop there, you can get exclusive access to discounts, newsletters, and great free content in your inbox daily.

Follow these simple steps to get the benefits:

1. Scan the QR code or visit the link below:

https://packt.link/free-ebook/9781837633289

2. Submit your proof of purchase.
3. That's it! We'll send your free PDF and other benefits to your email directly.

Made in the USA
Columbia, SC
30 November 2024

47934127R00148